TO

HADLEY CANTRIL

HARRY H. FIELD

GEORGE H. GALLUP

AND

ELMO ROPER

WITHOUT WHOSE PIONEER EFFORTS

THIS BOOK COULD NOT HAVE BEEN WRITTEN

MANDATE
FROM THE PEOPLE

MANDATE
FROM THE PEOPLE

JEROME S. BRUNER

DUELL, SLOAN AND PEARCE
NEW YORK

COPYRIGHT, 1944, BY
JEROME S. BRUNER

I

A WARTIME BOOK

PRINTED IN THE UNITED STATES OF AMERICA

ACKNOWLEDGMENT

TO those hundreds of thousands of Americans who patiently submitted to an examination of their private opinions and thereby made possible the measurement of public opinion I am most deeply indebted. This is their book.

The research of which this book is an expression was made possible by a foundation grant establishing and supporting the Office of Public Opinion Research of Princeton University of which the writer has been Associate Director. By collecting and analyzing public opinion material from all available sources, the Office has made it possible to give a running account of what America is thinking, what it is hoping. Other research organizations have been generous in making this work possible. Without the co-operation of George H. Gallup of the American Institute of Public Opinion and Harry H. Field of the National Opinion Research Center, the archives of public opinion at Princeton would still be only a fond hope.

To two men I owe a particular debt: Hadley Cantril and Gordon W. Allport—good friends, good critics—who, though by tradition not responsible for the views expressed in this book, are most certainly to be found walking through its pages.

The reader should be especially grateful to my wife, Katherine Frost Bruner, for it is she who has championed any felicity of expression to be found herein.

Hermine Hall has done the yeoman's job of preparing the manuscript and lightening the burdens of book-writing.

JEROME S. BRUNER

Princeton, New Jersey

TABLE OF CONTENTS

MANDATE
FROM THE PEOPLE

INTRODUCTION

THIS is a book about the future—about the peace. It is not a blue-print. The reader will not find here a summary of the requisites for either an enduring or a just peace.

It is a book about people or, more properly speaking, about "the public." Statesmen and the interests propose the shape of the future. But the people condone their chauvinism, deplore their cupidity, or glorify their idealism. In a democratic society, elections are the pay-off. But there are other more subtle means through which the public will is expressed. We write letters to our Congressman, to the newspapers; we roar approval or condemnation at mass meetings and rallies. Through these acts, we the people determine the climate of opinion. Statesmen and the interests may propose the shape of the future, but it is the climate of opinion which in the end makes one proposal flourish, another wither. People, then, make the future, decide whether it will be peace or war, abundance or poverty.

Lincoln once remarked, "What I want is to get done what the people desire to have done, and the question for me is how to find that out exactly." Perhaps it is an irony of democracy that leaders have found it difficult to discover just what it is that people want. Certain it is, however, that with the development of scientific surveys of public opinion, the task is becoming less difficult. Leadership does not, thereby, become nothing more than the ability to shift dextrously on every breeze of public sentiment. A leader is as good as his ability to understand what people want within the limits of what it is wise for them to have and of what it is possible for them to get. To attain that ideal requires more than a bowing acquaintance with the man in the street. It requires an exact appraisal of who wants what and to what end. That is what this book is about.

The task which is essayed in the following pages is easily outlined. For the last few years several research organizations have been collecting material on the kind of world the American people would like to see come out of this war. Using carefully refined sampling and interviewing methods, these organizations have compiled a rich catalogue of public opinion on the peace. That catalogue is the mandate from the people. This book is an analysis of it.*

There is, to be sure, more to public opinion than the findings of the public opinion polls. For in matters political, organization is as crucial as number. A highly organized minority group with vocal and determined spokesmen counts for more in our age than an inert mass. Polls do not measure the subtle factor of group organization, not even when they analyze returns in terms of Democrats, Republicans, union membership, or religion.

In the past, on the other hand, it has been the custom to discuss public opinion *only* in terms of organized groups. The Farmer became the American Farm Bureau Federation, the Businessman the NAM or U. S. Chamber of Commerce, the Worker the great international unions or the CIO and A. F. of L. Oftentimes, the Farmer and his spokesman, the Worker and his, the Businessman

* The public opinion polling organizations from which the material in this book has been gathered are the American Institute of Public Opinion (the Gallup Poll), the *Fortune* Poll, National Opinion Research Center, and the Office of Public Opinion Research of Princeton University. Where reference is made to poll data gathered in other countries, credit is due the Canadian Institute of Public Opinion, the British Institute of Public Opinion, the *Fortune* Poll of Britain, and the Australian Public Opinion Poll. Many of the polling results treated throughout this book have appeared before in the press releases of the Gallup Poll and other organizations. Such material is given new perspective by being brought together. A considerable part of the material presented has never, for various reasons, been released before. More particularly, the results of work done by the Office of Public Opinion Research is being presented here for the first time.

4

and his, were worlds apart. And so if polls err on the side of taking people in their abstract mass, the error has the virtue of egalitarian intent, of balancing one-sided impressions expensively cultivated by the "pressure boys."

A word about the general plan which this book follows. Roughly speaking, it is divided into two parts. The first part traces the outlines of American public opinion on international issues crucial for winning the peace. Here, in order, will be found discussions of (1) our ideological orientation toward war and peace; (2) the American conception of the role this country is to play in world politics when the shooting stops; (3) the place of America in world trade; (4) America's responsibilities in the social and economic reconstruction of the war-torn world; (5) the special case of Russia in the post-war period; (6) our relations with England after the war, and (7) the fate of the enemy.

The second half of the book looks to the post-war home front. Four central issues dominate the discussion: (1) freedom from want and the demand for security; (2) freedom of opportunity and the demand for jobs and a future; (3) the future of "free enterprise"; and (4) the task of demobilizing our two armies—fighting men and war workers.

To the average American, the domestic and international are far from equivalent in either personal significance or interest. In spite of the years of war, the events and problems which beset the world beyond our boundaries are of secondary interest to the man in the street. To him, the payoff is what happens right here at home— and what is likely to happen. A successful organization of nations is a hollow victory if it is coeval with unemployment on the home front. A good job is still the benchmark for the best of possible worlds even if two thousand miles away the subtle poisons of a new war are brewing beneath the surface.

Consider this question put to a cross-section of America during the winter of 1943-1944: Which kind of post-war problem interests you most—international post-war problems like setting up a new league of nations and police force, or domestic post-war problems like full employment and production? The answers tell their own story. Fifty-three per cent of the nation—better than fifty millions of Americans—choose domestic issues. Only 16 per cent consider international affairs as their first concern. The remainder can either make no choice or have no opinion on the matter.[1] *

If, then, the reader should be inclined to weigh the significance of the opinions reported in **Part I** and **Part II**, let him put the matter this way. Opinions on domestic issues are, more frequently than not, more personally relevant to people and more firmly based on conviction than are opinions on more distant international questions. A necessary corollary is that the American public is better informed about domestic issues.

But if there is a difference in emphasis, it is also true that none but the most insulated American believes it is of no import whether his country exists in a world threatening war or one pledged to peace. We have learned that a fire at the neighbor's threatens us too. The upshot of our lesser interest in international affairs is not that we don't care what happens to the world; it is, rather, that we are more willing to place international decisions in the hands of our leaders and their experts without exercising our critical prerogatives with the epic degree of fervor reserved for domestic issues.

* Numeral superscripts, "[1]," refer the reader to the Appendix starting on p. 229. To keep the narrative moving, the exact wordings of poll questions and the full results obtained have been relegated to an appendix. Here will be found wording, results, the date on which a question was asked of the public, and the name of the polling organization which asked the question. The Appendix is divided into sections corresponding to the chapters in the book. Questions in each section of the Appendix are ordered consecutively and marked with the same numbers as appear in superscript in the text.

Make of this what you will. But let it highlight the fact that there is a long way to travel before Americans become responsible citizens of the world. Americans are not, to be sure, different from others. The same can, doubtless, be said for Englishmen, Russians, Chinese, or Brazilians. Yet there is something beyond the fact of our relative insularity. We have grown up internationally with tremendous strides since the last war—our period of isolation notwithstanding. If we are not yet citizens of the world with the same ardor that we are citizens of the United States, at least it can be said that never has there been a period in our history in which the world has come in upon us as it has since 1933.

PART I: *THE WORLD SCENE*

CHAPTER I

OF WAR AND PEACE

TO understand fully what the American people want from the peace, we must know what they see in the war. What has the war meant to America? Has its meaning changed since its beginnings in Spain, Ethiopia, and China almost a decade ago? To the mass of Americans, is it a war of ideas? If so, what ideas? Is the war as close to us emotionally as it is to the Jew in the Warsaw ghetto, the bombed-out Londoner, the battered Rhinelander? Are we fighting because we were attacked or because we are redressing a more profound wrong?

These questions can be answered. But they cannot be answered adequately until we understand the context in which American opinion about the war has developed. If we are on occasion reluctant to grant the importance of co-operating with other nations in times of peace, how did we get that way? Is it that we feel secure about our ability to look after ourselves, or rather, that we are insecure about dealing profitably with other nations?

Such background factors—the "context of opinion"—mold opinions. When the background changes, specific opinions change. And so the first task in describing opinion is to sketch the context in which it grew. What is the context like?

Six cardinal convictions have probably played the greatest part in the growth of American opinion on foreign affairs.

The sense of geographical isolation
Faith in the nation's security
The feeling of political stability
Hatred of war
The humane point of view
Suspicion of foreign powers

A word about each.

The Sense of Geographical Isolation

Americans were, until very recently, convinced that other countries were a "long way off." The U. S. A. is an awfully big place;
there are oceans all around it. Everything from our schoolboy
geography to the legend of "America the refuge" has conspired to
keep wide the subjective distance separating us from the "old
world." Even so trivial a thing as the use of Mercator's projection
in teaching elementary geography has kept alive the legend of isolation. A geographer with a good sense of world politics has remarked,
half in jest, half in earnest, that American foreign policy during
the last fifty years would have followed a consistently different tack
had our State Department personnel been schooled not in the
Mercator's projection at the top, but in the orthographic projection
at the bottom of the figure opposite.

Recall Lindbergh's flight to Paris. The *leitmotif* of press comment was not the smallness of the world, but rather, the immensity
of the space traversed. Lindbergh was a hero not because he had
brought closer the old world and the new. Kudos were for his
bravery in flying that *far* alone. And is it not ironical that Lindbergh himself should have become a spokesman for isolation?

The frames of reference of the refugee—and most of us are less
than three generations removed from being refugees—have to a
large extent prevented distances from shrinking. Our reluctance to

TWO VIEWS OF AMERICA'S GEOGRAPHICAL POSITION

TRADITIONAL VIEW

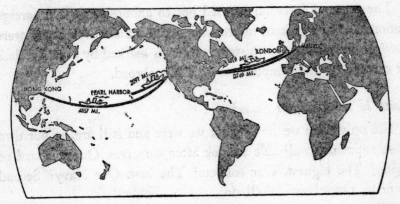

AIR AGE VIEW

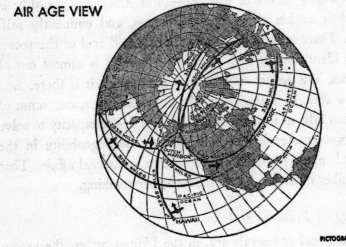

PICTOGRAPH CORPORATION

become embroiled in the strife that drove us from our homelands has invested an emotional tinge to our geography. We *want* to believe that Europe is a long way off. No surprise then that events in Prague, in Memel, in Manchukuo should seem like nightmarish shadow-play on a far-off screen.

The sense of isolation has led not to animosity toward foreign nations but to a lack of interest in foreign affairs. We never were *belligerent* isolates. Our history, rather, is marked by a passive lack of concern for the complexities of affairs abroad.

Faith in the Nation's Security

Not only were we far off, but we were and still are, in our own eyes, eminently well able to look after ourselves. Our standard of living? The highest. Our soldiers? The best. Our Navy? Second to none. Ourselves? We'll do.

Whatever may be said for the individual American—whether he be emotionally secure or insecure—most Americans are alike in fancying their nation as strong, prosperous, and eminently self-dependent. There is not, to be sure, the paranoid zeal of the young Nazi. Our identification with "mighty America" is almost out of consciousness. We do not talk about it much; but it is there. And its effect on opinion is profound. On domestic issues, our sense of security often lulls us into unreasonable faith in our capacity to solve economic problems easily. A belief in our impregnability in the international sphere parallels our confidence in internal affairs. That belief is weaker now. But it still looms in our thinking.

The Feeling of Political Stability

Violent political upheavals are, in the United States, the exception. Our system has never been threatened. Stability has been our bellwether. Our one Civil War—and what country in Europe has

12

been blessed by that few?—was in no sense a threat to American democracy. And the two-party system has helped. We have been spared the tragic political fragmentation so characteristic of continental democracies. Consider, too, that our parties have rarely disagreed on basic issues. To Americans "foreign" politics are incomprehensible and slightly mad. Here cabinets do not fall, elections are in November, political intrigue is assiduously kept from view, and assassination is shocking.

As a small example of the mildness of America's political temper, consider this question on which people were polled at the time of the 1942 elections. The question was asked at a time when interest in politics was high—a few days before the Congressional election. "Do you think it makes a great deal of difference or only a little difference which political party runs the country?"[1] These are the results.

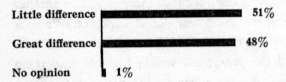

Little difference   51%

Great difference   48%

No opinion   1%

If, then, we find it difficult to understand the complex political struggles of Europe, fail, for example, to see any difference between Tito and Mikhailovitch, it is not because we have been misinformed. Our failure is one of unfamiliarity. To the city man, one bird's call is like another.

Hatred of War

A nation does not gain a unique distinction by hating war. Most civilized peoples hate war. America's hatred of it, because it developed into something akin to blindness, and may do so again, is of more than incidental cultural importance. Dismiss as typical of

13

our civilization the *mere* hatred of war and consider its peculiarly American manifestation.

No nation can exist which regards the absence of war as more important than any other national value. Hitler's expansion in Europe and Japan's in the Far East would never have reached their bloated proportions had that fact been realized by the Allied world sooner. America, of all the major United Nations, was the last to come awake to it.

We failed to come awake not because we despised values other than peace. Our torpor was born of blindness. And blindness was the child of a cynicism spawned during the years of disillusionment after the last war. While the second World War was making, our cynicism kept us actionless, annoyed. We thought war was a fraud, a means of making the rich richer, the poor poorer, the weak weaker. We hated war, were ashamed that we had gone into the last war, denied that it was necessary to consider that there might be another one. Without realizing it, we hated war out of existence. We took our psychological victory for the real thing.

And so we neglected the symptoms which, had we read them properly and in time, could have given us the power to stop the second war.

There was nothing inevitable about our cynicism. Emotional revulsion is perhaps a "natural consequence" of war. Cynicism is not. "Either war is a crusade or it is a crime. There is no half-way house." What we did here in America and what statesmen did abroad convinced the American people that the war *had not been* a crusade—and therefore had been a crime. From our high idealistic passion of "Making the World Safe for Democracy" we were cast down to a nagging partisan squabble about the League, a squabble in which all the earlier, noble issues got hopelessly lost. Naturally we were cynical. Had there been a palpable set of symbols upon

14

which the zeal for democracy could have been transferred at the end of the war—a real League, perhaps—there might have been no cynicism, no ostrich-like response to war.

Because we are, twenty years late, learning the meaning of the last war, our cynicism and its blindness can now be written off as yesterday's sleep-walking. In Figure 2, the number of Americans who thought it a mistake to enter the last war is plotted.[2]

Eventually polls will try to find out whether people think this war was a mistake. If, at any time in the future, six in every ten Americans believe that it was, then we may know we have lost the coming peace just as surely as we did the last. But whether there is cynicism or not, there will still be hatred of war. That hatred, fortunately, is our heritage.

The Humane Point of View

To us, the "humane view of things" is almost a substitute for a political ideology. Bloodshed shocks us. Our hearts and our purses are open to suffering at home and abroad. The moral and emotional value of the individual human being has always transcended the appeal of the political credo. Within a short period of time we gave for Finland and then gave for Russia.

So many things in our past have contributed to the humane quality of our thinking that it is almost impossible to know where to begin an account of causes. The fact that our population is an amalgam of those who have been economically and politically persecuted through the ages accounts for much. The frontier tradition—not dead by a far cry—in which neighbor helped neighbor is doubtless another ingredient.

Certainly religion is a factor. In October, 1942, 78 per cent of the adult population of the United States were members of a church.[3] We take our religion seriously. In the midst of the crisis

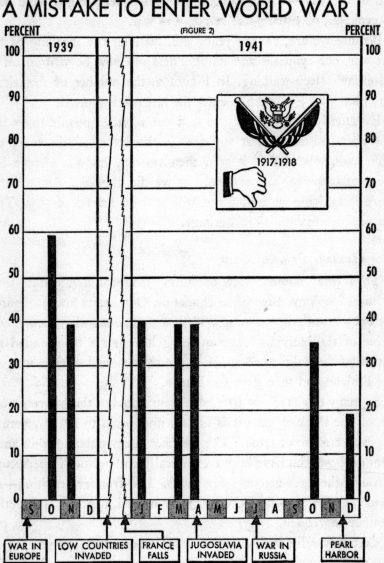

AMERICANS WHO THOUGHT IT
A MISTAKE TO ENTER WORLD WAR I

PERCENT   (FIGURE 2)   PERCENT

	1939		1941		

1917-1918

S O N D   J F M A M J J A S O N D

WAR IN EUROPE | LOW COUNTRIES INVADED | FRANCE FALLS | JUGOSLAVIA INVADED | WAR IN RUSSIA | PEARL HARBOR preceding Munich, this question was asked the American people: "Which do you think the world is most in need of today: greater economic security for the people of all nations, or more religion?" [4]

43%   felt that economic security was most important
37%   held the view that religion was of first importance
20%   had varied, miscellaneous opinions or were not sure

Suspicion of Foreign Powers

Suspicion of foreigners is natural in all communities. The very essence of social organization is that there is an in-group and an out-group and that the former is to be trusted and the latter not. So with nations. America being more isolated from contact with other countries—immigrants are not a substitute for day to day contacts with people of another nation—our suspicion of other countries was perhaps more distorting, less based on knowledge.

Specifically, our opinion of the future Axis and United Nations added an astigmatic blur to the world view which was to be our measuring instrument for assessing the chaos of the pre-war years. Of China we knew little—though we were sympathetic; certain it is that few considered her a great power. Our conception of Japan and her people was disdainful; they were ambitious imitators, energetic, secretive, and dangerous. Of Japan's war-like ideology we were only dimly aware. Our battleships could take care of Japan.

Our suspicion of the trio of Great Powers in Europe—Germany, Russia, and England—obscured our understanding of the part each was to play. The Hearst press and a generation of Red-baiters kept constantly alive the bogey of Communism and Russia. Toward England, the opinion of many years' standing prevailed: snobbish, imperialistic, out for her own ends. Hitler for a long time was either a matter of public unconcern or regarded as a foolish mountebank, presently to be overthrown by an indignant German people.

17

But again, our overall attitude toward the great foreign powers was more that of passive indifference than anything else. America was large enough to fill most of our minds. Interest in other countries, though in many cases it suffered from distortion, was not great.

Those, in brief, were the major dimensions of our thinking about international relations in the years which witnessed the incubation of World War II. Opinions are changing now. But they are not changing in a vacuum. Our new opinions are modifications of the old. We continue to reflect the American tradition—but in new ways. We are what we are for better or for worse. In the pages which follow we will be concerned with the specific manifestations of our deep-seated convictions and with changes in conviction. To understand American public opinion for what it is, the convictions behind it, its metamorphoses, the dimensions set down above must be taken as the bench marks by which permanence and change can be judged.

War Approaches

And so we faced the events that led to war. First came the Spanish Civil War—full dress rehearsal. In May, 1937, 79 per cent of the public felt that it made no difference to them which side won.[5] Nearly two years later, in December, 1938, when the Civil War had almost run its grisly course, 60 per cent were still indifferent about its outcome. The remaining minority was split three to one in favor of the Republic. After two years, then, only four in every ten Americans had taken sides.[6] Far from wanting to give aid, only 17 per cent of the voting public favored any changes in the Neutrality Act which might allow us to send arms to the Loyalists.[7] Spain was not the spark to set America off. Matters had not yet come close enough to home.

Spain was no special case. We were not ready to face the facts of Europe. The context from which our opinions took life was still

18

streaked with the hatred of war. The answer to the following question is characteristic of our thinking in the mid-thirties: "If one foreign nation insists upon attacking another, should the United States join with other nations to compel it to stop?" Does it seem out of character now that only slightly more than a quarter of us were prepared to see the United States join in sanctions against aggressor nations? [8] And of that minority who favored American intervention at that date, over two-thirds would have confined our activities to the non-military! [9]

The fact of the matter is, that of all the alternative ways of assuring our future national security, we were prepared to accept none of them. We did not want to arm; that smacked too much of war. We did not want to join the League, even if the League proved that it could work successfully. [10] We did not even believe, in 1937, that the dissolution of the League would make any difference to the future peace of the world. [11] We did not believe that it was the President's responsibility to try to interfere with the armament race going on in Europe. That was our feeling in 1937. [12] It was also our opinion in pre-war 1939. [13]

Looking back, there is something nightmarish about our reluctance to take action. We knew that Europe was heading for a showdown, that war was looming. We were refusing to take sides in the Spanish Civil War, but two-thirds of us were answering "yes" to the question, "Do you think there will be another World War?" [14] By the time we reached Munich, hardly more than a third of the nation thought that war in Europe could be put off for another year. [15] The pact at Munich only reinforced our conviction that a European war was in the offing. [16] Chamberlain may have believed Hitler when he said, "I have no more territorial ambitions in Europe." America did not. Less than one in ten were fooled. [17]

One myth had been shattered. We knew that there would be

war. But our blindness was too comforting to abandon. Yes, said America, war there will be, but not for us. That was the last barrier between inaction and action. In the relatively serene days of 1936, scarcely a third of the country thought that if there were another war the United States would become involved in it.[18] It was not until four months after the fall of France that the figure rose to the level of a majority. The story is told in Figure 3.[19]

Had we not been conditioned by our history to such a strong faith in our impregnability, in our geographical isolation, in the inherent stability of things political, perhaps we might have abandoned the notion that war did not threaten us. Because we did not see our own danger, we did not feel that the problems brewing in Europe needed a solution here. Why get entangled gratuitously in an affair which can only hurt one?

War Comes

And then war came. When it did, American sympathies were unerring. There had never been anything wrong with our sympathies where Germany was concerned. We hated the tyranny of fascism as we hated all tyranny. In spite of the best effort of the German Propaganda Ministry and its American outlets, no doubts about war guilt clouded the American mind. The overwhelming majority of the American people saw no justification in Hitler's claims to Danzig and the Polish Corridor; we were fed up with appeasement.[20-22] The fateful week of September 1, 1939, saw eight in every ten Americans place the blame for the war squarely on Germany.[23]

But sympathy is not action. After Poland we still did not want to get into the war.[24] Yet gradually, step by step, public thinking was changing.

What changed it? Certainly not Pearl Harbor alone. Was it a sense of military or economic expediency? Was it plain fright at

AMERICANS WHO BELIEVED
WE WOULD GET INTO WORLD WAR II

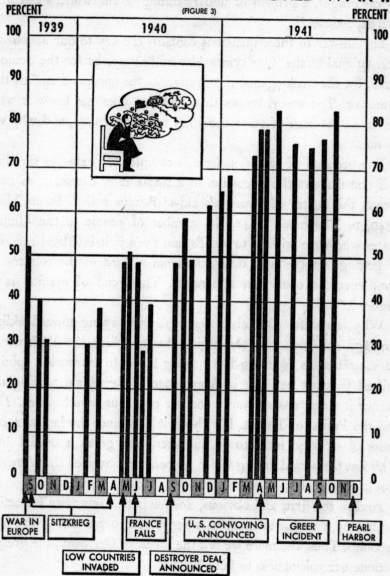

PERCENT (FIGURE 3) **PERCENT**

	1939	1940	1941	
100				100
90				90
80				80
70				70
60				60
50				50
40				40
30				30
20				20
10				10
0				0

S O N D J F M A M J J A S O N D J F M A M J J A S O N D

WAR IN EUROPE

SITZKRIEG

LOW COUNTRIES INVADED

FRANCE FALLS

DESTROYER DEAL ANNOUNCED

U. S. CONVOYING ANNOUNCED

GREER INCIDENT

PEARL HARBOR

what might come after a Nazi victory? Or was it a growth of ideo-logical insight, a growth of understanding of the world's essential interdependence?

The answer to these questions contains the key to our *actions* in international affairs. Our sympathies will always be for the democ-racies, for the weak against the strong, for the oppressed against the oppressor. The world knows that. What it does not know is why we act on the basis of our sympathies when we do act, and why we do not.

The problem of causation here is complex. It helps to simplify it if one narrows the discussion to a single case. Consider, as such a case, the matter of America's aid-to-Britain policy. From May, 1940, to November, 1941, the number of people in the United States who were willing to aid Britain even if it involved the risk of getting into the war, doubled—from a third of the country to some seven in every ten Americans. The trend of opinion is in Figure 4.[25]

Why the shift? One clue: the really big swing toward aiding England coincides with the period during which the Wehrmacht demonstrated its lightning-like striking power to the world; opinion shifted from 35 per cent in May, 1940, favoring aid to England even if it meant risking war, to 60 per cent four months later. This was the Period of Threat. For the first time since the last war, our sense of security, hitherto so unshaken, was given a crucial jolt. This was the period during which we became convinced that America would have to enter the war.

And so the first, and obvious, answer is that our taste for action catches up with our sympathies when we see our stakes in the pro-ceedings. Thus, the more we felt the threat of Germany, the greater became our willingness to help Britain.

Look inside the heads of those who favored and those who

22

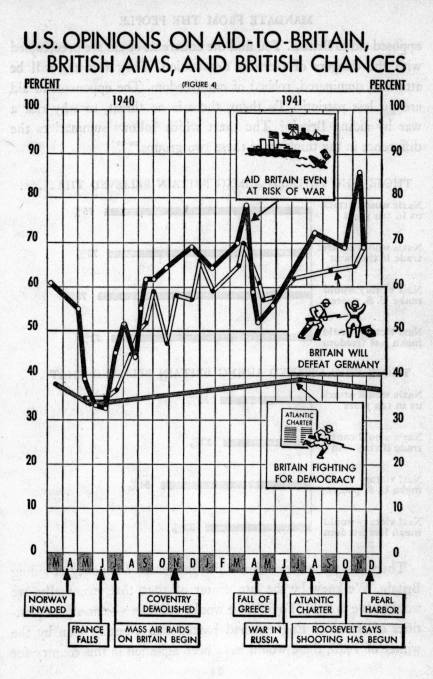

U.S. OPINIONS ON AID-TO-BRITAIN, BRITISH AIMS, AND BRITISH CHANCES

PERCENT   (FIGURE 4)   PERCENT

100   1940   1941   100
90   90
80   80
70   70
60   60
50   50
40   40
30   30
20   20
10   10
0   0

AID BRITAIN EVEN AT RISK OF WAR

BRITAIN WILL DEFEAT GERMANY

ATLANTIC CHARTER

BRITAIN FIGHTING FOR DEMOCRACY

M A M J J A S O N D J F M A M J J A S O N D

NORWAY INVADED

FRANCE FALLS

MASS AIR RAIDS ON BRITAIN BEGIN

COVENTRY DEMOLISHED

FALL OF GREECE

WAR IN RUSSIA

ATLANTIC CHARTER

ROOSEVELT SAYS SHOOTING HAS BEGUN

PEARL HARBOR

opposed aid to Britain. You find the adherents of aid are preoccupied with the dangers of German domination. They fear *we* will be attacked, dominated, robbed of our freedom. The opponents of aid are no less patriotic. To them, there is no threat, so why risk a war by aiding Britain? The chart which follows summarizes the difference in the thinking of these two groups.[26-29]

THOSE WHO FAVORED AIDING BRITAIN BELIEVED THAT . . .

Nazis would attack us in ten years	75%
Nazis would control trade if they won	73%
Nazi victory would make U. S. poorer	78%
Nazi victory would mean less freedom	72%

THOSE WHO OPPOSED AIDING BRITAIN BELIEVED THAT . . .

Nazis would attack us in ten years	33%
Nazis would control trade if they won	32%
Nazi victory would make U. S. poorer	54%
Nazi victory would mean less freedom	38%

There is a second condition which influenced our policy of aiding Britain. We knew by the late winter of 1940 that, eventually, we would have to fight. To fight we would need arms—enormous quantities of them. If England had looked like a beaten man by the winter of 1940, there would have been agitation in this country for withholding aid so that we might make ourselves stronger. Our concern was self-defense. Lindbergh and others among the isolationists tried to convince the public that the British were whipped, that our problem was to arm America. If they had succeeded, England might truly have been defeated. For, as Figure 4 illustrates dramatically, our desire to aid the British was firmly linked with our estimate of whether Britain was strong enough to help us— strong enough in short, to defeat the Nazis.[25, 30]

Thus far little has been said about Britain's war aims as a factor in hastening American intervention. Britain's ideological position in the war enlisted our sympathies; it did not, of itself, lead us into action. Certainly Britain's stated war aims had little to do with our willingness to aid her. In the crucial months during which we were rapidly becoming convinced that England must be helped, opinion on the nature of Britain's war aims changed not one whit (Figure 4).[25, 31]

Put it this way. Britain's war aims did not tip the balance of action. Yet had Britain not been ideologically what she is, nothing would have tipped it. From that point of view our action had its origin in sympathy; its catalyst was self-interest. Aristotle might have put it this way: ideology in American opinion is a material cause, self-interest an efficient cause of action. Ideological kinship was only one factor in the equation. Sympathy for England's plight during the blitz was another. But these need not be discussed here. They form the basis for a later chapter.

The best summary of why Americans grew to the belief that we must run the risk of getting into war by aiding England is presented by Americans themselves. In June, 1941, when the trend toward helping England had become well established, people who felt that we should aid England at the risk of war and those who were against such risks were asked for their reasons. Two facts emerged.

First, the majority of people who favored an aid-to-Britain policy did so for hard-headed, realistic, selfish reasons. Second, the non-interventionist sentiment was based primarily on traditional pacifist appeals that were applicable to any war at any time. But let the people speak for themselves.[25]

OF THOSE WHO FAVORED AID TO BRITAIN

5%	pointed to the economic advantages to us of an English victory
9%	talked about the ideological stakes in an English victory
68%	noted the military advantages of a "help Britain" policy, and
17%	gave other, miscellaneous reasons

OF THOSE WHO OPPOSED AID TO BRITAIN

2%	mentioned uncertain or questionable British war aims
9%	felt that aid was contrary to our economic self-interest
18%	contended that American isolation was the best policy for us
19%	pointed to the military disadvantages of aiding Britain
27%	based their position on a belief in pacifism as the best policy
25%	gave other, miscellaneous reasons

The case of England is not something special. It stands as an illustration of our hard-headedness in international affairs.

IN THE MIDST OF WAR

As we have gone deeper into war, have sensed its danger, our ardor for working with other nations against the common threat has increased. We have come a long way since 1936. But if we feel more strongly that we must stick together with our Allies, it is not the result of a new political philosophy of internationalism. The case of aid-to-Britain is applicable too to our new internationalism. If we have become convinced that our future security lies in a policy of collaboration with other countries, it is because of solicitude for our own security, not out of sympathy for others.

Our desires for action have changed much; our understanding of ideology has not. We have not repented for old sins. We still

26

think we were right. The difference is that the conditions which held in 1935 are no longer considered the conditions of the world today. Three years before Pearl Harbor only some two in every ten Americans, and these mainly the better educated, were willing to admit our failure to participate in the League as a cause of the European crisis.[32] Six months before Pearl Harbor the percentage was virtually unchanged.[33] One year after Pearl Harbor the same opinion prevailed.[34] We prefer instead the simple "devil theory" of war: the greed of Hitler and Mussolini caused it.[35] But that is the past. The present is different.

Today, we feel less secure, less isolated geographically. We know now that the safest protection is joint protection, collective security. But that is not, of itself, a new philosophy of internationalism. We still do not believe that there is something about internationalism which makes it *inherently* better than nationalism. Circumstances and not a change of heart have guided us.

What are we fighting for? People answer readily that we are fighting for freedom, liberty, and democracy. They say it with the sincerity of people who believe it. It is difficult to get behind the meaning of these words. It does no good to ask people what they mean. They have lived with the words so long that they can't define them any more. They feel them now as they have always felt them before—in the fringe of consciousness. The words are no longer revolutionary. They stand for the things we have had and want to keep. The same words were used by Americans in 1918, in 1898. They mean the same thing today.

But behind the words there is something else. We are not fighting for freedom and democracy and liberty because we want those symbols to be realized *everywhere*. We would be a happy nation if the world could exist as a free, equal, and democratic family.

27

But that is not why we went to war. We would not have waited for Pearl Harbor if that were the case.

We went to war because our security demanded it. To us this war is a crusade to regain that security and the freedom it gives us. We will not stop short at the end of the war. America knows now that it must work out a new formula for security at war's end. The old formula—staying out of world affairs—is no longer adequate. We are shopping for war-risk insurance and we mean to get it.

Our attitude toward the great "peace documents" of the war is symptomatic. We approve of all of them, to be sure; we are a people who believe in the extension of democracy. But none of the "documents" has captured the public mind. For none has been *the* simple guarantee of security.

Take, for example, the case of the Atlantic Charter. With the rest of the free world, America was thrilled by the epochal meeting at sea. It had élan. It captured our fancy. A few weeks after the meeting, in August, 1941, some three-quarters of the American people knew that a meeting had taken place and knew that a Charter of some sort had emerged.[36] Better than seventy million Americans had seen and heard. Five months later, polls discovered that less than a quarter of the American public claimed they had ever heard of the Atlantic Charter.[37] Tragically, only one in three of the enlightened few could name even one provision.[38]

This is not to say that we reject the Atlantic Charter. Decidedly we do not. The next two chapters will testify to that. Individual provisions of the Charter *are* supported by the majority—either because those provisions are humane or because they are convincing methods of ending war. But as for the Charter as a whole, we are not after an ideology; we are after the prevention of war. The document which will finally capture the American people is that one which spells out in simple terms how the next war is to be prevented. Such a document has yet to be written.

The same goes for the Four Freedoms—a simple credo in twelve words. Although only an infinitesimal fraction of the country would take exception to its four points, it has not, nevertheless, become a symbolic rallying cry for the future. It too was not a direct guarantor against war. Symbolically, freedom of speech and freedom of religion, though we believe in each deeply, do not have the freshness to kindle anew the convictions which by now are deep in our unconscious. Freedom from fear? Few of us have ever known the kind of fear to which the phrase refers. Freedom from want? It is what we want, yes, but neither it nor the other freedoms spell, in the mind of the average man, an end to wars.

The symbol which ignites us will have to be simple. It will have to be practical. It must not violate our humaneness. The manner in which we benefit will have to be crystal clear. It must spell the end of war. Anything short of that will have our sympathies, not our enthusiasm.

That, in bare outline, is the background to war, the road to peace, as we grasp it in America. It is a "majority" decision. It grows from the context of opinion which we were at pains to describe earlier in this chapter. Some of the details are unpretty. Some are not. Americans are not angels, nor are they profound scholars of political trends. If we count on them to be angels, we are fooling ourselves. Nor are the Americans any more selfish than other people. They are just people, suffering from all the shortcomings people normally exhibit.

To them, war is against something, not for something. The threat is the first mover. War is, straight and simple, a reaction to the threat. War accomplishes the removal of the threat. It is the last stage in a series of provocations; it is not the first step in a crusade. It is the denouement in a nightmare of insecurity. If there is an aim in war, it is a permanent removal of the threat of war.

When war is over, the task of removing the threat of war must continue. On that all are agreed. If the war itself is not a crusade, at least it is a lesson to us that past means of assuring peace have failed and that new devices must be forged. That is the task we must face when war comes to a close and the threat to our security is removed. Isolation, stability, security, morality—none of these is taken for granted as they were during the hypnotic '30s.

The war has convinced us that the world has shrunk and that there will always be threats—unless means are worked out to remove them. In lieu of a crusade for the international brotherhood of man, the war has created the conviction that all men—whether "international brothers" or not—must stick together for common protection.

How far that new realization has moved us will become apparent in the chapters which follow.

CHAPTER II

AMERICA IN WORLD POLITICS

IT is impossible to talk for five minutes about America's role in international politics after the war without bumping up against the urgent question, "But what about isolationism? Is America any less isolationist than she was before the war?" The question is misleading. There are as many "pure" isolationists now as there were just before Pearl Harbor. The bitter-end isolationists are still with us— still bitter though not so vocal. They never comprised more than 10 or 15 per cent of the American people. They are no more numerous now.

Nostalgic we were for the good old days when America was far removed from Europe's recurrent wars. And, likely, nostalgic we will remain. But once the majority of Americans realized that we must inevitably become involved in World War II, isolationism withered quickly. Be it recalled that well before Pearl Harbor we were ready and willing to use all means of war short of shooting.

The problem before Pearl Harbor and the problem now is not isolationism. It is, rather, the belief that we can be isolationists or interventionists—whichever is more expedient. In essence, it is the notion that we can be anything but internationalists. That pure and fervid isolationism which still burns so fiercely in men like Clare Hoffman and Hamilton Fish is not in the American people. When we are non-interventionists, it is for reasons of expediency. When we are internationalists, it is also for reasons of expediency.

31

And so if one should ask, "What are the dangers of the American people turning non-interventionist?" the answer is, "It depends upon whether we think it is worth our while to do so."

PARTICIPATION VERSUS NON-INTERVENTION

It can be said with as much emphasis as possible that *right now the great majority of Americans do not believe that it is to our advantage to be non-interventionist after this war.*

It can be said with equal emphasis that the props of non-intervention which sustained our pre-war attitudes are growing weaker with time. Two of those props—the belief in our impregnability and the sense of our geographical isolation—have been mauled by recent events to the point where they may be useless for the future.

There are auguries that our present position—"participationism" if you will—is growing stronger. Let us have a look at these signs.

1. Take first the matter of our appreciation of the role of other countries in fighting and winning the war. Were one to characterize a last-ditch isolationist, perhaps the first trait that would come to mind would be a callous disregard for what others are doing in the common fight. Strident voices of censure from the nationalist benches condemning Britain and Russia are too fresh in mind to need remark here. How far have we come? During June, 1943, when American armies were winning smashing victories in the Mediterranean and before Russia's 1943 Summer Offensive opened, three Americans thought Russia was doing most to win the war to every five who thought the United States was.[1] A nation of old-line isolationists just doesn't think in such terms.

2. Some will say, "Yes, the people are all in favor of joint action during the war and can be just as gracious as you please about the

work of their Allies. But what about after the war? How do I know they won't slide back into their old ways?" To this question there are several answers.

Given a new situation in which it appears to our self-interest to withdraw from the world, there is still much too good a chance that we *will* backslide. Right now, let it be said again and again, the bulk of the American people do not see the post-war situation in those terms. As *they* see the post-war world, our best bet is co-operation. The trend is clear-cut and requires no subtle interpretation. At regular intervals since Pearl Harbor, polls have been asking this question: "Which of these two things do you think the United States should try to do when the war is over—stay out of world affairs as much as we can, or take an active part in world affairs?" *Ever since Pearl Harbor, never fewer than two-thirds of America has favored taking an active part.* The trend can be found in Figure 1 on the page following.[2]

What people mean by "taking an active part in world affairs" has also gone through a healthy metamorphosis. In December, 1941, a cross-section of the country was asked whether they thought the United States should play a larger part, smaller part, or about the same part in world affairs as they did before the war. While Pearl Harbor was still smoking, 58 per cent voted for a larger part. A year and a half later, in June, 1943, the number of those voting for a larger part had increased to over three-quarters of the American public.[3]

Let it be said at the outset that as far as the will to take an active part in world affairs is concerned, there is no class, no region, which differs radically from the majority view. Political writers are too fond of talking about the "new nationalism" of the Midwest. The Midwest, to be sure, lags somewhat behind the country at large,

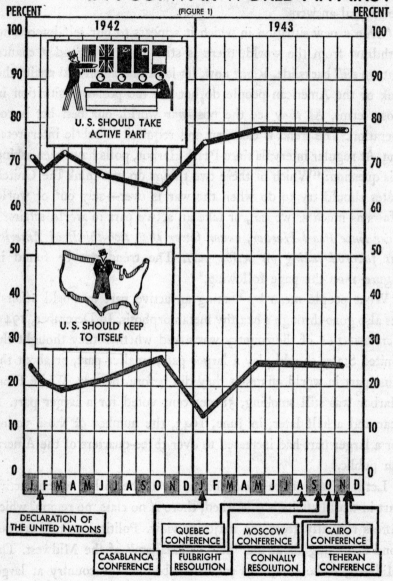

SHOULD U.S. TAKE ACTIVE PART IN POSTWAR WORLD AFFAIRS?

PERCENT   (FIGURE 1)   PERCENT

| 1942 | | 1943 |

U. S. SHOULD TAKE ACTIVE PART

U. S. SHOULD KEEP TO ITSELF

J F M A M J J A S O N D J F M A M J J A S O N D

DECLARATION OF THE UNITED NATIONS

CASABLANCA CONFERENCE

QUEBEC CONFERENCE

FULBRIGHT RESOLUTION

MOSCOW CONFERENCE

CONNALLY RESOLUTION

CAIRO CONFERENCE

TEHERAN CONFERENCE

but nationalism as it exists today is not isolationism. Consider these regional figures gathered during the early summer of 1943 in answer to the question whether we should take an active part in world affairs after the war.[4]

81% in New England favored taking an active part
80% on the West Coast
79% in the Mountain States
78% in the West Central States
76% in the South
76% in the Middle Atlantic States
71% in the East Central States

The same can be said for economic classes. The less well-off lag behind, but all are agreed. The poor too cast a majority vote in favor of post-war international activity for America.[5]

And what of Republicans and Democrats? The figures most emphatically do not bear out the traditional bogey of a rock-ribbed isolationist Republican Party. At no time since Pearl Harbor have Democrats and Republicans been on different sides of this issue. In Figure 2, on the next page, the trend of opinion among Republican and Democratic voters is compared.[6]

Opinions about our general role in world affairs are not, contrary to the fears of the faint-hearted, made of straw. People stick to their opinion even when you try to argue them out of it. In one survey during 1942 an attempt was made to do just that. Two arguments against post-war intervention were presented. Those who favored taking an active part were asked, first,

I. Have you ever considered the possibility that we might have to keep up a large army, navy, and air force at great expense to help police the world if we want to take an active part in world affairs? Do you think this expense would be justified?

And then, hitting below the belt,

PERCENT OF REPUBLICANS AND DEMOCRATS FAVORING POSTWAR INTERNATIONALISM FOR U.S.

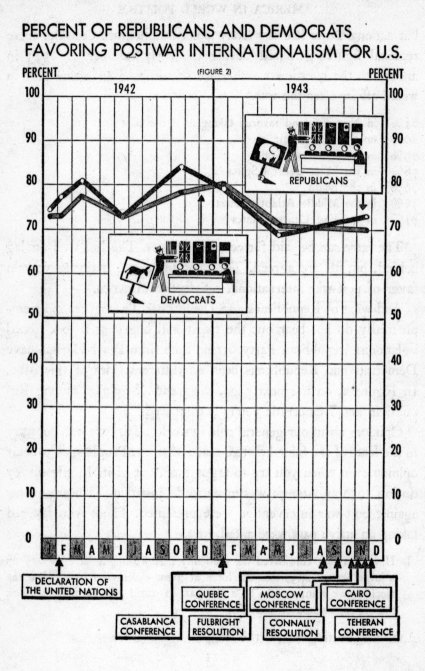

(FIGURE 2)

II. If our trade with other countries after the war gets us involved in entangling alliances and power politics, as Europe always has been, would
you still think it would be best to take an active part in world affairs?

What happens to those who favor taking an active part? [7]

93% still want to take an active part, regardless of the expense of an
international police force, and
61% still want international co-operation even if there is danger of "entangling alliances."

The same goes for those on the other side of the fence. Those
who favor staying out, favor staying out come hell or high water.
Two arguments against isolation were tried on the non-interventionists, with little success:

I. If it should happen that there is trouble and other nations get ready for
war, do you think we should stay out of world affairs then?
II. Suppose our standard of living is reduced when we try to get along on
what we grow and produce at home. Would you still think it would
be best to stay out of world affairs?

Here are the results of such suasion: [8]

57% of the isolationists want to stay that way even if a war threatens, and
61% still prefer isolationism even if it lowers our standard of living.

3. Finally, another clue to the fate of non-intervention. The very
essence of the isolationist dream is that everything will automatically
take care of itself if we just keep our fingers out of others' pies.
Translated into a post-war perspective, the frame of mind would
be that, quite passively, we should let the war come to an end and
then retire, by force of habit, behind the fences which shielded us
before. One need not stretch the argument to make the point that
the *one* thing a true isolationist would not want is action *now* to
commit us to international co-operation after the war.

Yet, in point of fact, the American people *do* want action now.

Attitudes have changed. Consider the difference in the climate of opinion of Summer 1942 and Summer 1943 as revealed by answers to the question, "Shall we plan the peace now or wait till after the war?" [9]

In Summer 1942 33% were in favor of planning the peace immediately
In Summer 1943 59% were in favor of planning the peace immediately

The desire for action is strong. Where there is a will to act, passive non-intervention cannot thrive.

Sentiment for immediate action has been validated in the voting booth. Although the event went unnoticed, in November, 1942, the voters in many of the counties of Massachusetts were asked to vote on this resolution:

> Shall the representatives in the General Court from this district be instructed to vote to request the President and Congress to call at the earliest possible moment a convention of Representatives of all free peoples to frame a Federal Constitution under which they may unite in a Democratic World Government?

Seventy-five per cent of those who voted did so in the affirmative. When a simplified version of the resolution was presented to a voting cross-section of the American public, 73 per cent of those with opinions were in favor of calling a conference now to plan the peace. Since that time, the figure has risen to 81 per cent.[10]

Finally, if further evidence of our desire for action before the end of the war be required, remember that months before Congress got around to voting on the Fulbright or Connally Resolutions, eight in every ten Americans had registered the wish that their Congressman vote for such resolutions.[11]

THE SHAPE OF INTERNATIONALISM

The question now is this: *How* will the United States participate in world affairs? It is no longer intervention versus non-intervention.

Will we participate as imperialists, as shrewd traders, as co-operators, as brigands, as suckers? How? Further, participate in what kind of international set-up? On what terms? With whom?

First off, it is important not to be excessively ambitious about an answer to these questions. Much of the press and radio discussion of "world plans" has gone unnoticed by the man in the street. As a nation we are not well-informed about the machinery necessary for a peaceful world order. Our habits of thought about foreign affairs are not guided by a long and honorable record of participation in world councils. In a very real sense we are starting from scratch, and, like most novices, are still learning the fundamentals.

One of the fundamentals which most Americans have learned—and apparently learned well—is that there can be no international order without some international body to compose differences between nations. Ask the nation whether it is better for two countries to try to settle their differences between themselves, or better to submit differences to some international body. Sentiment is overwhelmingly in favor of the latter.[12] Yet, only a few years ago, the majority of us believed that understandings between individual strong nations were a better guarantee of peace than an organization of nations.[13]

World Confederation

Today there is no doubt that, were a national referendum held, the American people would vote overwhelmingly in favor of American participation in some sort of league of nations. By the early fall of 1943 only 13 per cent of the American public were opposed to the idea of America's participating in a world confederation. The stability of American opinion during the year from September, 1942, to February, 1944, is shown in Figure 3 on the next page.[14]

SHOULD U.S. PARTICIPATE IN A POST-WAR INTERNATIONAL ORGANIZATION?

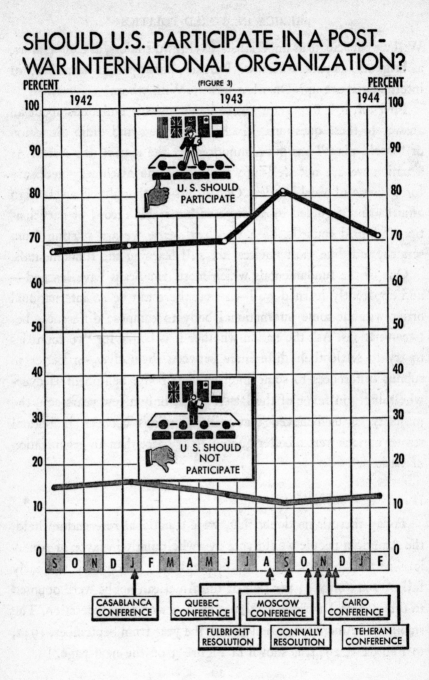

(FIGURE 3)

Although the better educated are considerably more internationally minded, the will to co-operate with a union of nations is predominant on all educational levels.[15]

92% of those with college education favor an international organization,
83% of those with high school training, and only
69% of those with grade school education.[15]

Of course, there are ways and ways of aligning oneself with an international organization. Someday some Senator will get up and say that the American people want to give the new world organization their moral support but abhor getting "entangled" with it. He will be wrong. Our people want real participation, not "moral" participation. When the public is given a chance to choose between moral and real participation, they go better than two-to-one for the latter.[16] The leaders of American industry commit themselves even more strongly on the issue—better than three-to-one.[17] We are not talking morals; we mean the real business.

Generally speaking, the conditions of power under which Americans would be willing to enter the league are not prohibitive. Although, as we shall see vividly later in this chapter, Americans ask for a big *quid pro quo* in their negotiations with other countries, they do not conceive of the league as an exclusive hunting preserve for America's international ambitions. In January, 1943, Americans were asked whether they would be willing to join on the condition that the United States had the same power as Britain, Russia, and Germany.[18]

62% favored joining even if Britain had as much say as the U. S.
55% favored joining even if Russia had as much say as the U. S. but only
28% favored joining if Germany had an equal say in the league's affairs.

Aside from the condition of equality with Germany (and only four people in ten would approve of Germany's immediate entry into the league anyway) the majority of the American public is willing to enter a world organization on equal terms with its major allies.

It is, to be sure, too early to find out in detail what the American people want from the new world organization. In large measure they don't know. How could they know? They have never been here before. But it doesn't take much questioning to discover that they want something with teeth. Regulation of armament? Emphatically yes.[19] Almost three-quarters of us are even willing to grant the union some power over the size of our own army, navy, and air force.[20]

Promulgation of international law? Again, emphatically yes.[21] Regulation of international commerce? The same thing.[22]

Does all this mean that we are as ready to yield on cases as we are on principle? Probably not. A realistic appraisal of opinion would have to include the statement that there is a long gap between principles and practice and that adherence to the former is not necessarily acceptance of the latter. We will kick when there is an attempt to regulate *our* armaments, *our* commerce, *our* habits of international intercourse. Of course. But bear one point in mind. *We do adhere to the principles.* There was a time not so long ago when we did not. The extent to which public information clarifies the meaning of principles in concrete terms will determine how ready we are to go along with the practices dictated by those principles. If information and education persist in being spotty and abstract and casual, the principles of internationalism to which we now adhere will have about the same meaning as "Love Thy Neighbor." Our leaders can inflame us to action. They can also let us slip back into sententious solipsism. Theirs is the burden of proof.

Critics of the public never tire of saying that Americans will favor a world league as long as the sailing is smooth and the sacrifices minor. We are, according to this school of thought, fair-weather internationalists. Any world plan which requires sacrifices on our part, the argument goes, will scare us off. At very best, this notion is but a half-truth. True, there are some sacrifices we are not yet willing to make—we do not understand the necessity of many of these. But the blanket statement that we will not sacrifice for international union is presumptuous. People all over the country have been asked whether they would be willing or unwilling to try out a league after the war if it meant doing such things as staying on food rations, paying higher taxes, having some of our army overseas for policing duties. These were the reactions.[23]

PER CENT OF AMERICANS WILLING TO MAKE THESE SACRIFICES TO HELP A UNION OF NATIONS GET STARTED

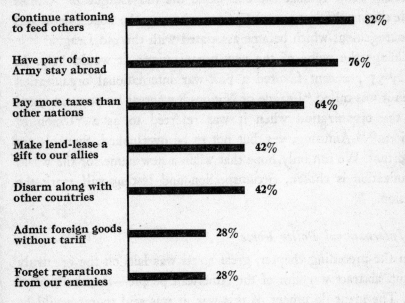

Continue rationing to feed others	82%
Have part of our Army stay abroad	76%
Pay more taxes than other nations	64%
Make lend-lease a gift to our allies	42%
Disarm along with other countries	42%
Admit foreign goods without tariff	28%
Forget reparations from our enemies	28%

Notice one fact about these figures. People are ready to make personal sacrifices—high taxes, rationing, having our boys stay overseas. But they are not yet ready to give up the traditional paraphernalia of international relations—war debts, reparations, tariff walls. Why not?

Reparations and war debts are the only terms in which Americans have been taught to think about immediate post-war problems. If our thinking about these problems is traditional, it is because nobody in a position of leadership has suggested an alternative. We will go on being traditionalists until someone thinks it worth while to tell us why the traditional methods have failed in the past. Certainly Germany can pay stiff reparations. Why not? Why should we let England keep all the money we've "given" her? Why should *we* make all the sacrifices?

The inevitable traditionalism of public thinking raises yet another problem. How combat the bad name the old League of Nations made during the last peace? Can we overcome the hopelessness and discouragement which became associated with the old League? [24]

Change the name of the new organization? It would help. In 1942, 55 per cent favored a post-war international organization when it was called "League of Nations," whereas 70 per cent voted for the organization when it was referred to as a "Union of Nations." [25] Amusing, yes, but not to be overlooked. Symbols are important. We can only hope that when a new name for the world organization is chosen, circumspection and testing will mark the occasion.

An International Police Force

In the preceding chapter, great stress was laid on the one truly potent, abstract war aim of the American people—the abolition of war. The great document of this war, it was said there, would be the one that contained the simple, classical formula for preventing war. It is, to be sure, too early to tell whether that formula has yet emerged. Such things have a way of coming into public consciousness gradually. The police force doctrine has undoubtedly come closest to it. It is simple. So familiar is it that people need hardly understand in order to approve. The very expression, "international police force," contains all the proper elements. It is "international" —affecting all nations. It is a "police," connoting an order more than casually enforced by good will. The police symbol implies keeping aggressors in line. It deals with the prevention of war in the concrete. It is active, American. It avoids the pitfalls of discredited disarmament. It is, in short, the most potent international symbol the American people have yet been shown.

By the end of 1943, three-quarters of the American public were ready to throw their support behind an international police force. The trend of opinion is shown in Figure 4 on the next page.[26]

The police force doctrine claims special support from no particular class. It has a striking universality.[27]

78% of the upper socio-economic class favor a police force,
80% of the middle class,
80% of the lower middle, and
74% of the lowest socio-economic stratum.

In the light of what has been said once in the course of this chapter about the insignificance of rank-and-file political differences on matters of international co-operation, it is not surprising that there is only a slight divergence in sentiment between Republicans and Democrats.[28]

80% of Democratic voters favor a police force, while
75% of Republican voters also favor it.

Again, we mean the real business. Most Americans have no very clear idea of how an international police force works, granted. Interviewers reports that fact time and again. Popular definitions of the term are vague. But we are for it in the same way as we

SHOULD UNITED NATIONS ESTABLISH POSTWAR INTERNATIONAL POLICE FORCE

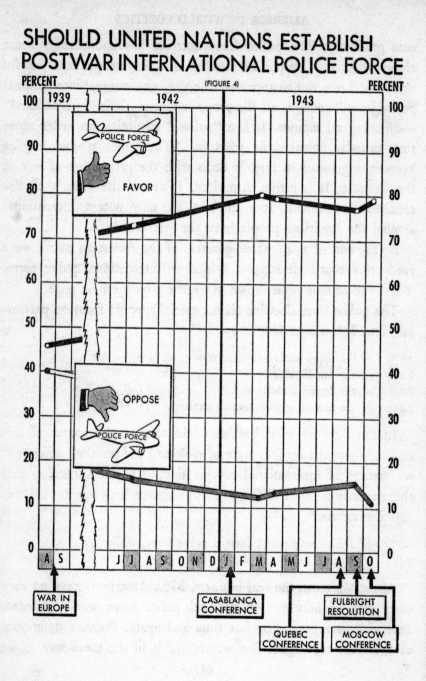

(FIGURE 4)

are for vaccination. Neither vaccination nor international policing is fully understood. Each in its own way, however, is a specific against an evil. Force stops aggression. Vaccination stops small pox. Never mind the niceties.

Consider this sample of what people envisage as a police force. People were given three alternative plans for policing—ranging from the innocuous to the two-fisted.

I. Police only the Axis.
II. Police the Axis and small countries.
III. Police all countries including the United States, Russia, and England.

Which one? The results leave little room for misinterpretation.[29]

Police Axis only	9%
Police Axis and small countries	11%
Police world including the U. S.	76%
No opinion	4%

Nor do we view the international police force as a combination of a few strong powers. It is more than that. All the countries must participate. This is a United Nations show. Ask people whether all the countries fighting the Axis should take a hand in policing or whether some countries should be excluded. This is what you find.[30]

88% vote for participation by all countries,
 7% would exclude some particular country (though not more than two per cent agree on any one country), and
 5% have no opinion on the matter.

But one cannot go far in a discussion of international policing without coming point blank to the problem of international versus national armament. Does a grant of power to an international police force mean that we must give up our own arms? If so, how do the people feel about it?

National Armament and International Police

If it can be said that the doctrine of international policing is a "natural" as far as American thinking is concerned, it can be said as flatly that the plea for disarmament is the black sheep among international plans thus far proposed. Stating the matter bluntly, the American people have no intention whatever of giving up the bulk of our massive armament after the war. When 87 per cent of a people are unanimous on a point, you can be sure they are serious. And 87 per cent of the American people want to keep a substantial Army, Navy, and Air Force after the war.[31]

Nothing attests better the strength of our desire to stay well armed than results obtained on a trend question asked regularly during the first half of 1943. Men and women all over the country were queried, "After the war is over, do you think every able-bodied young man should be required to spend one year in the Army, Navy, or Air Force when he reaches military age?" To those who still remember the stormy battle over the Selective Service Act in 1940, the proportion of Americans in favor of compulsory military service will come as a surprise (Figure 5).[32]

One need not hunt long for the causes of our grim will for preparedness. The unnerving effect of Pearl Harbor is too fresh in mind. The whole burden of criticism which befell our leaders in the dark year following Japan's attack rested on the charge of unpreparedness. We were, as many a person interviewed in the week after Pearl Harbor put it, "caught with our pants down." Our will to stay armed to the teeth now is, in large measure, the long shadow of December 7th.

SHOULD U.S. HAVE ONE YEAR COMPULSORY MILITARY SERVICE AFTER THE WAR?

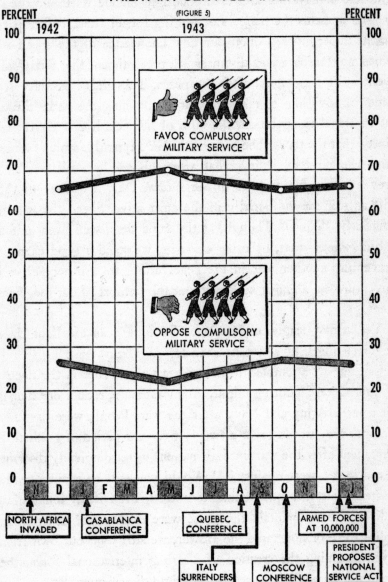

(FIGURE 5)

PERCENT — 1942 — 1943 — PERCENT

FAVOR COMPULSORY MILITARY SERVICE

OPPOSE COMPULSORY MILITARY SERVICE

NORTH AFRICA INVADED

CASABLANCA CONFERENCE

QUEBEC CONFERENCE

ARMED FORCES AT 10,000,000

ITALY SURRENDERS

MOSCOW CONFERENCE

PRESIDENT PROPOSES NATIONAL SERVICE ACT

More basic reasons compel us too. We have seen the world shrink.
The rise of airpower and breathtakingly mobile warfare have impressed upon us the dangers of waiting for an attack before parry-
ing it. Superimposed upon our new knowledge of the speed with
which war strikes across distances is a presentiment that today's dire
events will come again after the peace. Though, as we have seen,
America is willing to take a try at maintaining the peace through
international co-operation, the bulk of her people are not yet convinced that the try will be successful. Ask a typical sample of Americans whether they believe that after this war we will be able to
prevent other major wars in the future. Only a quarter of them
will answer unconditionally in the affirmative. Six in ten will tell
you flatly, "No." [33] Though, at the same time, well over half the
public believes that, by using our wits, we stand a good chance of
preventing another war in the near future, we are not yet ready
to venture out alone at night without the comfort of our own armament.[34]

Yes, a new league and a police force have an excellent chance
of succeeding. But why take chances?

One survey attempted to discover whether belief in the doctrine
of international policing might, in any measure, reduce our demand
for a large Army and Navy after the war. People were first asked
whether they would favor a twenty-five-year period of gradual disarmament after the war until all nations were completely disarmed.
Seven in ten were against it.[35] Would you still be against gradual
disarmament, the questioning continued, even if an international
police force to maintain the peace were established? International
police force or not, came the answer, we still want our own Army.
Even assuming the creation of a strong international force, then,
six in ten were still opposed to American disarmament.[36]

Is the American view of the matter a contradiction? Can you want a strong international army while wanting at the same time to stay armed to the teeth yourself? If that be a contradiction, then Winston Churchill is guilty of the same contradiction. Has he too not espoused both the maintenance of the armies we have built and the use of international force? The crux of the matter, I believe, is that nobody is ready to give up his nation's arms until some proven substitute for security against aggression is forthcoming. We expect other wars. We know that the weight of our arms saved us from disaster this time. We *do not* know whether an international police *can* turn the trick. We want to try it. But when you put up a new fence around a penitentiary, you put it outside the old one and tear down the old fence only when the new one is in working order. Can we be expected, the people argue, to tear down our inside fence first?

That is where we stand. Our position most emphatically does not mean that we don't want a police force, that we would prefer to rely on our own resources. Nor does it mean that we want to be the predominant military power with the police force in a secondary role. No, we want plenty of power everywhere so long as that power is pledged to the keeping of peace and not to the making of war.*

How else can you interpret people's opinions on the power of the police force? Adherents of policing, asked whether they thought the international police should be more or less powerful than the

* In the light of prevailing sentiment on the matter of national armament, it is probable that the most satisfactory policing arrangement would be one in which "national contingents" were pledged to the support of orders issued by a joint international council whose function was the enforcement of peace. Such an arrangement would satisfy our desire for national arms while, at the same time, serving as an international agency for preventing war. A suggestion such as this goes by way of being a hunch, for, in point of fact, the man in the street not only doesn't know what kind of police force he wants, but hardly knows what alternative plans are available.

armies of the United States after the war, gave the following answers.[37]

32% thought a police force should be stronger than U. S. Army,
25% thought it should be of the same strength as U. S. Army,
20% thought it should be weaker than U. S. Army, and
23% had no opinion.

If we were so hell-bent on looking after our own military problems unaided, surely more than a quarter of us would want to relegate the international police force to a position of power subordinate to our own. The figures speak for themselves.

America's Territorial Demands

So much for the organization of the peace. How about the "spoils of war?" How does America's rather common-sense internationalism based so strongly on practical self-interest express itself on the matter of territory after the war? The first thing that can be said—and with strong emphasis—is that when Americans think of our own territorial demands after the war, the major premise is military protection. There are two camps and two only—those who want island bases after the war as a protection against future attack, and those who think we should get no new territory at all after the war. *There is no major segment of opinion demanding territory for our economic gain.* The concept of warfare for expanding the size of empire is dead—in the United States at least.

Insofar as the demand for territory stems from a desire for military protection, it is a counterpart, an extension, of America's desire to keep a large army and navy after the war. In one major respect, however, the demand for new bases differs sharply from the dream of huge armaments: it is not nearly so strong nor so universal. New bases, unlike a large military force, do not loom as an obvious means of protection. The reactions of a cross-section of Americans to various territorial proposals appear below. At regular intervals for over a year thousands of Americans were presented with these four proposals for America after the war.

"Which of these four statements comes closest to what you think the United States should do about new land and possessions in the world after the war?"

  I. The U. S. should give up all land outside of the U. S. which is difficult to defend.
 II. The U. S. should be satisfied with the amount of land she had in the world before she entered the war.
III. The U. S. should try to get new military bases but nothing else.
 IV. The U. S. should try to get as much new land in the world as she can.

These are the results of the last questionings. They show no substantial shift from eighteen months earlier.[38]

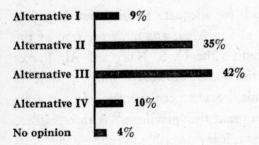

Alternative I	9%
Alternative II	35%
Alternative III	42%
Alternative IV	10%
No opinion	4%

To be sure, opinion on our territorial course after the war is far from crystallized. The issues are still vague. Yet there is good reason to believe that, at least as far as the Pacific is concerned, the demand for new bases may grow stronger rather than weaker. Bloody battles for Pacific islands, it is reasonable to believe, will make these islands symbolic of our struggle for security against Japan. Already Guadalcanal has become such a symbol. The majority of Americans do not regard it as part of the British Empire but as "our" Guadalcanal. Consider our bloody battles for Japanese mandated islands. It is doubtful whether we would be willing to give up the Marshalls to some other power after the war when we have paid the price of wresting them from Japan. Though opinion is not yet crystallized, it is likely that we will face a strong demand for Pacific bases after the war. The Cairo Declaration, unofficial statements by Secretary Knox and others, possibly "inspired" articles in the *Army-Navy Journal* about post-war bases in the Pacific—all these things make it seem unlikely that our demands will be frustrated.

At this early date it is, of course, impossible to try to gauge the reaction of other Pacific powers to our demands. The course of Pacific diplomacy is not, indeed, within the limits of this book. Yet, one passing comment on the role of public opinion in one of the Pacific powers is germane. Australia, at least, is relative sympathetic to America's demands for adequate Pacific bases. In a poll conducted throughout Australia in May, 1943, 77 per cent of the Australian public favored letting the U. S. Navy and Air Forces use Australian bases after the war.[39] However, when it came to *giving* these bases to the United States permanently only a quarter of Australians were ready to grant that privilege.[40] Although these figures are not easy to interpret, it is reasonable to suppose that Australian willingness to let America use her harbors and airfield augurs well for Australia's future reactions to America as a close island neighbor in the Antipodes—assuming, of course, that we demand no transfer of Australian territory to the American flag.

On the broader matter of American opinion on territorial readjustment elsewhere in the world, all that can be said at present is that we have not made up our minds one way or another on the complex issues involved. Detailed public opinion questioning yields only high "no opinion" returns.

What material there is, nevertheless, is interesting in one respect. It indicates rather clearly that in the realm of boundary disputes, most Americans have no axes to grind—not even the traditional one of autonomy for small countries. Late in 1942, Americans were asked whether they felt that the creation of such small countries as Lithuania, Latvia, Czechoslovakia, Poland, etc., was, in the light of subsequent events, a good idea or a bad idea. While six in every ten held that it was a bad idea, only three in ten stood up for the Versailles theory or small nation autonomy. The remainder had no opinions one way or another.[41] Americans, at least, will have few demands to make (see Chapter VI for a discussion of the Russo-Polish boundary dispute).

There is one influential school of thought which holds that American opinion on participation in world affairs can be turned very sour indeed at the first evidence of land-grabbing by a European power. Specifically, it has been said that if Russia is granted her demand for the Baltic states and Bessarabia, the old stereotype of wars as selfish European struggles for power would be reactivated and with the reactivation would come American disillusionment. No sane observer of the public would doubt that indiscriminate grabbing might turn us away from participation in world councils. That much, I think, can be taken for granted. But if a prediction on the basis of what we already know of public opinion is in order, it would have to take the form of a demurrer. The American ego is not involved in the "border-line" Baltic states today. Their disposition does not concern most Americans. What the faint-hearted should fear is that *any* territorial readjustment in Europe may be turned into capital by those who have been trying unsuccessfully for twenty years to find good occasions for souring us on world affairs. Russia and the Baltic states are no special case.

DOMINANCE AND SOVEREIGNTY

Thus far we have discussed the general trend toward international co-operation and the specific channels through which this trend has come to express itself. Two matters of the most vital importance we have touched scarcely at all. The first of these is the matter of dominance. Do Americans want to be top dog in the international order which they foresee after the war? Top dog in what way? Secondly, will our will to co-operate—even our will to dominate—be dampened by the fear that internationalism means the demise or lessening of America's sovereignty?

First, the matter of dominance. Any statesman who assumes that America will play ball with a world organization without wanting, at the same time, a goodly share of power is, to put it mildly, poorly informed. True, as the figures quoted earlier in this chapter indicate, we are willing to enter a new league on equal footing with Russia and England. But consider for a moment the role Americans expect to play in the post-war world.

First take the matter of which nation *should* play the most important part in world affairs after the war. Ask a typical cross-section of Americans the question, and then repeat it in the British Isles. This is what you will find.[42]

82% of the American public say that U. S. *should* play the leading role, and
43% of the British public say that Britain *should* lead.

So much for wishes. What about expectations? [43]

60% of the American public think the U. S. *will* lead, and
30% of the British public think that Britain *will* lead.

In short, to stretch a statistic into fanciful rhetoric, America wants to dominate twice as much as Britain and expects to twice as hard.

Consider the matter from a slightly different perspective. How do Americans think the four major powers will emerge from this war, stronger or weaker? Of America, three people in every four think we will be greater after the war than we were before it. Of Russia and China, about half foresee more power for those two nations. Where Britain is concerned, only a quarter of us see a more powerful Britain after the war.[44] Not only do we think that we should be dominant and that we will be dominant—we believe firmly that we will have the wherewithal to demand it.

It is, in a sense, vain to deplore this evidence of strong animal spirits in the American public. Traditionally, whenever America tackles a new task—and international collaboration is a new task for America—she sets her sights high. Doing a good job means playing a dominant role. Given the American competitive tradition, playing a leading role does not mean stepping on your neighbor's neck. It means a chance to have a real say, a chance to "show your stuff."

And, to be sure, we *will* be playing a dominant role after the war. Whether we participate intimately or not, our position makes such a role inevitable. From that point of view, there is nothing in the political future which spells thwarting of our desire to lead.

The question, then, boils down to the manner in which we will execute our part. Everything said so far in these pages indicates that, politically at least, we will want to play the lead within the framework of an organized world authority to which we will belong. Should such an organization fail to materialize, then our will to dominate—which will not be easily diminished—may take other, less collaborative expression. Of that we will speak in more detail at the close of this chapter.

Now what of "sovereignty"? Does our desire for dominance imply that we will jealously guard our "national sovereignty"? In the first place, it is doubtful whether the average man thinks in terms of national sovereignty. The "sense of sovereignty," like most political abstractions, is a subtle phenomenon when translated to the level of public opinion. Of our "sense of sovereignty" these things can be said.

1. The "sense of sovereignty" is not a conscious attitude in the same sense as is one's opinion of Russia. Under normal circumstances we take our sovereignty for granted and, unlike the fascist states, spend little time worrying about it. Properly speaking, the sense of sovereignty is a frame of reference, a background factor in our thinking, that rarely expresses itself directly.

2. The "sense of sovereignty" comes to the fore and dominates our thinking only when we are in an insecure position—attacked or threatened. Only when we feel that there is danger of losing them do we shout loud and hard about our sovereign rights.

3. The issue of sovereignty never appears in a vacuum. It is always related to some specific proposal—a joint board for the control of air commerce, an international police force, or what not. Where the merits and demerits of a specific proposal are known to the public in sufficient detail, the danger of a dispute entirely in terms of "sovereignty versus loss of sovereignty" is lessened. It is obvious that when an issue is debated in terms of keeping or losing our sovereignty, the first alternative will prevail. If, on the other hand, a proposal alleged to threaten our sovereignty can be discussed on its intrinsic merits and a good case made out for it, the question of losing sovereignty may never arise. And if it should, it can be counterbalanced by the benefits to be gained by adopting the proposal in question. Those benefits can be known only if the proposal is understood.

Sumner Welles spoke with common sense before the Foreign Policy Association when he remarked, "I can see no advantage to be gained at this moment by any general and theoretical discussion of the advantages or disadvantages obtaining to the United States by the limitations upon its sovereignty which it might undergo were it to participate in an international organization. Such a discussion, it seems to me, can only benefit those who are opposed to our taking part in any form of international co-operation and who desire by confusing the real issues, to engender public doubt and prejudice. Until we have determined exactly what form of world organization we believe should in our own interest be instituted, how can we tell what, if any, limitations such an organization might impose upon our sovereignty? . . . Would it not be wiser before entering into any impassioned debate upon the abstract question of sovereignty to wait and see what each proposed agreement involved and then weigh the advantages to be derived by us from such instruments against any attendant limitation upon our national freedom of action?"

The matter stands in just those terms. The crux is to weigh our specific self-interest against the abstract disadvantages of limiting freedom of action. Why the present concern? Have we not, after all, limited our sovereignty thousands of times during the last one hundred years with both broad and narrow treaties? Has the problem of sovereignty *per se* beaten us in most cases before?

Today, we want peace and order. We want it, and others who have been seared more profoundly by the war want it still more. The price we pay for the limitation of an abstract sovereignty is small compared to the gains. If the people of America are told that fact often enough and simply enough, there is no reason why the question of sovereignty should be any more serious than it has been in nine out of every ten treaties we have negotiated in the past.

Certainly every scrap of evidence that polls have collected during the past year indicates that the question of sovereignty is no particular obstacle to participation in a world order. Not only are the majority of Americans willing, as mentioned a moment ago, to back an international police force with power to police us; they are, moreover, willing to grant that police force at least parity with our own armed forces.

If that willingness does not clinch the issue of whether we fear encroachments on our sovereign domain, consider this. "Do you think a strong police force would be a threat to the United States," a survey asked a cross-section of Americans.[45]

26%   thought the police force might threaten us,
61%   could not see that a police force would be a threat, and
13%   had no opinion on the issue.

Sovereignty, for all that we have tried to make of it, is just not the bogeyman some have insisted.

Of course there are situations which will inflame our feelings of sovereignty. That much all will admit. The basic situation which can turn the trick is insecurity, nurtured by a background of ignorance of the issues involved. Should we feel threatened, it is reasonable to suppose that many will want to draw back to a sole dependence on our own resources. Consider the difference, for example, among those who, on the question discussed immediately above, felt that a police force might threaten us and those who did not. Of the small group of fearfuls, only 56 per cent favored establishment of a policing authority, in contrast to 89 per cent of the far larger group who disallowed a threat to the U. S.[46] Fear is what we must fear.

THE CANONS OF CAUTION

Thus far, the picture we have painted has been, by and large, a cheering one for those who believe that America's destiny lies with the world. It would be, however, a breach of caution and good sense to end on a note of optimism. Public opinion does not, *sui generis,* create its own laws. America wants a place in the world. That much is true. She will not be satisfied with a return to classical isolation—even if such a return were possible. But it is doubtful if America wanted the sort of post-war role wished upon her by a minority of senators after the last war.

Naturally, the gravest danger at war's end is that the leaders of the American people will block the public will. America has a group which makes up in vocality what it lacks in numbers. We know that it can muster support in the Senate dangerously close to "one-third plus one." If internationalism is defeated, the people are too. Public ardor is always at its maximum before an issue has been settled. After the fact, it has a way of dissipating. If the public will is thwarted, we will all regret—"but what can we do?"

The answer is not simple. The *New York Times* has committed itself to the position that our present system of treaty ratification is outmoded. The majority of voters in the United States would, if presented with the issue at the ballot box, vote to have a majority of both houses of Congress ratify treaties.[47] It is almost too late to set in motion the elaborate machinery by which we amend the Constitution. But if there is time, let us do it. If not, let us do it after the war anyway, so that the danger may be forever annulled.

But a senatorial reversal of the popular trend is not, by any means, the only danger. The American people can well undo themselves. Lacking a deep understanding of the mechanics of international collaboration, we can still be confused out of our present position. And there are many who will try to confuse us. War debts, international bankers, war guilt, perfidious Albion—the subtreasury of confusion is there for the using.

Were America's leadership more vigorous in combating the danger, the problem would be relatively academic. But virtually every opportunity to solidify and crystallize opinion for international participation has been missed. In place of a vigorous resolution on our post-war role, the Senate, with the implicit blessings of the other end of Pennsylvania Avenue, gave the country a watered-down statement that could mean all things to all men. Are we, as many fear, to wait till the last moment before organizing the public for the inevitable fight? If we are—and our past behavior affords no other hope—then the danger of a country confused to the point of apathy and disillusion is still real.

If confusion is a danger in the short-run, our greatest long-term danger is the failure of Americans to understand their self-interest in international collaboration. Public support for international issues stands or falls with our conception of the *quid pro quo*. To know that we want an end to war and that internationalism promises that end more plausibly than nationalism is only a beginning. The simple convictions of the man in the street may not be deep enough nor differentiated enough to withstand the assault of those casuists who are already questioning America's possible rewards from international participation. It is no accident that the bitterest scorn of the diehard isolationists who voted against the Fulbright and Connally Resolutions was reserved for the proposition that our self-interest lay in co-operation with other nations.

What of the much-talked-of "return to normalcy"? It too is a danger; but in no sense is it either inevitable or automatic. Regression to isolationism after the last war was not of the people's fashioning. Isolation was a legislative *fait accompli* which people accepted because there was nothing else to do about it. We were disillusioned. But it was not inevitable that we should have been disillusioned.

A "return to normalcy" is not out of the question this time. But it is wrong to assume that it *has* to take place. Regression can be accelerated by certain circumscribed conditions. So too, if these conditions are kept under control, the danger can be by-passed.

Perhaps the first condition, least controllable, is fatigue. We will be tired after the war. But fatigue is a relative thing. The business-man who is tired after a day's work suddenly finds himself fresh when faced with the pleasant prospect of a half hour of handball before dinner. In combating fatigue, the most important precaution is to see that there is a new and different and clearly defined activity to which to turn after leaving the old. If planning the peace can be made such a new, different, and clearly defined activity, the dangers of regression will be immeasurably decreased.

But peace planning cannot serve as an anti-fatigue measure unless certain psychological conditions are fulfilled. First, peace planning must not awaken the insecurity of the American people. We must not be made to feel that we are being threatened, economically, for example, by our former allies. As soon as insecurity enters, the will to co-operate with others, to participate in joint planning, will be sapped by the desire to withdraw to safety. Recrudescence of anti-Russian and anti-British propaganda at the end of the war is consummate psychological sabotage. To be brutally realistic about the matter, we had better expect that post-war anti-allied propa-ganda *will*, in some measure, dampen our will to work jointly and to try new solutions.

A second, extremely dangerous stimulus to regression is confu-sion. If post-war negotiations get hopelessly confused by a welter of incomprehensible issues (incomprehensible from the American point of view), the inevitable reaction will be a demand for the familiar. Crystal-clear information and a well-informed public are the two most dependable foes of confusion. It is hopeless to expect that both these conditions will be fully met. Realistically again, we can expect provocation to "normalcy" from this quarter.

The press has a grave responsibility in keeping post-war issues unmuddied. For it has within its power the means of confusion as well as the means of clarity. The lamentable journalistic practice, so often witnessed during the war, of creating "issues" and "conflicts" and "differences" for the sake of making news, can cause only harm. The task of the press, to be sure, is not to gloss over differences—nor is it to amplify them. Responsible journalism has as its primary duty, with respect to controversial issues, the reporting of differences in their proper perspective and the explanation of those differences in comprehensible terms.

A return to old pre-war squabbles at the peace table can serve as another motive power for a regression to normalcy. To move ahead, to map out new ways of preventing war, to work jointly with others—all these things require new frames of reference. Anything that drags us back into the '20s and '30s will serve to violate the new frames of reference that have been developing during the war. Let there develop a land-grab squabble, a welter of border disputes, bickering for commercial advantages, and the new will for internationalism may be quickly superseded by old ways of thinking. Again, some of the old disputes are, of course, inevitable; casualties among the ranks of the internationalists are likewise inevitable.

Finally, the longer we wait before entering into the problems of the post-war world with our allies, the greater the fund of fatigue to overcome, the better the chance of confusion, the more likely the old disputes, and the weaker the momentum of post-war planning. Every month we wait means weaker public opinion. Already the majority of the American people feel that planning should be under way. In many important respects it has already started. But, at that, we have probably waited much longer than it is safe to wait. Our delay means that the will for post-war pioneering has to some extent already been jeopardized.

These are some of the dangers we face. Let no one assume that, because opinion is favorable to internationalism today, there are no worries for the future. Other dangers can be outlined, ones which have only indirect bearing on public opinion. But let the list here suffice. The prospects are good now; but the future is not assured. In February, 1944, Mr. Anthony Eden spoke these words in Commons: "I can only promise the House plenty of difficulties, plenty of disappointments, and much deception in the times that lie ahead. I do not in my experience remember a period when foreign policy was so difficult to conduct as it is now." There is rough going ahead.

We have catalogued the grounds for despair. In summary, consider again the reasons for hope.

1. Right now, the country is ready to take its rightful place in world politics. If we fail to take that place, let our failure not be laid to the will of the people. The people need executors. The burden of our future history lies with these.

2. We wish to play our part in world affairs in the context of an authorized world organization that has scope and teeth and guts. Let historians note that too.

3. We wish to use force to keep the peace. We want that force under joint control and we want something more than token power. No statesman dare say that the American people are not ready for the controlled application of international force in the interest of peace.

4. We want our wishes to come true quickly. In short, we want the planning and execution of the post-war world to start now. If it has started, we deserve to know what can be told.

5. We wish no territorial aggrandizement for its own sake. If we feel that our security demands it, we will demand bases in foreign lands. Let other countries understand that our wish for new bases is not in the interest of commerce, or airways, or the Big Money. It is in the interest of preventing another Pearl Harbor.

Who misrepresents our wishes on this point—American or otherwise—is spreading falsehood for his own interests.

6. We wish to remain a free and sovereign nation—every nation always has and probably always will. Yet that fact need not be dust in the eyes of those who view the future hopefully. Of course we want our sovereignty. But we also want security and freedom from war. We are willing to "give up" some sovereignty if we are convinced that the reward is worth it.

7. Finally, we know one thing that we didn't know five years ago. America—or any nation—cannot live its life untouched by the world. We know that we are neither impregnable nor self-sufficient. In the momentous events of the last five years, the acquisition of that new knowledge has gone unchronicled. Yet in terms of America's future, it is doubtful whether there has occurred any event of deeper implications.

CHAPTER III

YANKEES TRADE WITH THE WORLD

TO an extreme measure America's history conditions her thinking about foreign trade. If there is any sphere of American public opinion which still breathes the spirit of the American Revolution, our attitude toward foreign trade is it. The practice of "protection-ism," which found its most fertile ground in the will to make in-fant American industries independent of England during the 18th and 19th centuries, is still the lodestar of popular thinking. Al-though our wishes no longer run in the direction of autarchy, it is no exaggeration to say that we would rather suffer the deprivations of complete economic self-sufficiency than face the hazards of com-pletely free and open trade.

That is our heritage. Though policy—particularly the trade pol-icies of Cordell Hull—has moved steadily away from the ideal of crass "protectionism," public opinion continues to lag behind. While Americans no longer worry about cutting aboriginal Anglo-Amer-ican apron strings, they do still worry about protecting American industry. The source of peril now is "cheap goods" made by "cheap labor." In a sense, the point of view is that of a producer. But it is also the point of view of the little man in fear of losing his job.

The fear of economic degradation is a generalized thing. When we view problems of foreign trade, we fall into the trap of for-getting that we are not alone. Our first thought is not whether others can help us. We worry instead whether others can or will hurt us. The benefits to be gained by gearing our unique productive capacities with those of other nations we ignore in preference to concentrating our attention on the dangers involved.

Why the lag in public opinion? Why a 19th century public for 20th century trade? Four forces, operating in the interest of backwardness, seem to be at work.

1. *The remoteness of the problems.* Trade over the oceans is a long way off. Its effects are mysterious and remote. Of only one thing are we sure: when foreign producers undercut our own products, it hurts. Of the specific ways in which foreign trade can *help* us we have been told little. Because the changing facts have been remote, America has been content to live with the stereotypes built up in the days when world trade was—or so we thought—a giant magic-lantern projection of the three little pigs and the wolf, with the U. S. playing the pigs.

2. *The millstone of classical economics.* In place of facts about trade stands the artificial economics of scarcity and demand—symbolized by the analogy of what happens when the famous marginal orange is brought to market. The model for international trade has been a storekeeper's model. Thanks to such doctrines, economics and social values have been left well apart. Asocial economics has performed the yeoman's job of keeping from schoolboys the basic meaning of economic life: the equitable distribution of as much of the world's goods as can be produced to as many people as possible in as great a volume as possible. Tragically enough, pints of milk for Hottentots and TVAs on the Danube were in 1943 still good for a laugh.

3. *The inadequacy of day-to-day reporting.* But most people learn their economics, not from the textbooks of classical economics, but from the newspapers. In their reporting and editorializing, newspapers have failed to present even the classical economics adequately. More important, the press, by its customs of reporting, has

left matters of international trade as remote as they ever were. Aside from a few major metropolitan dailies which have reported economic events in full, economic reporting in the American press has been lamentably shoddy. In lieu of simplification and dramatization of basic issues, the press has been content with either stuffy reporting of indigestible facts or a dress-up of irrelevancies. "Shall we call it bancor or unitas? Let's do a feature for page three." What difference that the reader has no more idea of what these amusing terms mean than the copy boy who rushes the half-baked blarney to the press-room?

For this practice we have paid an appalling price. The Reciprocal Trade Acts represent a cornerstone in our trade policy, an earnest of good will central in the structure of our international commitments. What kind of information job has the press done on them?

In December, 1943, six months after a two-year extension by Congress, a cross-section of Americans was asked, "What is your understanding of the term, reciprocal trade treaties?" The results are not unusual.[1]

3% defined reciprocal trade treaties correctly,
19% gave doubtful definitions, and
78% did not know what reciprocal trade treaties were!

Fewer than one person in every ten has a correct understanding of a seven-year-old fact which happens to be the central thread in the maze of American foreign economic policy.

4. *Economic insecurity*. Finally, there is the deadly fear of economic insecurity. The shoe—no matter how well made in Czechoslovakia—will pinch the foot that is pounding the pavement in search of a job. So long as a substantial portion of the nation dreads the consequences of even slight economic dislocation, a pioneering

policy of liberal trade will be appealing to few. Insecurity, except among the rare men of genius who prove the rule by their exception, is not a stimulus to enterprise. The small farmer, with artificially high production costs, the worker who can never be sure of his job in a marginal industry, the secure though poorly informed worker in an established industry—none of these is willing to see us take a chance with freer trade. In the end, they join with those to whom highly restricted trade is most profitable.

That is the background. Because our knowledge of the details of foreign economic relations is so sketchy, the background is almost more important than any specific opinions Americans may have. In the pages which follow, we will be talking about specific attitudes. They can be understood only if we bear constantly in mind the tree of protectionism from which the branches grow.

AMERICA'S FOREIGN TRADE

The Nature of Opinion

In spite of poor beginnings, our attitude toward American foreign trade has been growing in realism. At least we are moving away from a nostalgic attachment to pioneer self-sufficiency.

In September, 1939, a sample of Americans was asked: "Should the U. S. try to develop its own industries to the point where it does not have to buy any products from foreign countries?" Four years later, the question was repeated. Consider the change (Figure 1).[2-3]

Though the present split in opinion over the soundness of autarchy is small ground for rejoicing, it is nevertheless true that the old dogma of self-sufficiency is dying—albeit slowly. The growth of political internationalism discussed in the preceding chapter should speed its death.

SHOULD WE TRADE AS MUCH AS POSSIBLE WITH OTHER COUNTRIES OR NOT?

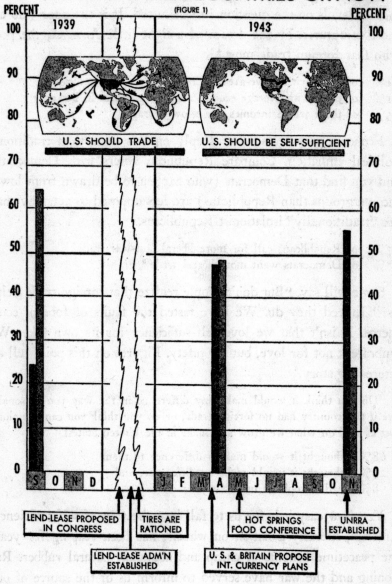

(FIGURE 1)

PERCENT — 1939 — 1943 — PERCENT

U. S. SHOULD TRADE

U. S. SHOULD BE SELF-SUFFICIENT

S O N D J F M A M J J A S O N

LEND-LEASE PROPOSED IN CONGRESS

TIRES ARE RATIONED

HOT SPRINGS FOOD CONFERENCE

UNRRA ESTABLISHED

LEND-LEASE ADM'N ESTABLISHED

U. S. & BRITAIN PROPOSE INT. CURRENCY PLANS

The role of economic insecurity in the psychology of self-sufficiency is nicely illustrated by a comparison of the opinions of three-income levels on the question just discussed. It is the poor who are most enraptured by the dream of a tight little America, the poor who fear foreign trade most.[4]

71% of those with above-average income oppose self-sufficiency
51% of those with average economic standing oppose it, but only
35% of those whose incomes are below average

Economic class cuts more deeply on this issue than traditional political affiliation. Compare Republican voters with Democratic, and you find that Democrats (who happen to be drawn from lower income groups than Republicans) are less opposed to autarchy than are "traditionally" isolationist Republicans.

57% of Republicans call for more liberal post-war trade
48% of Democrats want more liberal trade [5]

Some will say, "But don't people realize that foreign trade helps us?" Indeed they do. We have tasted the fruits of foreign commerce. It isn't that we love self-sufficiency for its own sake. We embrace it not for love, but for safety. Figures on this point tell an interesting story.[6]

"Do you think it would make any difference in the way you personally live if this country had no foreign trade, or do you think you can get along just as well on what we grow and make in the United States?"

68% thought it would make a difference to them
24% thought it would make no difference, and
8% had no opinion on the matter

Yet, how easy it is for us to fall into the trap of self-sufficiency. America, literally a nation on wheels, has been reaping for years the peacetime benefits of cheap and abundant natural rubber. Rationing and the war have served to inform us of the source of our rubber. Are we, at the end of 1943, looking forward to the return of cheap rubber and its benefits? Of course, but listen to the voices of protectionism. "Are you willing to pay higher prices for rubber after the war so that our synthetic rubber industry can compete with natural rubber from abroad?" Six Americans in ten are willing. "Home industry" is better than cheap rubber. Only two in ten relish the remembrance of $5.95 tires vividly enough to oppose a high-priced domestic product. The rest don't know.[7]

A more detailed picture of American protectionism comes to light in a survey conducted in Colorado. The first finding was this. The preferred method of "protection" is tariff. That is our compromise solution. It gives us the safe feeling of a weapon to be used against "cheap goods." Questioned on the best economic policy for America, 10 per cent were in favor of complete autarchy, 12 per cent for free trade, and the great bulk, 71 per cent, for tariffs. A handful had no opinions.[8]

To get at basic attitudes, those who favored either complete economic isolation or a tariff system (81 per cent) were put through a grilling that went something like this.

"In peacetime, do you think we have so much of some products that it helps to sell or trade them to other countries, or not?"

Seven in eight of the adherents of trade restrictions agreed that we did have surpluses and that it did help to send them abroad. And four out of that seven even went so far as to admit that other countries had to send us their products, some of which competed with our own, in order to be able to buy the things made in the U. S. A.[9] So far so good.

"For most of the products we send to foreign countries," ran the cross-examination, "do you think it's generally better to sell them for money or credits, or better to trade them for products we need?"[10]

54%   thought product trade better than cash sales,
33%   thought cash sales better than product trade, and
13%   had qualifications or were not sure.

"When another country produces a good quality product cheaper than Americans can," came the final question, "some people say it'd be better for everybody in the long run if we let it come into the United States without any tax or tariff and turned American production to some other product which we can make cheaper than anybody else. Do you agree or disagree?" [11]

62%   of the restrictionists disagreed,
28%   agreed to this long-run proposition, and
10%   were not sure whether they agreed or disagreed.

The skeleton on which opinion is hung looks something like this: We favor restriction of imports into the United States, and our preferred method of restriction is the tariff. That much is traditional.

Most of us believe that in order to have a healthy economy, we must sell our surpluses abroad. That, too, is traditional.

Traditional likewise is the majority belief that it is better to trade goods for goods than goods for gold.

Now leave the traditional realm. Do others have to sell to us if they are to buy our product? Only half believe it. When we move beyond the realm of our immediate interests, the public does not see the problem.

Go one step beyond to the level of revolutionary free trade—each making the things he can make most efficiently. Support breaks down completely, and only a small minority remains.

The Stability of Opinion

There we have it. What next? Will our post-war economic commitments be such that public opinion will refuse to support them? How strong are our convictions? Can we be swayed?

Thus far we have spoken of opinion on these matters as if it were strong and crystallized and ready for action. As far as the background factors are concerned—our traditional protectionism—that is true. But opinion on specific matters is anything but crystallized. It may go as well in one direction as another. By placing foreign trade in the context of *political* internationalism, it is possible to make public opinion more liberal. The appeal of international collaboration has that much potency. But appeal to the old shibboleths of "foreign labor" and you swing it just as far in the opposite direction.

A few examples of the instability of opinion on foreign trade. Link liberal trade with political internationalism and see the result.

"Here are two plans for the United States to follow after the war. Which one do you like best?"

PLAN A

The best way to make sure of prosperity in this country after the war is to make sure that other countries are in a position to buy goods from us. We should co-operate with them by joining some sort of League of Nations backed by an international police force to prevent a new war every twenty years. There just can't be prosperity in one country for long unless all countries are prosperous.

PLAN B

The second plan takes the view that Europe and Asia will always have their problems which are none of our business. We should try to make America prosperous whether other countries are prosperous or not. Instead of depending on a league of nations to keep us out of war, we should build up an army and navy so strong that no one would dare attack us. We should trade as little as possible with other countries so that we would not have to depend on them for anything.

The vote differs quite strikingly from the 50-50 balance obtained at about the same time in early 1943 with the neutral wording discussed earlier in the chapter.[12]

65%   choose Plan A—thorough-going political and economic internation-
      alism,
27%   choose Plan B—thorough-going political and economic isolationism,
      and
8%   have no preference.

Now link free trade with the importation of goods made by foreign labor living on a sub-American standard of living.[13]

"Because of cheap labor, the people of Europe can make shoes and other
such products for much less than our workmen. Should we let these goods
enter the country to compete with similar products which we make here?"

68%   vote to keep out foreign goods,
23%   vote to let in foreign goods, and
9%   have qualified and no opinions.

This question, to be sure, does not cover all foreign goods; it
names only those which would compete with goods made by "our
workers." Yet, one must be realistic. Against liberalized trade, this
particular appeal—any appeal—will be used to cover the whole
gamut of imports which might conceivably, now or in the future,
compete with what America can make.

Perhaps the instability can be described most concisely in terms
of a confusion between general and specific, or abstract and particular objectives. There can be no doubt that we like to talk of liberal
trade—so long as the talk is kept on a high plane of abstractness.
In January, 1944, for example, America gave its blessings to these
three trade principles.[14–16]

After the war, would you like to see the U. S. increase its foreign trade
over what it was before the war?

62%   said yes, only
10%   said no, and
28%   were without an opinion.

After the war, should the United States try to *sell* more goods to foreign
countries?

76% were willing, only
12% were opposed, and
12% were without an opinion.

After the war, should the United States *buy* more products from other countries?

68% were in favor, only
19% were opposed, and
13% had no opinion.

Our *abstract* willingness to trade should not, of course, be taken too lightly. It is, after all, an improvement over the state of opinion in, say, 1939. But, alas, acceptance of general principles does not necessarily spell acceptance of the consequences. During the very same week in January, 1944, these questions—spelling out the consequences of liberal trade—were also put to a cross-section of America.[17-18]

If European countries can make shoes more cheaply than we can, should we buy most of our shoes from Europe and try to employ our workers in making other things that we can produce more cheaply than Europe?

46% were opposed to such a plan,
32% gave it their support, and
22% had no opinion.

If foreign countries can grow and sell certain farm products more cheaply than we can, should we buy these products and get American farmers to raise other products which we can grow more cheaply than foreign countries?

32% were opposed to such a plan,
44% gave it their support, and
22% had no opinion.

And at that, farmers were 4-3 against the latter plan.

Yes, we like general principles—but not their consequences.

When opinion is that unstable, it is ripe for a leader. It cannot be counted on to lead on its own. So the question is this. Who, or which group, has the best chances of swinging public opinion behind it? What view of international trade is likely to prevail?

Consider first the alternatives among which the public will be asked to choose. On the one hand, there will be the inevitable high tariff advocates and their spirit of autarchy. From them will come powerful, nostalgic appeals. But the one weapon which they cannot use and which their opponents can is our new belief in political internationalism. The American people do not want political isolation. Only the fear of economic dislocation at home can make them abandon it. People with jobs and secure futures don't turn to the tariff battle.

Far to the other extreme will be the appeal of those who favor a liberalization of trade restrictions with an eye, in the long run, toward their complete removal. To the majority of Americans, such a long-run policy is soft-headed. We are neither politically nor economically mature enough to consider such a proposal now.

Midway between the two extremes lies a third view—one which is being advocated widely by many leaders of American industry. The position is not one of economic isolation. Rather, it envisages a vigorous economic policy in the field of foreign trade. Its enemies call it militant economic nationalism; its friends prefer the label "opportunity for American enterprise." In essence, it represents a rejuvenation of the Yankee trader spirit.

Whether or not this view proves in the long run desirable, certain it is that some of its expressions have been most unfortunate. Admiral Vickery, speaking in London, "warned" the British that America would be a maritime nation after the war. The *Manchester Guardian* voices the fears of those who foresee a cut-throat America when it points to a hopeful but not inevitable corollary of a vast American merchant fleet. Will the bottoms of American ships be as filled with imports as with exports? In the same category is the re-

quest by the U. S. Chamber of Commerce that American businessmen be allowed to travel in military territory before war's end in
order, so the implication goes, to get the business before others
arrive.

A saner expression of the new approach to foreign trade appears
in the Department of Commerce report, "The United States in the
World Economy." In essence this report, and others like it, calls
for vigorous trade within the context of the Reciprocal Trade Acts.
It envisages as much foreign trade as possible and on the best terms
possible. Tariffs are to be kept, but wherever feasible they are to be
lowered, in return for a lowering of barriers on our own goods. Although no statement has been made officially, not a few adherents
of the policy favor, where necessary, the intervention of the Government in the conduct of commerce—as in the case of overseas air
transport.

This middle view is completely compatible with the stable background of American thinking on questions of foreign trade. It has
the further virtue of making political internationalism consistent
with a reasonable desire for economic protection. If, in the post-war
years, America's policy with respect to trade hangs on the balance
of public opinion, support will most probably go to the middle view.
For it is the middle view alone that combines the virtues of political internationalism with moderate protectionism.

But a word of caution. It is foolish to suppose that the public will
oppose excesses committed in the name of this middle view. If
American interests try to, and succeed in, grabbing better air facilities than other nations, the imperialists who are responsible will,
likely, be toasted as exponents of American enterprise. The extent
to which we manage to "corner" markets will not be regulated in
any way by public indignation. The American people do not yet
understand the economic needs of other nations. Indeed, according

to a survey cited earlier, only half of those who favor trade restrictions are willing to admit that others have to export to us in order to import from us.

In a very real sense, then, the American public is completely open to suggestion on the extent to which the vigor of our middle-way economic policy shall become oppressive to others. Final control cannot rest with the people.

So, remembering the last chapter, we are faced with a dilemma. For all America's willingness to participate in international politics, the sad fact is that we, as a people, are not ready to implement our political commitments with corresponding economic agreements. We do not yet realize that one without the other is the first down payment on the third world war.

The Economist of London sums the matter up tartly: "In political matters, the tide [in the United States] is flowing toward Wilson; but in those questions of economic cooperation which are the lifeblood of an enduring settlement, there are signs of a return to the big stick and the ideology of McKinley."

THE TASK AHEAD

Public education is sorely needed. Our knowledge of the economic facts of life lags too far behind our political wisdom. A program of education is needed. Four points can guide it.

1. We can take for granted that the people have not been told, or, if told, have not understood the most basic principles upon which today's international trade operates. Because they have not been told, they have persisted in believing the "truths" of the 19th century. They must be told what 20th century reciprocity means to them. But they cannot learn unless they be motivated. Motivation can come only when people see their stake in the matter, understand their self-interest. Motivation and the facts can be combined.

It is not difficult to write a headline which, in essence, proclaims, NEW TARIFF BILL UPS GROCERY BILLS THREE DOLLARS A WEEK. Time is running short. If those who aim to *inform* the people do not get there first, others will.

2. Though we are internationalists in a political sense, our economic thinking is dominated by the doctrine of protectionism. Because the principle of protectionism strikes so close to a man's sense of security in his job, because it has, indeed, become a part of our folklore, the only way to counteract the influence of the doctrine is to adopt it. He who would explain reciprocal trade to the people can best succeed by using the doctrine of protection in its broadest sense—"reciprocity is the best form of protection."

3. Opinion, being uninformed, is easily pushed around by the appeals of propaganda. As long as such instability exists, the danger of demagoguery will be acute. With momentous decisions to be made soon—indeed, already being made—we can hardly afford the danger of a propaganda *tour de force* by special interests. The time to start working is now.

4. Finally, there is a happy sign. The trend in public thinking is toward more liberal world commerce. That trend is healthy. It is consistent with our desire to participate in the world's political affairs. Public education must capitalize on the trend. The relation of liberal trade policies and political security must be writ large. We want no more war. We know now that political collaboration can help prevent war. That economic collaboration is an even surer preventive, we have yet to learn.

CHAPTER IV

WORLD RECONSTRUCTION

WHEN the war comes to an end, the United States will be in a unique position, a position not designed to make others feel kindly toward us. In the first place, we will be the greatest creditor nation in the world. It will be within our power to squeeze or not to squeeze the debtor members of the United Nations.

Second, and of no less importance, ours will be the only country with sufficient reserves—spiritual and material alike—to aid other nations to their feet after the war. America's great industrial plant is the only one in the world that has not felt the disastrous impact of bombs and fire. It is not inevitable that debtors should dislike their creditors, nor that the hungry resent the well-fed. But that these conditions provide fertile ground for resentment, nobody will deny.

A third factor in the equation of post-war good will is the attitude of our allies toward our role in winning the war. In 1943, for example, only a handful of Britishers thought the United States was doing most of all nations to help win the war.[1] While Russian opinion cannot be judged by statements in the official Russian press, yet there is reason to suppose that the Russian people as well as the press believe our contribution in terms of lend-lease and fighting does not match the bloody contribution to victory that Russia herself has made.

If, then, the war should end with America in a highly favorable economic position, and with our allies feeling that we have got off cheaply, America can again become Europe's Uncle Shylock. A few irresponsible statements in high places, evident reluctance to help our allies when war ends, a scattering of unreasonable demands on debtor nations—any of these things can precipitate a "blood versus dollars" dispute of ugly proportions.

That is how America's post-war position can look to outsiders. To the bulk of the American people, it does not, naturally, look the same way. In this chapter we will confine ourselves to the American view. To what extent will the pressure of public opinion on matters of war debts and reconstruction force policy toward or away from hard-cased "bill collection"?

First, a word about policy. Our lend-lease agreements are such that the "payment" for goods shipped to other countries is not rigidly circumscribed. It was never intended that we be paid back completely in cash; nor was it ever intended that we be paid back "in full" with new materials. A good case, for example, can be argued by advocates of the view that the man-hours spent by other countries in using American lend-lease equipment can be counted as part payment. The flexibility of lend-lease is such that "repayment" can, in some as yet undefined instances, take the form of returned equipment. Indeed, the President's original description of lend-lease as lending your garden hose to a neighbor whose house had caught fire can well be taken as a symbol of the absence of defined repayment policy.

To go beyond lend-lease, the lack of clarity attaching to our role in post-war reconstruction matches the uncertainty of our prerogatives as a "war creditor." In spite of the food conference at Hot Springs, and the deliberations of UNRRA, the field is still wide open.

Few of the precedents that have guided us in such matters before are relevant today. Lend-lease is not war debt pure and simple. Reconstruction of a continent smashed almost to matchwood has no parallel in the devastation, picayune-by-comparison, after the last war. Policy will, in large measure, have to start from scratch. In such cases, it is inevitable that leaders will look to their peoples for guidance. They will, to be sure, look elsewhere as well. But with our official intentions still so uncrystallized, public opinion is in a crucial position to tip the balance of power. Consider, then, the state of public thinking on the important questions of reconstruction.

REPAYMENT OF LEND-LEASE

As far as the public is concerned, it is axiomatic that we *should* be repaid for lend-lease after the war. Upward to three-quarters of the American public held that view in the fifth year of war.[2]

In many ways, our present view is conditioned by our past experience with "war debts." The American public never did give up the idea that we should be paid back by the defaulting nations of World War I. As late as August, 1938, with the shadow of a second world war hanging darkly over Europe, the demand for repayment was such that only nine per cent of the American public favored the cancellation of our old war debts.[3]

But if our past conditions us to demand payment, it also leads us to the belief that payment will not be forthcoming! While three-quarters think we *should* be paid back, only three in ten think we *will* be.[4]

In very general terms, then, that is our view of the situation. The past lies heavily upon it. But what about the present? Do the American people understand the difference between "lend-lease" in this war and "loans" during the last, and does knowledge of that difference affect thinking about repayment? Further, to what extent is our present view of lend-lease open to change as a result of new experience?

On the first count, whether we understand the workings of lend-lease, the answer is a mixed yes and no. Though the reciprocal *spirit* of lend-lease is grasped by some half the population, few indeed realize that England, for example, is actually paying us back in fairly good measure with goods and services during the war. A national cross-section was asked whether the United States was receiving anything at all in repayment for shipments sent to England. While 54 per cent granted that we were receiving something, less than half of these (some 20 per cent) knew that we were receiving anything by way of material payments. The others were thinking of payment in terms of help and friendship. The rest of the population—almost half the country—considered that we were getting nothing at all, material or otherwise, in return for our shipments to England.[5]

What does knowledge of reciprocity do to attitudes on lend-lease? Do the people who know about current repayments still want to get "paid back"?

Consider these figures. Of those who know that we are receiving goods and services in return for lend-lease shipments, 28 per cent insist that we be paid back more after the war. Of those who do not know that there is any reciprocity involved in the lend-lease program, *74 per cent insist that we be paid back more after the war.*[6]

Knowledge of the reciprocity of lend-lease does, in other words, give pause to would-be advocates of reckless collection. Doubtless anything that weakens the analogy of lend-lease and the monthly bill from the corner grocer would do the same.

Failure of our information services to reach deep in the population with an explanation of reciprocal lend-lease stands out sharply when figures for three educational levels are compared.[7]

72% of those with college training think we are getting something in return,

59%   of those with high school backgrounds, and only
40%   of people who never went beyond grammar school

There are other facts which, if known to the public, could reduce the grip of the past on our thinking about debts. A state-wide survey in Colorado, experimenting with various methods of weakening the desire for repayment of lend-lease after the war, came up with some interesting results.

All those people who insisted that we should be repaid for lend-lease in part or in full—some two-thirds—were asked, first, whether they would still insist on payment if collection caused a depression in England after the war, and second, whether the fact that lend-lease saves American lives would influence their desire for payment.

The results are striking. Both appeals reduce the desire for repayment. On the matter of saving American lives, the response was not so great as one would expect. Though nine people in ten know that helping our allies takes some of the burden of fighting off us, the fact has only a small influence on our thinking about payment.[8]

70%   would not consider lend-lease paid in full even if our shipments did save some American lives
19%   would consider it paid in full if American lives are saved, and
11%   aren't sure

That our equipment saves American lives is no reason why Britain should not repay us for that equipment.

More successful is the appeal that forcing collection may cause a depression in England. We are too close to a recent depression ourselves to wish one lightly on others.[9]

37%   say collect even if it causes a depression in England,
46%   change their minds about collecting if it causes a depression in England, and
17%   aren't sure

These are only two appeals. If people can be taught about reciprocity, about the savings in American lives brought about by lend-lease, about the dangers of depression inherent in a policy of tough collection, they will be on the road to learning the facts. Knowledge of the facts, in this instance as elsewhere, is a good insurance against reckless public opinion.

What we have been saying here is not designed as an appeal for leniency toward debtor nations. The problem, pure and simple, is one of bringing the American people face to face with the facts and consequences of America's lend-lease policy. Whatever we do about the settlement of war debts after this war, it is fairly clear that we will break many precedents. The breaking of precedent will not, in itself, cause alarm in America. Resentment will come only if people are allowed to keep their rigid convictions, given life during the last war, about "cash payment in full." The safe course, it seems to me, is to prepare people for the future with a realistic picture of the present.

To sum up, the American people in their present mood are the pawns of a traditionalism compounded of our experiences with debt in the last war. To the people it is axiomatic that we be "paid back." It is also regarded as a near certainty that we probably won't be paid back. Surely the inference is that our faith in the old axiom is not so strong as it once was.

With that as the background, we are ready to be educated in the meaning of lend-lease. Education in reciprocity is wanting. But effective educational techniques are not. We know that there are ways to reduce the fever of "creditor psychosis." We also know that the fever will have to be reduced if we are to avoid the danger of incurring the ill will of those who have fought with us in the war's common cause and who will have to work with us in the cause of peace afterwards.

Relief and Reconstruction

But the problem of debt repayment is the negative side of reconstruction. Whether our demands are so severe that we leave others hamstrung financially, or lenient enough to permit our allies to get back on their feet without the added burden of an enormous mortgage, there still remains the positive side. The positive side is our readiness to help in peace as we have in war.

Relief and reconstruction, as far as public thinking is concerned, have two sides. One is best called "disaster aid," the other is long-run reconstruction. Each, because they have different roots, should be treated separately.

As far as relief from disaster is concerned, we feel as strongly now as we ever have about feeding the hungry and aiding the sick. The immediate problems of relief continue to touch us deeply. The Red Cross and the Community Chest are very much in the American spirit.

The point need hardly be "proved." A few figures throw the matter into its proper perspective. "If in some countries of the world people are short of food at the end of the war, should the United States help feed them?" went one question. Only five per cent dissent.[10] "Would you be in favor of continuing food rationing if this were necessary to feed people in countries hard hit by the war?" Nine in ten agree.[11] "Will it be necessary to continue food rationing here for a while after the war?" Almost two-thirds answer in the affirmative.[12] We can take for granted that, after the war as before, Americans will want to help the unfortunate, may even demand that the unfortunate be helped.

But how far beyond such relief are we ready to go? How willing are we to continue giving or lending help after the more patent evidences of suffering are no more? What terms will we demand?

How likely are we to dismiss the rebuilding of, say, Dnepro-petrovsk, as just another "TVA on the Dnieper"? These are the real problems.

The matter probably boils down to our view of reconstruction. Interpreting reconstruction as charity is one thing. Seeing the world in reconstruction as a market, is another. So long as we foresee a huge market for American goods in devastated areas, enthusiasm for continuing material aid will doubtless prevail.

In the fifth year of the war, the "producer's view" is dominant. This question was put to the American people:

"After the war, do you think we should or should not plan to help other nations get on their feet by sending them money and materials?"

Sentiment is unequivocal.[13]

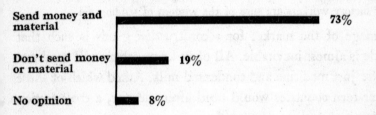

But willingness to aid in reconstruction is not a perquisite of the producer alone. Men at the bench as well as men in the front office cast majority votes in its favor.[14]

86% of executives favor aiding with money and materials
70% of factory workers also favor aid in reconstruction

And even those arch economic isolationists, America's farm proprietors, go along. Seventy-five per cent give their assent.[14]

Though moral responsibility, to be sure, influences our opinions, it is not the prime mover. We feel deeply the moral compulsion to help. But in themselves, morals do not guarantee a thorough-going program of post-war aid. Inquire whether Americans think the United States has the *moral* responsibility to see that the people of other nations are well fed, and you will find that only four in ten agree with you.[15]

Our view of reconstruction is hard-headed. Self-interest buttresses our humane feeling, and self-interest is a potent force. If you ask people over the country whether they think our aid in reconstruction will make us prosper or lower our standard of living, this is what you will find.[16]

59% see prosperity as the outcome of a policy of aid
22% say that our living standard would be lowered, while
19% are not sure which would happen

Again, worker and executive see eye to eye: [17]

68% of executives foresee prosperity deriving from aid, while
61% of factory workers are sure of the wisdom of sending aid

Our image of the market for reconstruction goods is such that brisk trade is almost inevitable. All of us know others will need our help.[18] Not just medicine and condensed milk. Asked which of these things war-torn countries would need after the war, a cross-section of Americans gave these answers.[19]

96% said food,
84% said medical supplies,
81% said clothing,
72% said machinery,
70% said building materials,
56% said household furnishings.

That we should produce more of these things to have enough to supply the needs of others is taken as axiomatic by the public—nine in ten agreeing on the point.[20]

But it is a mistake to assume, on the basis of these figures, that the American people expect our role as supplier of reconstruction materials to be all velvet. Most people realize that sending aid will mean a heavier tax burden in this country, at least until the world gets back on its feet.[21] Yet, the fact remains that *only one American in ten is deterred by that fact.*[22] We still want to supply aid, on credit if need be.

Even in reconstruction of *enemy* countries, the majority of Americans are eager to lend a hand. Here, however, a considerable minority draws the line.[23]

35%   would bar Axis countries from receiving American aid, and
 3%   would exclude certain allied and neutral nations.

Yet, large minority opposed or not, it is significant that still in the midst of war, a majority of the American people are willing to give material aid to our enemies when the fighting is done.

THE PROSPECT

If an Englishman or a Russian or even a German should ask me whether I thought that the American *people* could be depended upon to give other countries a break during the period of post-war reconstruction, I should answer, "Yes."

As far as debts are concerned, it seems doubtful that the American people will clamor for a cut-throat policy of "collect and be damned." Though we have much to learn about "two-way" lend-lease—and the newspapers could do far more than they have in advancing our knowledge—a slow beginning has been made. To understand reciprocity is to abandon the model of the past. Nor will the majority of Americans push collection willy-nilly if it becomes clear that such collection can set off depressions abroad and rob us of the customers on whom we are counting. The question is whether people can be informed in time and in sufficient measure to allow them to act in their own best self-interest.

As far as relief and reconstruction are concerned, the case is open and shut. Disaster relief we will give because to do otherwise is to negate one of our deepest ideals. Long-term aid in reconstruction we will give too. We see it as our own best interest: it is, in simple terms, the sort of policy that pays off economically.

What remains is the question of "official" policy. People alone do not write the peace. No official policy on debt collection has even been intimated. That field is wide open. But in the field of relief and reconstruction, past actions already indicate that the official will and the popular will are not likely to be out of phase. The spirit of UNRRA suits the American temper.

In a very real sense, however, the problems of relief and reconstruction are subsidiary to our more basic economic and political intentions. We are, to be sure, sympathetic toward the immediate needs of devastated Europe and Asia, and we do see a chance for prosperity in the reconstruction market abroad. Unless something sours us on world co-operation in general, we will very likely remain so. But if and when we grow sour, demagogues will be heard on every hand proclaiming the malicious intent of UNRRA and the rest.

Put it this way: American sympathy and American self-interest —a magic combination—are on the side of this country's full participation in reconstruction. But such sympathy and such self-interest have their roots in our new internationalism. Let internationalism wither, and our role in reconstruction withers with it. The war-torn world will need our goods, but our good will must determine the shipments.

92

CHAPTER V

AMERICANS AND BRITAIN

MUCH nonsense has been written and much spoken about Anglo-American relations. The bulk of it has come from two groups of extremists—each intent on making of Britain a passion. On the one side are the defamers of perfidious Albion; on the other, the adherents of "Britain can do no wrong." Each has done a yeoman's job of obscuring basic truths about American opinion on Britain. To each, the forest has been a few stunted trees.

In spite of the bitter screed turned out daily, it is still true that England is the country with which we feel the greatest kinship. We speak the same language, share the same traditions, enjoy the same food, tell the same jokes. So much in our own image is she, that England is not considered a "foreign" country. Our ways are the same ways. That is the first fact.

The second fact is even simpler. We like England. We like her better than any country save our own. When Americans are asked to choose their favorite nation, England leaves competitors well behind. Here are some figures.

WHAT COUNTRY DO YOU FEEL FRIENDLIEST TOWARDS? [1-4]

Year	Leading nation		Second nation	
1935	England	29%	France	5%
1936*	England	56%	France	11%
1937	England	31%	France	6%
1939	England	43%	France	12%

* The figures for 1936 are based only on those people able to name a favorite country and consequently are higher than for other years. Data on those not able to choose was not available.

After four years of war, we still like England. In 1943, American workers were asked to name their favorite among England, Russia, and China. Of those who could choose, better than half named England.[5]

The combination of communality and liking makes our opinions of Britain different from opinions about other countries—different not only in degree but different in kind.

Because we are akin to the British, know what they are up to, and take an interest in their doings, we are far better able to assess their merits and demerits. Our criticisms of things British, based on greater familiarity, are more trenchant, more precise. And because we like the British we can carp and blame without renouncing a friendship and dependence which we have come to take for granted. No matter what any American says or any Britisher says, all of us know that the consequences will not be war—nor even a serious strain on diplomatic relations. We are in no more danger of a breach with England than is Texas with the rest of the United States.

Into that background fits the recent history of our opinions. There have been irritants—some of them important, some ephemeral. The irritants are important only because they illustrate something about the surface of our opinions and not because they indicate their depth. A full pharmacopoeia of irritants would be both tedious and of questionable relevance. But, by way of background, it is valuable to review some recent specimens which can, likely, become operative again.

England's conduct of the war is the first. Our feelings on the subject are notoriously mercurial. As of 1944, with a better military situation, we think that England is doing a good job. Let her make a major mistake, and the barbs will fly again. The trend of American opinion on Britain's war effort is interesting—if only for the violence of its fluctuations (Figure 1, next page).[6]

Though military bygones may be written off as bygones, they may well stand as reminders of the fact that the future is not without its hazards. The last stages of the war, fraught as they will be with fatigue, hardship, and the legacy of Britain's colonial policy in the Far East, will provide ideal conditions for a renewal of denunciation. As a background for peace-making, such denunciation will, at very least, be a serious nuisance.

But more important than our habit of questioning British war conduct is our sub-surface suspicion that the British are trying to take advantage of us. There is nothing sinister about it: older brother trying to do us out of the family car on Saturday night. Thus, we are still able to embrace as our favorite ally the nation believed by four in ten Americans to be chiefly to blame for getting us into the last war! [7]

True to form, we expect England to try to get the better of us at the end of this war. Almost two-thirds of the country believes that England will try to have more to say about the peace than we will. That suspicion cannot be written off as an omnibus opinion of all foreign powers. A comparison of opinion on Britain's and Russia's post-war intent is food for thought.[8-9]

62% think Britain will try to have more to say about the peace than the U. S., only

31% think Russia will try to have more to say than we do.

Again, there is no reason for alarm. Our expectations are standard Americana. They are a natural hazard to post-war amity, a hazard which will be overcome because we all want it to be overcome. What is important is that we not be trapped into drawing invalid conclusions. We believe Britain will try to have more than her say,

IS BRITAIN DOING ALL IT CAN TO HELP WIN THE WAR?

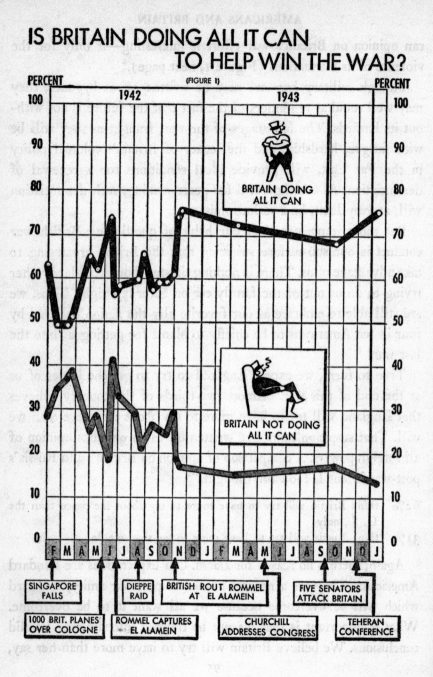

(FIGURE 1)

PERCENT — 100 90 80 70 60 50 40 30 20 10 0

1942   1943

BRITAIN DOING ALL IT CAN

BRITAIN NOT DOING ALL IT CAN

F M A M J J A S O N D J F M A M J J A S O N D J

SINGAPORE FALLS

DIEPPE RAID

BRITISH ROUT ROMMEL AT EL ALAMEIN

FIVE SENATORS ATTACK BRITAIN

1000 BRIT. PLANES OVER COLOGNE

ROMMEL CAPTURES EL ALAMEIN

CHURCHILL ADDRESSES CONGRESS

TEHERAN CONFERENCE

but we are still willing to play ball with her—hoping that we will be able to keep her in her place.

Cut from the same pattern is our estimate of what Britain's real aims are in this war. Because we know her so well—and, likely, because one's intimate friends are rarely angels—we persist in holding the realistic view that England is fighting to preserve her own place in the world as much as she is fighting to preserve democracy. We like her no less for it. Events have altered our convictions little. In the darkest days of the blitz, as many Americans thought she was fighting to preserve her power and wealth as thought her chief aim was the defense of democracy.* Three years later, the picture was unchanged.[10]

Finally, we are ever obsessed by the image of Britain as the Colossus of Empire, an exploiter of backward peoples. The stereotype doubtless had its roots in the American Revolution. Britain's imperial era kept it alive. Today we are still willing to agree with the blanket charge that Britain oppresses her colonies. These are the reactions of a cross-section of Americans to the accusation.[11]

"The English have often been called oppressors because of the unfair advantage some people think they have taken of their colonial possessions. Do you feel there is any truth in this charge?"

56% think there is truth in the charge,
33% do not agree with the charge, and
11% have no opinion on the matter.

Those, in brief, are four specific irritants, none of them designed to make post-war negotiations easier: Britain's conduct of the war, her habit of trying to take advantage of us, her basic aims in the war, and her tradition as a colonial power. We are fond of none of them.

* See Chapter I, Figure 4.

The Will to Co-operate

That is the background. There is plenty we do not like, and plenty we admire. What about the future?

The first premise of the public is that England *will want* to co-operate with us and can be depended upon to do so.[12]

The second premise is that the United States *should* co-operate with England after the war.[13]

The final premise, as clear-cut as the first two, is that America *will* co-operate with Britain after the war.[14]

These are the figures.

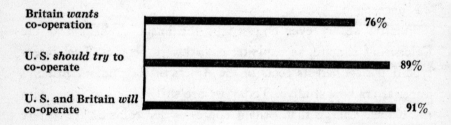

Britain *wants* co-operation — 76%

U. S. *should try* to co-operate — 89%

U. S. and Britain *will* co-operate — 91%

There is more than sentiment in our desire for Anglo-American collaboration. It is based on the sort of self-interest of which enduring foreign policy is made. The course of the war has confirmed us in what we already knew: that England shields us from European assault. This time she blunted Axis aggression before it reached us. And in the economic sphere, trade with Britain and traffic in British products are familiar enough to have the sanction of usage. All these things add up.

What form shall Anglo-American co-operation take? A permanent mutual assistance pact with England is one aspect of the problem which has occurred to many.

In the fall of 1943, the country was asked:[15]

"After the war should the United States and Great Britain make a permanent military alliance, that is, agree to come to each other's defense immediately if the other is attacked at any future time?"

61% favored a permanent military alliance with England,
27% opposed such an alliance, and
12% had no opinion on the matter.

An alliance with Britain is not, to be sure, first choice among plans for international co-operation. Though two-thirds are ready to endorse such an alliance, only a small number would choose it in preference to an international organization or a four power pact (see Chapter II). Sum it up this way: if all else fails—and few believe that all else will—we will accept an alliance with Britain as a minimum program, accept it gladly. We would, of course, prefer, insofar as our opinions on the matter are crystallized, an alliance which fits into a broader framework of general international security.

But there is a quarter of the population opposed to an alliance with Britain. An analysis of how they vote and where they live provides a kind of anti-British map of the United States.[16]

Region	Per cent opposed to an Anglo-American alliance
New England	27
Middle Atlantic	31
East Central	30
West Central	29
South and Southwest	15
Rocky Mountain	26
Pacific Coast	33
Political preference	
Democrats	24
Republicans	33

Though there are differences, the country seems pretty much of one mind. An opposing minority is inevitable. Brendan Bracken, speaking before Commons, once remarked that in America there is a minority inalienably addicted to Anglophobia. In his opinion, little could be done about it. Probably Mr. Bracken is right. Still, majorities in all groups and sections are willing to endorse an Anglo-American alliance.

But if a majority of Americans is ready to join with Britain in a military alliance, that same majority is hardly ready to relinquish old economic doctrines in England's behalf.

There is, for example, the matter of free trade with Britain. On that issue, America is split. Ask a cross-section of the British public, on the other hand, whether England should level all trade barriers against American goods, and the result is strikingly different. These are the figures.[17]

42% of Americans want Anglo-American trade barriers abolished,
69% of Britons want Anglo-American trade barriers abolished;
35% of Americans want trade barriers maintained,
13% of Britons want trade barriers maintained;
23% of Americans have no opinion on the subject,
18% of Britons are without opinion.

Nor are we any more eager to lift immigration restrictions in behalf of the English. For every two Americans who would vote to remove bars against British immigration into the United States, six would vote against the proposal.[18]

Britain, obviously, is a partial exception to the American rule of economic protectionism. Because she is like us, because her standard of living is not so far below our own, we are not so fearful of a British economic threat. Even so, the country is not *for* free trade; it is split on the issue. It is not *for* free immigration; a majority is opposed. But we are progressing. That only 35 per cent of us do favor trade restrictions against Britain is something of a tribute to growing flexibility in this country. Yet here as elsewhere, the same truth holds: Americans do not see the connection between political and military collaboration on the one hand, and economic collaboration on the other. The chances are that, when the post-war sniping at Britain gets started, the relation will be still further obscured. Accusing fingers pointed at Britain's dickering in oil, in rubber, in tin, can only make more difficult the task of bringing the two countries closer together economically.

By Way of Prediction

Extrapolating American opinion into the post-war years is a dangerous but irresistible kind of chess. The temptation is too strong to pass by.

1. It is vain to hope that our mild but chronic case of anti-British allergy will disappear overnight. We criticize and pick at England; but we don't break diplomatic relations with her. In a very real sense, opinion reflects our "informal" alliance with the British. It will, doubtless, continue to do so.

2. There is a widespread belief in the United States that England has passed her zenith, that she will come out of this war materially weakened. While this view prevails—and facts will likely confirm it in shorter time than we suspect—our fear of England as an economic threat may lessen considerably. Of the four Great Powers of the United Nations, it is generally agreed in America that Britain will be most weakened by the war.[19]

America's position *vis-à-vis* Britain after this war may well be similar to the position of England *vis-à-vis* France after the last. A weakened Britain will evoke greater American sympathy than she ever enjoyed as a "top-dog." In a real sense, the economic decline of Britain after the war may spell the beginning of the end of Britain-baiting in the United States. And if economic decline

STRENGTH OF BIG FOUR AFTER THE WAR

United States

Stronger ████████████████████████ 73%

Weaker █ 4%

Same ██████ 17%

Russia

Stronger ████████████████ 57%

Weaker ██ 7%

Same ██████ 17%

China

Stronger ███████████████ 55%

Weaker ██ 8%

Same ███████ 21%

Great Britain

Stronger ████████ 25%

Weaker ████████████ 34%

Same █████████ 28%

were accompanied by the demise of highly placed Tory mentality in Britain, resentment would dissolve that much faster. The rise of a British liberalism at home and abroad would bid fair to capture the sympathy, even the enthusiasm of America.

3. Our demands for post-war trade will be loud and strong. It is ridiculous to expect that American public opinion will permit our own trade expansion to be curtailed in the interest of helping Britain. It is certainly doubtful, for example, whether public opinion would

oppose a subsidized merchant marine of immense tonnage even if such a merchant marine might ruin Britain's chances as a carrier of world sea-borne commerce. The same goes for other fields of commercial endeavor. And so, while Britain can count on friendly opinion, she had best not look forward to economic mercy. There is no sizable segment of the American public which can be counted on to brake our rush for the world's goods and markets. If the United Nations fall short in their efforts to establish effective machinery for the control of world commerce, America can be a party to the possible undoing of Britain.

4. One last speculation about the impact of public opinion on economic relations between Britain and the United States. Most Americans, we have seen, still believe that lend-lease to the British is a one-way street. Barring any radical change in American information policy, there is a good chance that the American people will have no different view by the end of the war. Debate on repayment at war's end may, consequently, make many an American feel like a sucker. Already attempts to build such feelings are on display. The globe-girdling Senators of 1943—wittingly or unwittingly—did their utmost. To put it very mildly, the "war debt" problem where England is concerned is packed with potential dynamite. That dynamite may well explode any sympathy in America which Britain's weakened condition might otherwise arouse.

5. In the political sphere, the situation is not nearly so tense. Americans will not, as we have seen, oppose an alliance with Britain —though they would prefer a more comprehensive international alignment. There is no question but that the war has brought the two countries closer together politically and militarily than they have ever been before. That much is so clear that certain American politicians who have previously been reluctant to make *any* statement about post-war foreign policy at all are now "committing

themselves" in favor of Anglo-American alliance. Mr. Churchill sensed the depth of the accord when he pulled out all the stops and stated bluntly at Harvard that our fates were bound together. Given practice in close political collaboration with the British, our feeling of political kinship will grow. Whether it will ever reach the point of "union" is something which cannot be foretold.

CHAPTER VI

RUSSIA: FROM TEHERAN TO THE FUTURE

WHEN the rocky and hazardous road of Russo-American relations finally wound into Teheran in December, 1943, the American people were heartened. But they were not deceived into thinking that from Teheran to the future there led a paved super-highway of amicable diplomatic relations, that the periodic hairpin turns and sheer cliffsides had been permanently left behind. In spite of Moscow and Teheran, America is still sensitive to the delicacy of relations between Russia and the West. The most optimistic statement about public opinion is that it has passed that critical stage in which doubts of Russia's intentions still weighed more heavily in American thinking than did our hopes of enduring rapprochement with the Soviets. But even such a statement would be giddily reckless were one not to add in the next breath that there are still unsettled issues which in the future can and may upset the new balance of public thinking.

For who will deny that there still exists a strong undercurrent of suspicion of Russia? Public opinion figures show it; casual conversation among friends underlines it. Yet beneath the suspicion—bred largely in the past—there is something new, something of the present which augurs well. When the Nazi armies stormed into the Soviet Union on June 22, 1941, three new sets of attitudes had their birth in America, each in its turn a backfire against the old blaze of suspicion and doubt.

One set of attitudes had to do with the Russian people. The Finnish war, with its lurid tales of Russian officers driving their men into battle with guns at their backs, put a final touch on the then widespread belief that the Russian people would, if given a chance, be well rid of Communism. Our image of Russia's people was that of a depressed, inert, and driven mass, lacking the gumption to be rid of their tyrannical leaders.

The war against Germany has changed all that. Our admiration for the fighting spirit of the Russian people is enormous. We take in them the same pride we do in any people who will fight courageously—and successfully—against a more powerful adversary. The people of Russia have a clean bill of health where we are concerned.

By their fight, the Russian people have done something else to American public opinion. We have not, to be sure, become convinced that Communism is a good thing. But we have adopted a new and tolerant view of its Russian manifestation. If a people are that willing to fight and die for it, it must be what the people want. In American thinking, nourished in the lore of democracy, the will of a people is not a chimera but a living, palpable thing. If a people want a particular form of government, they should have it. It is extremely difficult for us to believe that people can be wrong about what they want. We even try to argue away fascism as something which the German people do not *really* want. So Russia's Communist form of government has been graduated from something despicable in and of itself, to a system which we dislike but which we will tolerate in Russia because Russians like it.

Finally, Russia's position as an underdog *vis-à-vis* Germany has broken the spell of the idea that Russia is the power that has always had designs on others, always in the role of the bullying and devouring bear. Her call to the West for help was the tacit, though tenuous admission that the Russians could not be completely independent of the rest of the world, could not always be a prowling bear. As time has gone on, that first feeling that there was something in common has grown steadily. Moscow and Teheran brought it to a new stage of maturity. Now most of us are convinced that there *is* a common bond between the Soviet Union and the democracies. The big question mark is whether Russia will want to see that bond strengthened or not. But let no critic minimize the importance of the new belief that Russia shares with the West a common fate. That is new. It is, perhaps, one of the great turnabouts in the history of American public opinion.

A quick sketch of poll results on American opinion concerning Russia illustrates vividly our feeling for Russia as an ally in war.

When, shortly after the Nazi invasion of Russia, a cross-section of America was asked whether we should send help to the Russians, some eight people in ten were for it.[1] Few indeed were those who did not want Russia to beat the Germans—in spite of "bleed-each-other-white" propaganda.[2]

The change made itself felt in other ways. For some time before the start of the Russo-German war the American public had been polled at intervals on whether, if forced to make the choice, they would choose to live under Communism or Fascism. The trend in Figure 1 on the next page needs little comment.[3] The meaning of such figures as these must not be mistaken. They do not indicate that the average man is ready to welcome Communism here at home. Actions speak more clearly than opinions. The American Communist "Educational Association" still has less than 300,000 members. Our opinions do, however, tell something about the increase of tolerance for Russia as a Communist state.

But the courage of the Russian people has done all *it* can do to improve American opinion. And the fact that the Russians like their form of government has done all *it* can do to make us tolerant of Russia. What remains now is for the newly realized bond between Russia and the West to be strengthened.

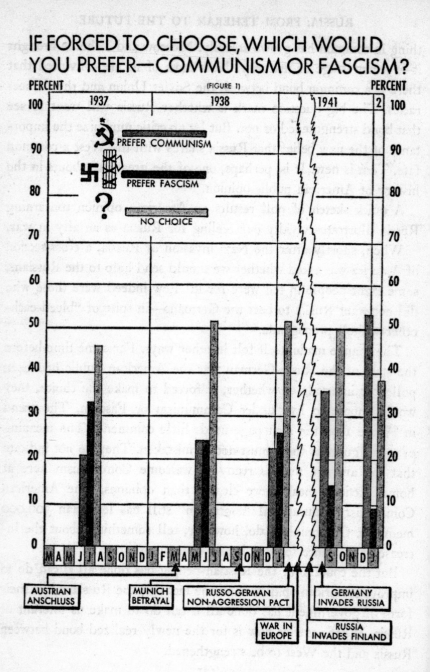

IF FORCED TO CHOOSE, WHICH WOULD YOU PREFER—COMMUNISM OR FASCISM?

(FIGURE 1)

PREFER COMMUNISM

PREFER FASCISM

NO CHOICE

AUSTRIAN
ANSCHLUSS

MUNICH
BETRAYAL

RUSSO-GERMAN
NON-AGGRESSION PACT

GERMANY
INVADES RUSSIA

WAR IN
EUROPE

RUSSIA
INVADES FINLAND

Were it only a matter of strengthening the sense of common cause, the task would not be so urgent. It is more than that. Today, public opinion on Russia is, and probably will remain for the next few years, in a delicate state of equilibrium. On the one side are fears, on the other hopes. Failure to realize the hopes can only make them diminish and give to the fears the power they once exerted on our thinking about Russia. If then Russo-American relations do not improve, if promises and implied promises are not fulfilled, opinion must inevitably worsen. The past and the future are in conflict for dominance in our thinking. One must win. In history there are no tie scores.

In a sense, then, these pages record not an accomplished fact, but the elements of an equilibrium. We are concerned here with both the symptoms of future collapse and the possibilities for future accord. To the latter we turn next.

The Chances of Success

One premise for the future on which most people agree is that we *should* co-operate with Russia after the war is over *if we can*. That is the view of eight in every ten Americans.[4] As many believe that the United States will make every effort possible to achieve accord with Russia.[5] We should and will try to co-operate. That much is hopeful. But what about Russia? Will *she* make every effort to co-operate? That is the crucial question. For as far as America is concerned, the burden of proof is not on us, but on Russia.

And so the crucial question for public opinion is this one: "Do you think Russia can be trusted to co-operate with us when the war is over?" The question has been asked the American people by the polls repeatedly—in moments of hope and moments of despair. Figure 2 following sums up the trend of opinion during the last year and a half.[6]

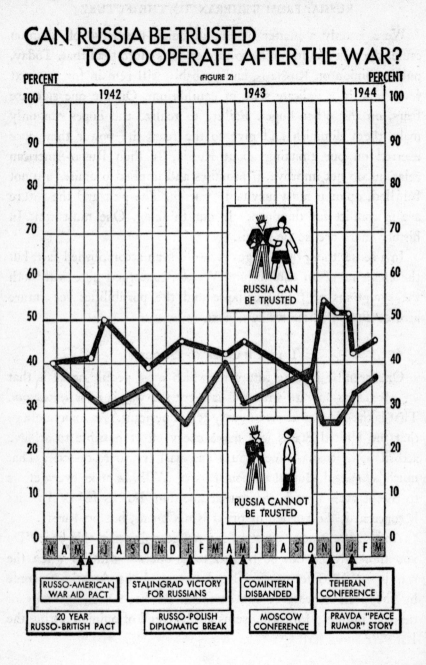

CAN RUSSIA BE TRUSTED TO COOPERATE AFTER THE WAR?

(FIGURE 2)

This is the fever chart. Russian offensives, the dissolution of the Comintern, the Moscow Conference, Teheran—none of these things has had a spectacular influence upon it. Roughly speaking, of every one hundred Americans, forty think Russia will co-operate, forty think she will not, and twenty have not made up their minds one way or another. In periods of smooth sailing, the balance shifts a little; it shifts too when things get rough. But generally it has remained at the same level. Perhaps Moscow and Teheran have served to raise the level of confidence. That remains to be seen. By late January, 1944, much of the effect of the conferences had already worn off.

The cleavage over Russia in the population at large does not, contrary to the belief of many, reflect a struggle between definite, clearly delineated groups in the country. Group differences there are, to be sure, but these cannot obscure the basic fact that all Catholics are not opposed to Russia, nor all Protestants for her. Republican and union member, Negro and Italian, urbanite and farmer, Catholic and Protestant—they can be found on either side of the fence. The rather elaborate table which follows is a catalogue of the opinions of the major population groups in the United States. It is well that it be on the record.[7]

CAN RUSSIA BE TRUSTED TO CO-OPERATE AFTER THE WAR?
(January, 1944)

	Russia can be trusted %	Russia cannot be trusted %	No opinion %
The nation as a whole	41	35	24
Economic level			
Above average	51	32	17
Average	47	34	19
Below average	38	36	28

	Russia can be trusted %	Russia cannot be trusted %	No opinion %
Educational level			
College	47	37	16
High school	41	33	26
Grammar school	40	30	30
Region			
New England	41	38	21
Middle Atlantic	39	38	23
East Central	37	37	26
West Central	43	30	27
South and Southwest	47	27	26
Rocky Mountain	43	37	20
Pacific Coast	43	37	20
Occupation			
Executive and professional	52	31	17
Farmers	39	35	26
White collar workers	44	32	24
Service workers	35	35	30
Skilled workers	35	41	24
Semi-skilled workers	37	39	24
Unskilled workers	32	36	32
Type of community			
Large cities (100,000 plus)	42	35	23
Medium cities (10-100,000)	45	33	22
Small towns (under 10,000)	40	35	25
Rural	39	35	26
Sex			
Men	45	36	19
Women	37	34	29
Age			
20-29	38	35	27
30-49	41	37	22
50 and over	43	32	25
Union affiliation			
Union workers	36	40	24
Non-union workers	36	35	29

	Russia can be trusted %	Russia cannot be trusted %	No opinion %
Politics: 1940 vote			
Democrats	44	32	24
Republicans	40	41	19
Color			
White	41	35	24
Negro	24	38	38
Religion			
Catholic	31	44	25
Protestant	42	33	25
None	43	34	23

A few words in passing about the "catalogue." Several bare facts are worth recounting. First, if there is any "class" difference in opinion on Russia—and it is, in fact, only negligible—it goes counter to what the Marxist textbooks would predict. Not the proletarian masses, but the well-educated, the economically well-off, the executive and the professional are the most confident of Russia's good intentions. So much for one shibboleth. Another has to do with the implacable hostility of Catholics for Russia. Leaving aside for a moment the question of the Catholic hierarchy, the difference in opinion of Catholics and Protestants on the question of Russia-after-the-war is not striking. Difference there is, to be sure, but it is not of the magnitude which spells a sullen Catholic population bitter over American "overtures" to the Soviet. Finally, the professional Red-baiters who despair of the "Red unions" are true to form as ever: considerably wrong. Belonging to a union has no effect, one way or another, upon opinion toward Russia.

Though the country feels that the burden of proof is on Russia and though many still doubt that she will be able to prove herself, the outlook for public opinion is more than hopeful. *We are* ready to do our part. Though, in early 1944, as these words are written, the promises of Moscow and Teheran look not quite so heartening as they did. Those conferences did have a salutary effect. Consider, for example, what the Moscow Conference did to the public.

In the first place, its effect was widespread. Virtually eight in every ten Americans heard of it.[8] In itself that is an encouraging fact, for even "historic" conferences have a way of slipping by the public's attention. Particularly to the poorly informed, more firmly wedded to the older animosities of Russia, the fact that the three great powers were sitting down together and talking about their common problems was of tremendous importance. For these are the people who, not being abreast of current developments, had understood least what Russia and the United States shared in addition to a common enemy.

A second result of the conference was that it shocked and surprised the public into a realization of how much could be accomplished by the three powers acting in political concert. Suspicious of Russia, we were not prepared to see anything very much more than political double-talk and goodwill as the fruits of the meeting. When, consequently, the results were announced, full 43 per cent of those who knew a meeting had been held confessed that more had been accomplished than they had expected.[9] Scarcely ten in every hundred Americans expressed any disappointment. Nothing can be better for international relations than shocks like these.

All of this is not to say that the great mass of Americans learned in detail what went on in Moscow. In point of fact, only about half of those who had heard of the conference were able to tell interviewers a week or so later what some of the specific decisions of the conference were.[10] That, to be sure, is regrettable. It is also inevitable. What is more important is that people had the feeling that things were accomplished and lasting peace brought that much closer.

A final augury of the good which the conference created was the faith of the country in the promises made by the conferees. A majority of the country felt that the three nations would stick to the agreements; less than a quarter thought that one or more of the three powers would not.[11]

The preparation for accepting Russia had, of course, been progressing apace before Moscow. Moscow gave it new impetus. If, before Moscow, some three-quarters of the country thought it just that Russia have as much say as we do in deciding Germany's postwar fate, it may be taken as axiomatic that such feelings have been deepened.[12] If half of those with any opinion on the matter thought before Moscow that an alliance with Russia for mutual protection would be a wise move for the United States, that conviction is, doubtless, stronger now.[13] In short, America wants to co-operate with Russia. No survey of opinion on the matter shows the contrary. Any move which brings the two nations closer together will strengthen that desire. It is no longer a matter of convincing the American people that it is to our best interest to have a strong Russia as our friend. The task now is to convince the public that Russia *can* and *will be* such a friend.

The chances of a successful Anglo-Soviet-American future reached a high point, as far as the public was concerned, immediately after Teheran. We heard the promises and were impressed. But promises for the future may also be a boomerang. To promise and then not to deliver is far worse than not to promise and not to deliver. The drawn-out crisis over Poland, Russia's recognition of Badoglio *sans* prior consultation, the bizarre needlings of England and America in the Soviet press—none of these things, coming after Moscow and Teheran, can do anything but disillusion us. Trend figures of Russia's trustworthiness in the months following Teheran only bear out the point. We are still not out of danger.

115

But the chances of success are still good. They will not, however, become better *automatically*. If, as Anthony Eden has put it, there are "many difficulties, many disappointments, and much deception" still to be faced, the future will require from us the greatest restraint, the least passion, and the sagest understanding. That is the minimum price.

The Chances of Failure

What specifically is it about Russia's post-war intentions that people do not trust? The question is a difficult one. Most of the suspicion is vague and rooted in the past.

First of all there is the feeling that Russia is in this war primarily to solve her own difficulties—defeat the Nazis—and not to aid the democracies as such. Right now the two tasks happen to be parallel. That a nation should be fighting primarily for its self-interest does not, in itself, shock us. Many of us hold that England has the same motivation. The difference is, perhaps, that we are convinced of the underlying community of American and British self-interest, but have yet to be convinced of the community of interest between ourselves and Russia. There is, for example, the matter of Russia and Japan—a typical stumbling block. When Germany is defeated, will Russia help us in the war against Japan? [14]

49% think Russia will help us against Japan,
31% think she will not help us, and
20% aren't sure whether she will or not.

That part of America may have to eat crow some day for its misgivings that Russia will not help us against Japan—if that day should come about—is no answer to the questioning voice of suspicion. Even if Russia does join in the Pacific war, Americans probably will not eat their crow wholeheartedly, with the relish of men assured of the folly of their earlier doubts. For it is not alone

Russia's role in the Pacific war that is at stake. It is the enigma of Russian policy as a whole that troubles us. No single act can strike to the core of the enigma. It is too deeply set in our thinking, too protected by tributary suspicions. Should Russia join against Nippon, our anxieties will be allayed to some extent. Yet some of the enigma will still remain. Somebody will worry aloud about the intentions of Russia in the development of China, in the control of the northern sea lanes to the Orient, in something. Overcoming misgivings toward a powerful nation upon whose designs a large measure of our own security depends is not a task to be done in a day. A long and difficult road lies ahead.

Suspicions of Russia's demands at the peace table are of the same intricately woven cloth. Will Russia want the same kind of peace that we do or will she make demands to which we cannot agree? [15]

30% say Russia will want the same kind of peace as we do,
48% say she will make difficult demands at the peace, and
22% are not sure.

Yet it will take more than Russo-American felicity at this peace conference to banish completely our misgivings over all future conferences. But advancement will have been made. In public opinion as elsewhere, Olympus is best reached by making progress in that direction.

So too, the spread of Communism in Europe—another topic capable of stirring our fears. Will Russia try to bring about Communist governments in other European countries after the war? [16]

41% say that she will want to bring about Communist governments,
31% say that she will not want to, and
28% aren't sure.

Yet Communist-inspired governments or not, we will persist in looking for the Red hand in Europe for some time to come.

In spite of all this, Goebbels would be foolish to assume that his propaganda-line had wrought the results intended. Though many believe, for one thing, that Russia will want to foster Communism in neighboring countries, far fewer believe that she will bring it about. If Russia is largely responsible for Germany's defeat, people were asked, will Europe go Communist after the war? [17]

25%   say that Europe would go Communist if Russia plays the lead in defeating the Nazis

70%   do not believe that Europe will go Communist under those circumstances, and

5%   aren't sure

Nor have our suspicions, egged on by "anti-Bolshevik" propaganda, softened our hardboiled attitude toward the nonsense of a German-dominated *cordon sanitaire* around Russia. "If you were sure," one poll queried, "that Communism would be a strong force on the continent after the war, would you like to see Germany remain a strong power to offset Russia's influence?" [18]

28%   would vote for a strong Germany under the circumstances,

68%   would vote against it, and

4%   have no opinion.

Thus far we have been dealing with the specific manifestations of a more basic and pervasive doubt. In a very real sense, specific issues are only the rods down which the lightning of suspicion travels. The lightning itself is vague. Attempts to describe it have been made but rarely with clarifying success.

One such attempt in 1943, asked the 34 per cent doubtful of Russia's post-war intentions why they held such an opinion. [19] Whether such a point-blank approach to the problem is as fruitful as more subtle techniques is, perhaps, doubtful. But, at least, it does yield some outlines of the nature of suspicion.

Answers, generally, fell into three distinct categories. First, there were those *who do not believe that Russia is really interested in* having relations with other countries after the war. Some pointed a finger at Russia's failure at that time to sit in on military and political councils of war. Others stated rather flatly that Russia is interested only in Russia. Some quarter of those distrusting Russia's post-war intent fell into this category.

A second group was concerned with the *vast ideological and political differences* which stand between the two countries. Can two countries as different as the United States and Russia really find enough in common to cement their collaboration in peace as in war? That was the question which preoccupied a fifth of those who did not believe that Russia will co-operate with us after the war.

If the statements of these first two groups of doubters can be taken at face value, there is hope that events alone will dissolve their suspicions. The misgivings mentioned above were expressed in 1943. Since then, there have been Moscow and Teheran, proving presumptively, at least, that Russia *is* interested in co-operating. We have heard much talk, too, of the common economic interests of the two countries. Talk, to be sure, will not be enough. But if parleys lay a solid foundation for future action, they are also the opening guns in the fight against suspicion of Russia. It will, at least, be more difficult to charge either that Russia has no interest in real co-operation or can find no sufficient basis for accord which would make it worth while.

The task of convincing the remaining doubters is less easy. For the third and largest group—close to half of those who do not foresee post-war Russo-American co-operation—is even less concrete in their suspicions. To them, Russia is just a bad moral risk. Her past sins, the Red menace, her "double dealing," the degradation of Christian ideals—all of these are currency in the treasury of hatred which we have inherited from the past. By far the most emotional of all doubters, these people are not interested in hearing facts—or, at least, not facts on the other side. The conviction of evil comes first; the details have meaning only in terms of it. These are the real victims of hate propaganda. In the same role as our rabid Anglophobes who see only evil in Britain, our minority of Russophobes will be a vocal and dangerous obstacle in future relations with Russia. That is our fee to the pipers of hate, many of whom are still amongst us.

How summarize our chances of failure? There are still tendencies to negativism. It will be many decades before they are stamped out. While they are alive, the public can be convinced that Russia is not for us. Distrust of the Soviet Union is not merely a case of suspended judgment. We are still ever ready to have proved to us that our new-born confidence in the Russians is misplaced. Conviction is on the side of distrust. What we must remember is that there are years, perhaps decades, in which the public's sympathy for Russia must not be taken for granted. Irresponsibility of action or expression in either country is, in the light of that fact, an act of treason against the cause of peace.

The Balance Sheet

Early in this chapter it was remarked that opinion on Russia had passed the critical stage, that the arguments in favor had attained more weight than the arguments against. Were the problem of Russia not an ever-changing one, that statement would be enough. A true balance sheet of opinion on Russo-American relations must also include a record of transactions in the immediate offing.

Such impending transactions cannot, of course, be spelled out in detail. Only two of them—one fraught with dangers, the other pregnant with possibilities—need be noted here. Consider first the more hopeful.

The Allied assault on Europe has brought into closer concert the military plans of Russia and the Western democracies. The armies of the coalition are working in greater strategic unison than they were ever able to do before. Opinion toward Russia must inevitably be improved thereby. The closer the battle of Europe approaches the final decision, the more obvious becomes the co-operation between the two countries. Aid to Russia, formerly thought of in terms of how many tanks and planes and tons of beef had been supplied through Lend-Lease, is now more obviously aid to Russia to help us. In this atmosphere the barrier of remoteness is slowly being torn down.

Russia's intentions toward the countries of Eastern and Central Europe is the transaction most fraught with perils. Putting the matter thus is to narrow it too much, to remove it from its broader political perspective. Yet narrow it we must. For to the American people, anything which gives the appearance of a post-war land-grab is the signal for cynicism. We do not deny to Russia or to any other country the right to "legitimate" territory. Legitimacy means many things—strategic frontiers, land formerly taken from a country, etc. It is a flexible concept. So too, as we saw in Chapter II, is our whole outlook on boundaries. Yet if boundaries should become the trigger for "interregnum" acrimony within the family of the United Nations, we may get sufficiently fed up with the family to hold back from full participation in it.

But the prospect is not so alarming as some would make out. Those who claim the first "official" Russian demand for territory will set off a whirlwind of reaction against her in this country are talking well beyond the facts. Some six in ten Americans believe that Russia will want more territory after the war.[20] On *general principle*, to be sure, the country is against the idea of expansion through conquest. Russia is not an exception to the principle—27 per cent think she should have more territory, 56 per cent that she should not.[21] But there is reason to believe that the general principle of "anti-expansion" does not cover completely the problem of Russia's demands for so-called legitimate territory.

Even on the touchy question of Poland, fully half of those with opinions on the matter believe that the United States and her allies should make no effort to stop Russia from getting what she wants.[22] If the continuing crisis between Russia and Poland over borders is settled within the framework of the United Nations and if Poland is given a say in the matter, many of those who would have the Allies intervene in behalf of Poland would, doubtless, be satisfied.

That is why it is the spirit rather than the content of boundary settlements which is of the greater importance. *Terra irredenta* and continuing boundary disputes have rarely been a function primarily of the lines drawn on maps but, rather, of the spirit in which the lines were drawn.

There are two transactions already under way—the coalition warfare in Europe and the settlement of boundary questions. What else may come up in the future lies beyond the scope of this book. Only one prediction need be made. If there is machinery for the settlement and adjudication of future differences—whatever their nature—the chances of a debit piling up in the balance sheet of opinion will be minimized. We do not fear the problems we face. Americans are almost exasperatingly cocksure of their ability to solve any and all of them. What we must have to keep that cocksureness alive is the means for settlement—a working and effective international organization.

WHAT REMAINS TO BE DONE

What remains to be done? Certainly it would be as foolish to try to ram pro-Russian propaganda down people's throats as ever it was to play the same game with anti-Russian propaganda. The final form of our relations with Russia has not yet been determined. Of one thing we can be reasonably sure: relations with Russia will, at least for some years to come, be a very difficult problem in public relations. We are going to make demands; so is Russia. A cool-headed public opinion—cool-headed no matter what happens—is the safest public opinion. We have seen in this chapter what the sources of distrust are, where the foci of friction. What remains to be done?

Put the matter in terms of problems. What are the problems of Russo-American relations as reflected in American public opinion?

1. The first problem—and the biggest one—is proving that we can co-operate with a country with which we had been at logger-heads for some twenty years. We are a practical people. Our only proof that we can co-operate with others is that we *do* co-operate and *continue* to co-operate. A good-sized chunk of America is ready to be convinced that it can be done. Events will convince them. If events do otherwise, all that follows is idle advice.

2. America and Russia are different, granted. Until very recently, virtually every scrap of information released on Russia was devoted to proving that point in rather ugly detail. Even now there is a tendency to present Russians and Russia as part of a different world from ours. Yet observers who have stayed in Russia for more than the perfunctory month's tour come back feeling how alike is the Russia of today and the America of fifty years ago.

To explain Russia to America (and vice versa) one must start with similarities. Without an account of similarities, Russia and

123

Russians are abstractions. Americans must know more about Russians and their country. Not in general terms, either. Tell the wheat farmer of Kansas about the wheat farmer in the Kuban. Let Pittsburgh know about its twin city of Stalingrad in peacetime as in war. While Russia remains an unfamiliar abstraction, noted primarily for "differentness," somebody or something can always, in a moment of crisis, turn her into a dark threat. Familiarizing people with Russia is no sinister propaganda campaign. Russia is an important fact. It is just plain horse sense to know that fact.

3. Americans are uneasy in their foreign relations unless they sense a good, simple *quid pro quo*. In a formal sense, we do not yet know what the Russo-American *quid pro quo* is. But we do know, in broad terms, what the advantages are of being on good terms with Russia. Progressive executives are not unmindful of Russia as a customer. None but a fool would deny that it is better to have Russian arms with us than against us. It would take a political casuist to doubt that a peaceful Russia is a guarantor of peace in Eastern Europe and, hence, in the world at large. Finally, we all know that, come what may, Russia will be a powerful nation whether we like it or not. It is to our self-interest to try to get along with her, just as it is hers to try to get along with us.

Those are the terms in the equation of "mutual self-interest." People have been told the terms, but not often enough and not enough people. If and when full peacetime collaboration between this country and Russia matures, the task of explaining the advantages of co-operation will be lightened. In the meantime, there is enough to be said that is not being said to warrant a good deal of reflection by the press, radio, and movies.

4. Finally, from the long-term point of view, there is much to be done in the schools. It is high time that the Russian government

stopped being dismissed as "Communism with a few bureaucratic frills." Russia, its people, and its government are engrossing subjects. In all fairness to our youth, we should start teaching these subjects. The prospect of another generation of badly informed Red-baiters is almost too discouraging a prospect to ponder.

CHAPTER VII

THE FATE OF THE ENEMY

CONCERNING the fate of our enemies after the war, we Americans have few definite ideas. What notions we do have are guided by simple convictions: we must be humane to enemy people, ruthless with enemy leaders, and see to it that our enemies cannot rise up to strike us again in twenty years. America did not go into this war hating her enemies.

THE BACKGROUND

Consider first the matter of hatred. We do not, as yet, "hate" our enemies. We are, to be sure, hostile. But the gap between hostility and hatred is a broad one. Hatred, psychologically, is an enduring and consuming thing which outlasts the situation that creates it. Hostility is a function of a situation. Those who hold that we should "hate" our enemies and everything connected with them are playing with dangerous words. The consequences of hatred are long-lasting and emotionally degrading. "Hating the enemy" *in toto* means rejecting Bach along with Hitler. That we have not yet done. In this war sauerkraut is still sauerkraut, and no move has been started to "abolish" kindergartens. Our enduring hatred has been reserved for enemy leaders, not people.

In 1942, a cross-section of Americans was asked whether they, personally, hated the German and Japanese people. The consensus was clear-cut.[1]

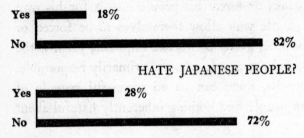

People, to be sure, are not good judges of their own emotional state. Hatred may mean different things to different people. Yet always it has the core of bitterness. That three-quarters of the nation have escaped such bitterness is what counts. In the end we may be an island of sanity in a bitter world.

Compare our attitude toward German culture in this war and in the last. During the First World War we drove a distinguished conductor from the podium of one of America's great symphony orchestras because he was a German. Wagner was, by common consent, banned. In the present war, fewer than one person in ten contends that we should bar German music.[2] The German language was struck from the curricula of leading schools and universities in 1918. During the Second World War, only a handful would vote in favor of such a step.[3]

All this in spite of the fact that nothing during the last war could compare with the bestial atrocities of this one. Slave labor, the Gestapo, the torture of Bataan's defenders, Lidice, the carnage of occupied Russia, the strafing of packed highways to deepen civilian confusion—the list is unique in the history of evil. Yet in spite of the truly visceral provocations to hatred, we still do not hate. Why?

Several factors are at work. In Chapter I, an effort was made to outline the popular view of war's cause. Ours is the "devil theory." Hitler caused it. War comes, according to current folklore, when a leader hoodwinks or forces his people into it for his own ends. Although the people who allow themselves to be forced or hoodwinked are, to be sure, guilty of warlike impulses, yet it is the leaders, nevertheless, and not people who are primarily responsible. While that view prevails, there can be no successful crusade of hatred. The American people find nothing inherently hateful about the German people.

The capacity to hate, although it may appear unexpectedly in any group, is usually the manifestation of a cultural tradition. In America, in spite of the fact that we have had our share of race riots and lynchings, that tradition is not a salient characteristic of the culture. True, we hated hard during the last war; but that is a complex story. It is worth noting that, in this war, the one section which stands out above the rest of the country in its hatred of the enemy is the section where hate—race hatred—is always just below the surface. The South makes an interesting contrast when placed against the rest of the nation.[4]

33%   in the South hate the German people; only
14%   of the rest of the country feel the same way.

Still another consideration. In the pages of our newspapers, from the pulpit, on the screen, over the radio has come a picture of innocent Germans victimized by Nazi villains. Dick Tracy and Superman trap Nazi spies, destroy Gestapo sadists. When the ordinary German is involved, he is pictured not as an object of hate, but of sympathy. Hollywood has dramatized the Underground or the little man or the tortured prisoner in the concentration camp. Even in real life, we have, since 1933, been face to face with the victims of Nazi terror to whom America has been a haven. By identifying ourselves with these victimized Germans we have made it difficult—if not impossible—to achieve the total emotion necessary for consuming hatred. In the presence of such distinctions hatred cannot flourish. We know that it is a group and not a people against whom we fight.

That we hate a group, not a people, is evident. Ask the nation whether they consider the German people or the German Government, the Japanese people or the Japanese Government our chief enemies. Answers interpret themselves. Shortly after Pearl Harbor, three-fourths named the German Government; two-thirds the Japanese Government. The trend of opinion has changed little since then. As of this date, the trend of opinion on Germany has changed little. The same can hardly be said of opinion on Japan. The story is told in Figure 1 on the following page.[5-6]

But it is wrong to assume that we consider the people of enemy nations blameless. Compassion is not forgiveness. If the German people and the Japanese people let themselves get hoodwinked into war as often as they do, there is something wrong with them. Take first the German people. How do we describe them? A sample of the nation was given a list of 23 adjectives and asked to pick those that best describe the Germans. Here is a profile, as we see it, of the people of the Reich.[7]

	Per cent		Per cent
Warlike	68	Honest	10
Hard-working	62	Unimaginative	8
Cruel	59	Ordinary	8
Treacherous	43	Artistic	7
Intelligent	41	Aristocratic	7
Conceited	33	Dull	6
Arrogant	31	Religious	6
Progressive	31	Rude	19
Brave	30	Ignorant	12
Quick-tempered	26	Radical	24
Sly	22	Lazy	1
Practical	21	Can't say	5

ARE WE FIGHTING AGAINST GOVERNMENTS OR PEOPLES?

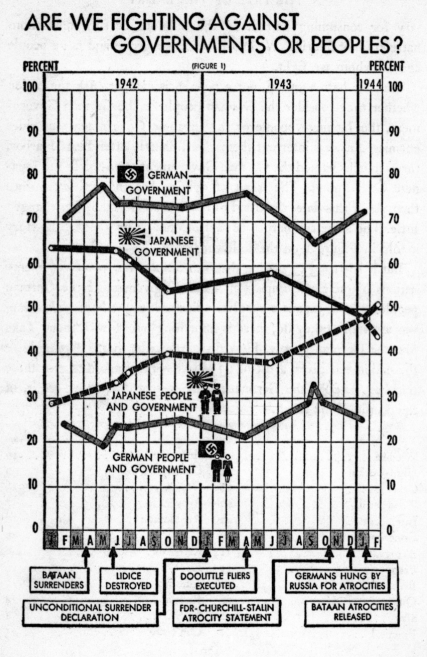

(FIGURE 1)

In our eyes the German people are warlike all right. Any nation that can breed that many disturbers of the peace that often must be warlike. That is the common-sense view. It should be proof that our humaneness is not predicated on the assumption that Germans are angels. If anything, our opinions derive from the realization that Germans are people—not angels. It happens that we respect people.

The Japanese people fare less well. Their "profile" is more jagged toward the top—more people gang up in agreeing about their negative traits and fewer say kind things about them.[8] *

	Per cent		Per cent
Treacherous	73	Religious	18
Sly	62	Ignorant	16
Cruel	55	Rude	12
Warlike	46	Radical	12
Hardworking	39	Practical	9
Conceited	27	Unimaginative	7
Intelligent	24	Ordinary	6
Brave	23	Dull	4
Arrogant	21	Aristocratic	4
Progressive	19	Lazy	3
Quick-tempered	19	Honest	2
Artistic	19	Can't say	7

But our opinions of the two peoples are more profoundly different than their profiles. Figures collected between 1942 and 1944 tell a more complete story. People were asked at different times during that period whether they felt the German (Japanese) people would always want to go to war for power, whether they were too easily misled into war, or whether they were peace-loving and forced into war (Figures 2 and 3).[10]

Two things stand out. As far as the Germans are concerned, we

* To check against an "oriental halo" people over the country were asked to describe the Chinese people as well as the Japanese. The sharp difference in results indicates that "Japaneseness" and not "orientalness" is what is being described.[9]

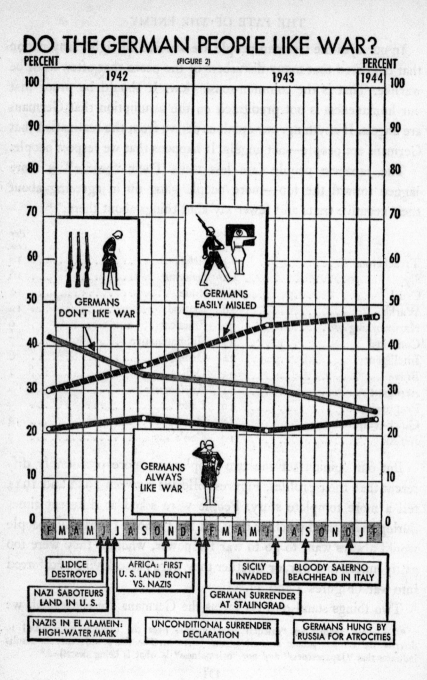

DO THE GERMAN PEOPLE LIKE WAR?

PERCENT (FIGURE 2) **PERCENT**

GERMANS
DON'T LIKE WAR

GERMANS
EASILY MISLED

GERMANS
ALWAYS
LIKE WAR

LIDICE
DESTROYED

AFRICA: FIRST
U. S. LAND FRONT
VS. NAZIS

SICILY
INVADED

BLOODY SALERNO
BEACHHEAD IN ITALY

NAZI SABOTEURS
LAND IN U. S.

GERMAN SURRENDER
AT STALINGRAD

NAZIS IN EL ALAMEIN:
HIGH-WATER MARK

UNCONDITIONAL SURRENDER
DECLARATION

GERMANS HUNG BY
RUSSIA FOR ATROCITIES

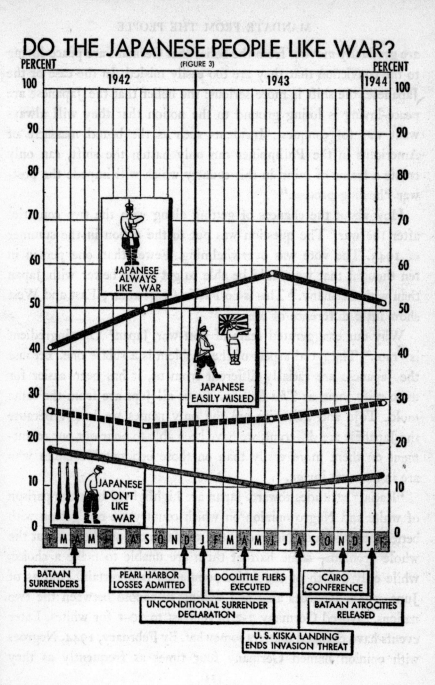

DO THE JAPANESE PEOPLE LIKE WAR?

PERCENT (FIGURE 3) PERCENT

JAPANESE ALWAYS LIKE WAR

JAPANESE EASILY MISLED

JAPANESE DON'T LIKE WAR

1942   1943   1944

BATAAN SURRENDERS

PEARL HARBOR LOSSES ADMITTED

DOOLITTLE FLIERS EXECUTED

CAIRO CONFERENCE

UNCONDITIONAL SURRENDER DECLARATION

BATAAN ATROCITIES RELEASED

U. S. KISKA LANDING ENDS INVASION THREAT

are gradually moving from the belief that Germans are peace-loving to the conviction that they are too easily misled. In the case of the Japanese, the shift is more serious: the belief that the Japanese are peace-loving is losing ground to the notion that they will always want war for conquest. Incidents such as the brutal massacre of Americans in the Philippines can only hasten the shift, can only create a frame of mind in this country which will impede the post-war "healing process."

How about the chances of getting along with the two countries after the war? The question was put to the nation in the summer of 1943. The vote was overwhelming. Fewer than one person in ten thought that we would be able to get along better with Japan than with Germany.[11] This is no Pacific Coast affair; East and West show little difference of opinion.[12]

Why our exaggerated fears of post-war Japan? One ingredient is "race." The racial aspect of the problem is a subtle one. Because the Japanese are racially different from us, it has been easier for us to reify them as *The Enemy*. To us all Japs are from the same mold. Tojo and Hirohito are the only names we know. Because the Japanese are different, we have been able to pour out our resentment on them more easily than on those occidental enemies who are in our own image.

"Racial" attitudes toward Japan are highlighted by a comparison of white and Negro opinion on which country we can get on with better after the war. Negroes, first, are far more apathetic about the whole problem—some half of them are unable to make a choice, while only a fifth of the white population is uncertain. And as of June, 1943, Negroes able and willing to choose between the two nations, favored Germany 3-2 in contrast to 10-1 for whites. Later events have changed matters somewhat. By February, 1944, Negroes with opinion named Germany four times as frequently as they named Japan. But during the same period, the balance of opinion among whites had jumped to 19-1 in favor of Germany.[13]

Not only is Japan different. It is unknown. Who are Goebbels' and Goering's opposite numbers? Few of us could answer. Having known so little about Japan, we have for the most part been without opinions. Our feelings have been neutral. In 1937, for example, two-thirds of America, when asked to characterize their opinions about Japan, could say only that they felt neutral.[14] Our intercourse has always been one-way. While the Japanese came to study at our universities, we did nothing but buy the gimcracks labeled "Made in Japan." Even after Pearl Harbor, fully half the nation thought that Japan had gone to war against us because urged by Germany—the villain in the piece.[15] Since that time, we have added to that picture some important and some irrelevant details. Japan, we know now, is out to control as much of the world as she can grab. If events have not made that abundantly clear to us, the Cairo Declaration has. We have also come to look upon Japan, not as something out of Gilbert and Sullivan, but as a formidable power with resolute and fanatical armies. Aside from these two bare facts, we know only that the Japanese General Staff is addicted to imaginary sinkings of the United States Navy about four times a year.

Race hatred and our fear of an enemy we hardly know have been aggravated by Japan's mode of warfare. The fanaticism of her soldiers has been weird and not a little terrifying. What manner of man is the Japanese soldier who fights savagely to the last, and crowns his achievement with suicide? Atrocities against Americans have sealed our belief in the uncanny cruelty of our Pacific foe.

ARMISTICE AND NEGOTIATION

When shall we make the peace? With whom shall we negotiate? And what shall be the nature of the armistice that precedes final peace making? A simple answer would seem natural: make peace when the enemy is defeated; make it on the basis of unconditional surrender with the commanders of the enemy armies; and let there be an armistice until an adequate treaty can be strung together. But this is not a simple war, nor is the process of negotiation unmuddied by precedent. The Unconditional Surrender Declaration is deceptively simple even to the American people.

First of all, with whom shall we deal and when? Although in this country there has never been any sizable copperhead group advocating a negotiated peace, nevertheless there has been considerable confusion over what represents an absolute surrender and a negotiated peace.

In November, 1942, and twice previous to that during the year, the American public was asked: "If the German Army overthrew Hitler and then offered to stop the war and discuss peace terms, would you favor or oppose accepting the peace offer of the German Army?" In January, 1942, some 30 per cent were ready to accept such a peace offer. Thirty per cent is no majority—but it is some 28,000,000 people. By November the figure had changed little, 33 per cent. The Casablanca statement, had it been elucidated properly, should have knocked the bottom out of support for "peace talks" with the German Army. It did not. Two weeks after the pronouncement of Unconditional Surrender, the figure was hovering around 28 per cent, a drop barely outside the range of sampling variance to which polls are prey.[16]

Granted, majority sentiment is sound and sufficiently wary of talking business with an intact Nazi military machine. It grows more so with time. But the confusion of the minority is worth noticing. Two things seem to be operative. One is a misconception of the German Army. Even in 1943, a fifth of the nation believed that the German Army is, like the armies of the United States and

Britain, a people's army, that the German Army *is* the German people.[17] What Casablanca did not explain was the meaning of peace with German militarism.

Since the days of Casablanca, the Americans have learned the importance of not compromising with German militarism.[18] But a second point remains. We are still a long way from having any specific ideas of which other groups would make dangerous fellow-negotiators. A book published in the fall of 1943 suggested, for example, that none other than Hjalmar Horace Greeley Schacht would be a rather ideal person with whom to talk peace when Nazism is defeated. Do the American people know about the role of German banking and big business in the rise of fascism? I bring the matter up here not to criticize the American people, but to point to a serious information problem. A democratically oriented public opinion might go a long way toward steering us from the temptations of expediency. Remember, when the dispute over the appointment of Giraud to head the French in North Africa was at its hottest, only four people in ten knew who de Gaulle was, and three in ten Giraud.[19]

But the American people do realize that grievous mistakes can be made in the period immediately following the shooting. If they, through their lack of knowledge of enemy countries, are in danger of making mistakes in haste, they are wise enough to provide safeguards against repentance in leisure. The majority of Americans are in favor of postponing final peace discussions for sometime after the war. Only a third of the nation opposes a cooling-off period during which we may consider with circumspection our best course of action.[20] Such a transition period is doubtless contemplated by the United Nations. If we do not know the intricacies of enemy nations now, a cooling-off period may provide an ideal interval for learning.

The Treaty and Its Consequences

The average man has thought little about the problem of punishing the enemy, because the problem is still remote. When he is asked specific questions about how we shall treat our enemies, he is able to come out with a coherent answer only because that answer is based partly upon the background of thought and emotions already described in this chapter and partly upon a few very basic ideas about the proper handling of enemies in general.

What are these basic ideas? I should list these.

1. The enemy must be punished severely for breaking the peace. The punishment must be in full. Whatever our opinions about enemy people, however much we feel compassionate toward them, our sympathies must not deter us from setting stiff terms.

2. In providing for punishment of enemy nations, we must be careful that our treatment of enemy *peoples* be humane. "Treat them kindly" is our motto.

3. The leaders of enemy nations, the dictatorial men responsible for starting this war and for prosecuting it with ruthless savagery, must be dealt with severely—that means prison if we are kindly and death if we are just. Hitler particularly must be shown no mercy.

4. On what shall become of enemy nations as political entities—and this does not mean empires—we are not yet decided, though we rather favor letting them exist whole. We are sure, however, that they must not remain strong nations after the war. They have, in essence, read themselves out of the councils of the Great Powers. Until they can prove that war is not their only means of dealing with international problems, they should have little voice in international decisions.

5. Above all things, the enemy should be stripped of every vestige of military power, be completely disarmed.

6. The best way of seeing to it that enemy nations do not rise to attack us again in the near future is to police them.

7. One feature of the treaty must be reparations. The enemy has caused death and destruction to others and must be made to pay until it hurts. That is only just—an eye for an eye.

8. The Axis nations must be stripped of the land they have gained through conquest.

Those are the eight cardinal points. Whether they change in specific detail or not, their meaning is likely to remain constant. Many important matters are not included—re-education, the form of government in enemy territory, the nature of new leaders in Germany and Japan, United Nations aid in reconstruction, etc. Although we have opinions on these matters too, such opinions, still uncrystallized, are notoriously subject to the impact of events.

First we must turn to the meaning of the eight points.

Severity of Treatment

Popular reappraisal of the treaty that ended the last war has it that the Treaty of Versailles was not hard enough on Germany, that it allowed Germany to grow strong again. In 1937 and again in 1942, people were asked whether the Versailles Treaty had been too harsh, too easy, or about right. The results each time were similar. At both dates, more than four in every ten of those Americans with opinions on the matter charged that Germany had not been handled firmly enough.[21-22]

What about the treaty to follow this war? Shall it be harsher or not so harsh as the one that followed World War I? Between 1939 and 1944, we have begun to approach unanimity—on a tough treaty. The trend is given in Figure 4 on the page following.[23]

In the sections which follow, the meaning of a "tough treaty" will become apparent.

SHOULD TREATY OF WORLD WAR II BE MORE OR LESS SEVERE THAN VERSAILLES?

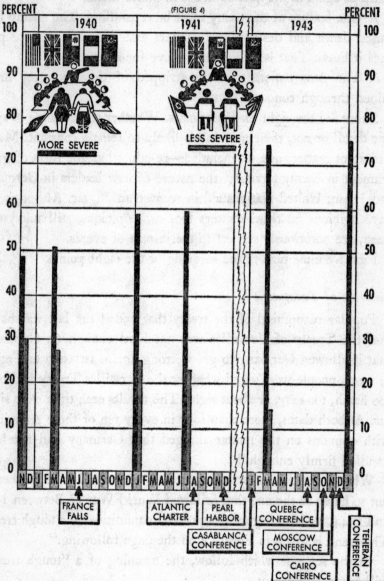

PERCENT   (FIGURE 4)   PERCENT

FRANCE FALLS

ATLANTIC CHARTER

PEARL HARBOR

CASABLANCA CONFERENCE

QUEBEC CONFERENCE

MOSCOW CONFERENCE

CAIRO CONFERENCE

TEHERAN CONFERENCE

Disarmament of Our Enemies

Most of us are firmly convinced that Germany, given half a chance, will start preparing for another war if she loses this one.[24]

70% believe that Germany will start preparing for war if she loses,
17% believe that she will not, and
13% are not sure about it.

Given such a conviction, we do not, naturally enough, want to see our enemies well armed after the war. Recall too our conviction that the German and Japanese people cannot be trusted with armaments; these people either like war for itself or are too easily led to it by their leaders.[10] So long as our major war aim remains negative—the prevention of future war—we can be sure that disarmament of our enemies will always be a big item on our post-war agenda. It is now. We believe firmly that the German army must be disbanded and kept disbanded, that Germany must be occupied, and that the seed of the trouble—the Nazi Party—must be stamped out.[25]

Humaneness toward the German and Japanese People

Opinion on treatment of the Japanese people is still uncrystallized, and few surveys on the subject have been made. The end of the war in the Pacific is sufficiently remote and fraught with so many possibilities for the fanning of hatred that figures gathered up to this time may in a few years have little relevance.

About the handling of the German people, however, we have definite and firm notions, having fought two wars against Germany in one generation. Humane, yes. Ask people how we should treat the German people after the war, and the answers divide somewhat as follows.[26]

61% say that we should treat them kindly and with consideration
19% want kindness backed by firm treatment

12%   advocate an "eye-for-eye" revenge on the Germans, and
9%   are indefinite or unsure.

Our perspective is not a bloodthirsty one. Shall we, for example, protect the German people from the possibility of bloody revenge by overrun countries? Yes. The proposition that a Nazi be killed for every person killed by the Germans in occupied territories meets with the approval of only four in one hundred Americans.[27] Indeed, in October, 1942, some 63 per cent of the population were willing to have our Government make the promise that we would protect the German people from the revenge of occupied Europe as a means of getting Germany to stop the war.[28]

On the surface the picture seems contradictory: a treaty more severe than last time; suspicion that the Germans and Japanese like war too well; yet a humane point of view toward enemy people. But the puzzle fits together.

We are, to be sure, humane. Yet our humaneness is neatly divided from our understanding of the way in which treatment of Germany and Japan as nations will affect the German and Japanese people. The contradiction is not one of intent; it stems from lack of knowledge. That story can be told next.

Reparations and Economic Revenge

Ask people how much we should make Germany, Italy, and Japan pay toward the cost of the war. The answers are somewhat out of line with the humaneness with which we propose to treat enemy people.[29]

	Germany %	Japan %	Italy %
Collect as much as it is possible to get, even if it breaks them.........	43	45	41
None of the cost of the war........	9	8	9
Something in between...........	38	37	40
No opinion....................	10	10	10
	100	100	100

During the spring of 1943, a survey in Colorado attempted to get at the anatomy of our economic bloodthirstiness toward the enemy. How reconcile it with our humane sympathies? How square it with our avowed wish to give enemy peoples a hand on the road to peaceful and democratic reconstruction?

First of all, people do not see the connection between economic revenge and its consequences, hardly realize, for example, that our insistence on reparations after the last war created the conditions of misery which permitted the rise to power of Hitler and the Nazis.[30] Asked whether reparations were one of the main factors contributing to the rise of Hitler,

19% agreed that reparations were,
63% disagreed with the idea, and
18% were not sure.

It is no surprise, then, that 52 per cent of the Coloradoans polled held out for trying to collect as much as possible from the Germans, even if it breaks them.[31]

But the Colorado survey also showed that there were ways in which the spirit of economic revenge could be modified. Various methods were tested. Those who felt that we should collect till it hurts or at least collect something from our enemies—some 82 per cent—were put through a systematic grilling to see if their minds could be changed.

First, they were asked, if collecting caused a severe depression in Germany, would we be wise to collect and run the risk of hurting our international trade, or wiser to forget collection and hope that trade would improve? [32]

Then, if we punish Germany's leaders and take away all the land that Germany has gained since the rise of the Nazis, should we still try to collect more in the way of reparations? [33]

This is what happens.

82%   want to collect to start off with; only
55%   want to collect when the danger of hurting our trade is mentioned; and only
38%   still want to collect after the danger of depression is pointed out and the provision made that Germany will be stripped and punished in other ways.

The optimist will immediately say, "Ah, see, the American people will not make fantastic demands for collection when the facts are shown to them." But optimism here is misplaced. What guarantee have we that on an issue such as this the facts will reach the American people? During the war they have not. At the very time when there has been the greatest moral compulsion to bring all important available information to the people, survey after survey has indicated that facts such as these are not, except in distorted form, reaching the bulk of the American people.* And, too, the optimist reckons without that spirit of economic adventuresomeness which may well blossom after the war. Likely enough it will serve to hide under a bushel rational arguments for intelligent economic treatment of Germany rather than allowing them to shine through. There is still little support for wild theories of economic revenge.[25] But if our current information policy of keeping all cards close to the chest before they are played continues, the facts are not likely to reach the American people soon enough to forestall such support. If that happens, the consequence is clear; a frame of mind best described as "revengeful collectionism" will prevail when decisions come to be made.

* A long exposition of this point is out of place here. For two succinct demonstrations of vital gaps in American information and what can be done about them, see Gerard B. Lambert and Hadley Cantril "Informing the Public: A test case," *Public Opinion Quarterly*, Vol. 7, No. 3, 1943, and Jerome S. Bruner, "OWI and the American Public," *Public Opinion Quarterly*, Vol. 7, No. 1, 1943.

And so there indeed is the rub in humaneness. To put it concisely, we are abstractly humane, economically tough.

Germany as a Post-war State

No strong body of opinion in favor of rendering Germany and Japan into a checkerboard of petty principalities exists today. A sample of the nation was given the choice of seeing Germany broken up so that she could never rise as a unified nation again or seeing her remain intact, with present leaders deposed and punished.[34]

30% voted to have Germany broken up into small states, but
64% preferred to have her continue intact under a new government;
 6% had no opinion on the matter.

The same spirit was shown in a later survey in which various methods of dealing with Germany after the war were outlined. Faced with the choice of seven alternative methods of dealing with Germany, only one person in ten chose dismemberment.[27] We share our attitudes with the other English-speaking countries. The same view prevails in England, in Canada, in Australia.[35]

What then? What do we wish? Merely that our enemies get rid of their leaders and their dictatorships and live like decent human beings again. We will be the regulating guardian until that is accomplished. The matter is simple. The public has no comprehensive formula. Details can come later.

Will enemy peoples want a change from dictatorship? On the whole we are pretty well convinced that in the case of Germany and Italy, at least, people will want a change after their debauch of *Uebermenschlichkeit*. About the Japanese people, we are not so sure. The question was put this way: "In your opinion, after the war will the German people (Japanese people) want the kind of Government they have now, or some other kind?" These are the results.[36]

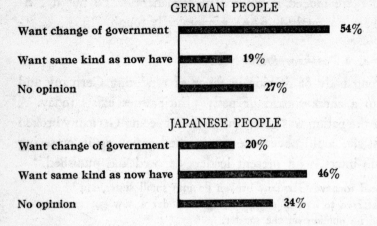

GERMAN PEOPLE

Want change of government — 54%

Want same kind as now have — 19%

No opinion — 27%

JAPANESE PEOPLE

Want change of government — 20%

Want same kind as now have — 46%

No opinion — 34%

But will the American people demand that democracies be set up in all enemy countries? An answer to the question is still impossible. That we will demand the uprooting of war leaders and dictatorship is certain, but opinion is not crystallized on the form of government to fill the vacuum.

And what about reconstituted enemy nations in the large context of a world organization? Where do they stand? In one survey, 73 per cent of the American people who had expressed a willingness to see the United States join some projected union of nations were asked whether they would approve letting Germany, Italy, and Japan into the union.[37]

52% approved letting Italy join the union,
44% approved German entry, and
40% were willing to see Japan become a member.

Aside from Italy, obviously, none of these countries could count on support from a majority of the American people; even Italy's majority is slim. If one remembers, however, that these questions were asked in the midst of a war, the percentage of approval is strikingly high. If one were forced to a conclusion on the basis of this survey, it would be that strong opposition to incorporation of enemy nations—on a limited basis—will not develop.

Limited basis? Decidedly. Let them join, say many, but curtail their power within the organization. If, for example, you ask all those not opposed to the United States joining a confederation whether they would still approve if *Germany* were allowed to have the *same* power as we do, then the number of supporters dwindles to a weak minority.[38] Let them in, yes, but keep them in their places until such time as they can prove their trustworthiness.

Treatment of Enemy Leaders

On the matter of enemy leaders and war criminals public opinion is vigorous and clear-cut. Our very conception of the origins of war underlines the overburdening guilt of these men. So, when you ask a sample of the country what should be done with Nazi leaders, you get answers like these: [39]

36% say they should be killed summarily,
25% recommend exile or imprisonment,
13% state merely that they should be punished harshly and severely,
 6% recommend deposing them and keeping them from power in the future,
 2% favor torture,
 2% say that they should be court-martialed,
 2% say they will be killed before we get there,
 2% recommend leniency,
 2% claim that what happens to Nazi leaders is none of our business, and
10% have no opinion.

The catalogue is on the bloodthirsty side. So is our temper. By war's end there may, of course, be a hopeless beclouding of who is a Nazi and who is not a Nazi (vide Italy). Barring such confusion, the case will be open and shut. Americans will demand the heads of war criminals.

Policing the Enemy

We believe strongly that force is the best instrument through which to keep the peace. That means some form of policing. Through policing, the Axis nations—indeed, any potential aggressor nations—are to be kept in line. The details are still not clear in American thinking—nor in the thinking of American officialdom.

Occupation of enemy territory—the first form of policing—is, of course, taken for granted. Scarcely one American in ten would oppose it.[25] Indeed, more people want occupation to continue for a ten-year period than would have it end when the Nazis are tamed.[40] We are talking tough on this point and we mean it.

Axis-held Territory

To date no major polling organization has spent the money necessary to test questions on whether the enemy should be allowed to keep lands conquered since the beginning of the war. Polling is too expensive a procedure to use on obvious issues. One semi-controversial issue which approaches the question of Axis-plundered territory was asked a few months before Italy's capitulation. It is an augury of opinion on the broader question of Axis-dominated Europe.[41]

"If we make peace with Italy, would you be in favor of returning all or nearly all the possessions Italy held in Africa at the start of the war?"

17%   favored the return of Italian pre-war African territory,
61%   opposed it, and
22%   had no opinion on the matter.

THE PERSPECTIVE

Those are the broad outlines. They are vague. Many details are still in the air. But details, as far as the man in the street is concerned, are for the future; they can wait. Even when the issues are before the public, many vital questions will be left to the experts for settlement.

In spite of everything, public opinion is going to be faced with hard decisions, once the enemy is defeated. If it is to be a responsible force in influencing the shape of our policy toward the enemy, it must be maximally informed. Where does it fall short now, and how can it be improved?

The American people, clearly, have a much oversimplified picture of the way in which Axis countries can be deterred from further aggression. The idea in substance is "Treat 'em rough." The enemy must be dealt with severely, more so than "last time." On only one point do we discriminate: that we be humane to enemy people in the abstract. Severity, to be sure, is richly deserved. Yet it is admittedly insufficient as a guiding principle in treating erstwhile enemies. To the whole question of ways and means whereby Germany, Italy, and Japan can assume gracefully their places in the concourse of nations, the American public has most certainly given little thought. If our leaders have ideas on the matter, those ideas have yet to be aired in public.

Some will say that talk now of our treatment of Germany, Italy, and Japan after the war may serve to stiffen the morale of the enemy. That depends upon what is talked about and in what tone of voice. Lest we forget, Wilson's Fourteen Points, whether adequate or inadequate as a diplomatic blueprint, were one of *the* most powerful propaganda weapons in bringing about the collapse of German morale in 1918.*

We are left with the feeling that American thinking on the prob-

* An able discussion of the role of the Fourteen Points in speeding the downfall of Germany can be found in G. G. Bruntz, *Allied Propaganda and the Collapse of the German Empire in 1918*, Stanford: Stanford University Press, 1938.

lem of the enemy is traditional in the extreme: tough treaty, reparations, punish the leaders. The model is obviously 1918. But 1918 applied to 1948 may well be disastrous. Europe after this war will be a study in exploded social institutions. Class lines in Germany and more particularly in German-occupied territory have been smashed by the exigencies of administration by plunder. The church, the labor movement, the educational system, the system of justice—all these things have been so mercilessly supplanted by *ersatz* Nazi models that when the fascist regime collapses, little will be left to take its place, save the AMG administrators who move in *pro tem.* At very best, the transition from a Nazi Europe to post-war non-Nazi Europe—whatever its form—will be stormy, possibly bloody. The revolutionary turmoil will make virtually impossible the application of traditional sanctions against defeated enemies, large and small. Putting the load of revenge-motivated reparations on the shoulders of people who have suffered as Axis satellites or who, as citizens of the Reich, have felt the weight of Allied bombs will be salt in wounds that in the interest of general European reconstruction had best be healed as quickly as possible. Even the conservative National Association of Manufacturers has realized the dangers inherent in reparations and has publicly questioned their wisdom. To date, no effort has been made to inform the American people of the likelihood of seething chaos in Europe after the war. Without such information, it is futile to hope that public opinion will be in a state of readiness to understand the issues as they arise. Our traditional thinking may be our undoing.

England, in the front line of battle and more keenly aware of the realities of modern warfare, seems readier to accept new economic formulae for the peace than are we. We have had no unseating blitz. A sample difference of opinion illustrates the point. It has been proposed that three or four million Germans be sent to Russia at war's end to rebuild demolished cities. It is not a traditional idea. Opinion in America, though favorable, is hardly enthusiastic—50 per cent in favor, 30 per cent opposed. Compare Britain: 70 per cent for, 15 per cent against.[42]

The place of enemy nations in the jigsaw puzzle of post-war economic life is another problem on which public information is wanting. In a sense, this problem is part of the broader one discussed in Chapter III. The majority of the American people want to see the world back on its business legs after the war. There is no reason to doubt that the enemy is included in that wish. Yet it is abundantly clear that in the matter of enemy economics after the war, the American right hand knows not what the left hand does. We want to help Germany get back on her feet; we want to collect reparations; we want to protect our own trade. Each of these contradictory programs occupies a separate pigeonhole in our thinking. No leader of real stature—and the President would be the obvious candidate—has had the forethought or courage to tell the American people how all of these masters can be served at once, or if not served at once, which will have to be slighted. Time is running perilously short.

Thus far we have been talking almost exclusively of Europe. More can be said of the problems of the Far East. But what is most important about public opinion on Far Eastern post-war problems is not that we have vague opinions, but that we have virtually no opinions at all. Probably never has a modern nation fought an enemy about which she knew so little as we do of Japan. It is admittedly important to prepare guide books for soldiers going overseas so that they may know of the customs and problems of the countries in which and against which they will fight. The War Department in collaboration with other agencies has done a splendid job with these guide books. But why has nobody thought of the need for providing guide books on our enemies for the civilian? A guide prepared, let us say, in conjunction with the editors of *Life* or other magazines expert in the pictorial presentation of fact, would still appeal to a broad audience. Nor is there any reason why the written guide could not be supplemented with well-constructed movies and carefully produced radio shows.

The picture as a whole is not too discouraging. Americans have not thought in much detail about "disposing" of the enemy after the war. Unmotivated by real hatred, they profess to humane sentiments about the peoples with whom we are at war. The prevalent view is probably simpler and more traditional than the post-war situation will allow it to remain. But, given the proper handling of information, we can learn. That we do not as yet see the constructive problem of rehabilitating the enemy is, perhaps, the most dangerous aspect of American opinion. The public may be satisfied merely to see the punishment of German leaders and the slapping on of heavy "fines." It may lose interest after that and leave the matter to the proverbial experts. The time to start informing the American people about the issues which will have to be faced in post-war Europe was last year. The time at which machinery for handling these problems should have been tentatively blueprinted (with the full knowledge of the public) was yesterday. It takes time to inform a people. In this area as in others, time is running out.

PART II: *THE HOME FRONT*

CHAPTER VIII

SOCIAL SECURITY: AMERICAN VERSION

THAT the American people want a sound and humane social security for this country goes without saying. Who denies it flies in the face of the evidence.

But it is a mistake to think that, because we as a people favor social security, we are at the same time giving homage to the ideal of a social-service state. Social insurance is for a rainy day. In the eyes of most Americans, the worst thing that could happen is too many rainy days for too many people. The popular idea of an economic heaven is not the assurance that we will be looked after in misfortune, but that we will have jobs and self-respect, *and* generous provisions for those who, through temporary bad luck or infirmity, are not able to share fully in the vigorous and expanding economic life of the nation.

FREEDOM FROM WANT

That is the context in which the concept "freedom from want" exists in the American public mind. It is a context which derives from our frontier tradition, from our belief that, "really," each man can and should look after himself. But "really" means "ideally," because none but the most hide-bound individualist would claim that our economic difficulties today are as easily overcome as they were in the days of the frontier. The crux of the matter as far as public opinion is concerned is this: people see the changes but nevertheless believe—or, perhaps, hope—that the old frontier individualism is still a possible, still a desirable pattern.

Yet the fact that people see social security as only the negative side of a more adventurous freedom of initiative should give small aid and comfort to those breast-beaters who oppose comprehensive social security as "coddling." The danger of post-war unemployment—a bitter lesson learned after the last war—has made America more security-conscious today than it has ever been in a period of prosperity. Terminate that period of prosperity, and the popular cry for adequate social insurance would be the political *lingua franca* of two-thirds of the nation's popular vote.

Turning from tradition to the soberer facts of expectation, one might ask first, how optimistic are we about freedom from want? We are a practical people. Americans do not see freedom from want as an easy ideal. Freedom from want is, rather, one of those goals always to be fought for but never attained. It ranks with "honesty," "goodness," and the other social ideals. To sense this pragmatism, one has only to ask a cross-section of the country whether, in their opinion, there will always be people in America who do not have the kind of food, clothing, and housing they need. No fewer than eight people in every ten you talk to will agree that such people there will always be.[1]

The roots of our feeling go deep. They take their life from our faith in individualism. Men have unequal endowments; the world's goods come to one according to endowment. Blame is rarely attached to the "system." There will always be want simply because some people just do not have the initiative or ability to escape want.[2] That is the prevailing view in America.

But though Americans expect no millennium we are, neverthe-less, sold on the "ideological" as well as on the practical necessity for social security. There is no better earnest of our convictions than a summary of opinion on some typical measures of social security. The figures which follow are a sample: [3-7]

OPINION FAVORING SOCIAL SECURITY MEASURES

Old-age pensions	94%
Job insurance	84%
Health insurance	83%
Aid for students	79%
Works relief	73%

If a "plebiscite" on social security were to be conducted tomor-row, America would make the plans of our social-security prophets look niggardly. We want the whole works.

THE SPECIFICS OF SOCIAL SECURITY

A word more about specific kinds of social security. Practically any reasonable proposal for social security can, doubtless, count on majority support from the American people. But that is not the whole story.

Take first the matter of political support for specific measures. Though the principle of comprehensive, cradle-to-grave security is, as we shall see, a bone of contention between Democrats and Re-publicans, the same cannot be said for party sentiment on *concrete* measures. In the figure which follows, five specific social-security measures are presented, along with the support they muster among Republican and Democratic voters.[3-7] The meaning is self-evident.

VOTER SUPPORT FOR SOCIAL SECURITY MEASURES

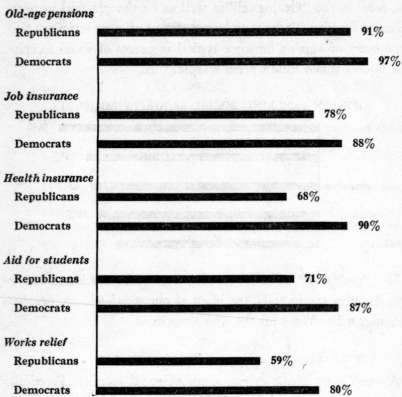

It is not correct to assume, however, that the public feels equally agreeable about all forms of "civilian" social security. Our tastes are fairly well differentiated. A poll once asked this question of the public: [8] "If the Government had only a limited amount of money to spend for social security after the war, which one of these social-security programs do you think would be most important?" Four kinds were named: old-age pensions, medical care for those who need it but cannot afford it, unemployment insurance for those who lose their jobs, and aid for children who cannot be completely supported by their parents. The replies afford an interesting glimpse into the American mind.

The measure which polls twice as many votes as any other is old-age pensions. The "want" which moves us most deeply is one which visits all equally, has its roots in nature, and is *least* amenable to the control of man—old age. Of those who can choose among the various forms of social security, 40 per cent place old-age pensions first. The closest competitor is unemployment insurance at 23 per cent. Medical care and dependency allotments bring up the rear with 18 per cent and 19 per cent respectively.

But the country as a whole is an abstraction. What counts are the groups which make it up. A summary of their opinions looks like this: [8]

	Old-age pensions %	Medical care %	Unemployment insurance %	Child assistance %
Age				
Under 40........	29	23	28	20
Over 40.........	47	22	12	19
Economic Status				
Above average	37	30	15	18
Average	40	22	22	16
Below average	43	20	17	20
Sex				
Men	38	22	19	21
Women	42	23	17	18

By and large the American people agree about the specific kinds of social security that are most urgently needed. What differences there exist are easily understandable. The young man at the peak of his earning period naturally rates unemployment insurance higher in the scale of significance than does the oldster. Conversely, people over forty consider old-age pensions more urgent than do most youngsters. The differences are inevitable. Yet they are small enough to indicate that serious public controversy on details is unlikely.

One field in which the American people have very definite prejudices is unemployment relief. We may have had our plethora of WPA jokes, but when it comes down to cases there are few Americans indeed who would not rather work on a governmental works project than receive an out-and-out relief check. Work, whether on WPA or not, is better than sitting around—even if both be equally paid. The matter was put this way to the American people: "What do you think is the best way of providing help for unemployed people—for the Government to pay them an unemployment compensation until they can find a job again, or for the Government to provide a job on some kind of public works project?" Seventy-six per cent choose public works. The poor see eye to eye with the rich; Republicans with Democrats.[9]

The question whether people are willing to pay for the social security of which they so heartily approve is quickly answered. Yes, emphatically. Workers have been asked whether they would be willing to pay three cents on every dollar of their paychecks to match a corresponding three cents put up by their employers. Two-thirds are willing.[10] In the bad year of 1938 some six Americans in ten were willing to pay $2.00 a month for complete medical care for themselves.[11] Two dollars is a lot of money at 1938 buying power; it is, at any rate, probably a good deal more than enough as a monthly contribution to a national health plan. Thumping majorities, too, express themselves in favor of adequate taxes to provide such things as medical care for the needy, job insurance, old-age pensions, and work relief.[12]

A Case Study in Opinion

A concrete case study of American opinion on social security throws our way of thinking into somewhat sharper relief. In March, 1943, to the accompaniment of mixed cheers and catcalls from the press and commentators, the President sent to Congress an omnibus plan for social security after the war: the badly battered NRPB Plan. For the first few days after its appearance, the Plan held the center of the stage; indeed, quickened the hope of millions. But no effort was made either on the part of the Administration, Congress, or the press to keep interest in the Plan alive. That in itself was typically American. How different the treatment of the Beveridge Report in Britain. Consider, however, the nation's reaction.

One week after the Plan was announced, 58 per cent of the nation had heard of it.[13] That, in the midst of war, while other, more dramatic news was appearing under bigger headlines in parallel columns, is something.

Two weeks later, as a result of sloppy publicity, the number of people who said that they had heard of the Plan dropped to 35 per cent.[13] By now the Plan is all but forgotten. The decline is dramatic. In England enthusiasm grew with time; here it fizzled out.

Was the principle of the new Plan approved by the people? A week after the announcement of the NRPB Report by the President this question was put to the American people.[14]

"According to a new plan for social security announced by the President, the government would provide higher social-security payments to everybody, young or old, who is in want because of unemployment or illness or disability after the war. Would you approve or disapprove of such a new social-security law?"

76% approved
15% disapproved
 9% had no opinion

It is, of course, no surprise that greatest support for the Plan came from those most intimate with the sting of want.[15]

58% of the upper income group favored the Plan,
73% of the middle income group, and
83% of the lower income group.

All income levels, to be sure, poll majorities in favor of social security. Yet it would be political blindness not to take cognizance of the fact that it is primarily the little man in America who appreciates social insurance as his more fortunate brethren cannot.

If there is a deepening difference of opinion between the rich and the poor, that difference is also making itself felt in the political arena. The Democratic Party with its great following in the urban industrial areas is far more security conscious than the rank and file of Republicans. While

83% of Democrats favor extended comprehensive social security, only
57% of Republicans give their approval.[16]

Any difference of opinion between the rich and the poor is magnified manifold when one goes to the leaders of the two ends of the economic hierarchy. In a survey conducted about a month after the NRPB Plan was announced, representative leaders of business, the CIO, and the A. F. of L. were asked whether they thought Congress should act now on the NRPB social-security proposals or upon some substitute, or whether it would be wiser to wait till the end of the war.[17] The sharp difference in leadership opinion leaves one not a little worried about the future.

29% of business leaders voted for immediate action
84% of national, regional, and state A. F. of L. leaders voted for immediate action, and
97% of national, regional, and state CIO leaders voted for immediate action

As far as business leaders are concerned, the issue goes beyond whether Congress should act immediately or not. In the Fall of 1942 the nation's business leaders were asked whether the Federal government should provide for medical care for the needy, old-age pensions, and job insurance. Did they think the Government *would* provide these things? The picture that emerges is one of almost sullen dissent.[18] On the matter of job insurance, for example, only

35%   thought there *should* be provision for job insurance, but
84%   thought the Government *would* provide it

Medical care for the needy?

24%   thought there *should* be such provision, but
60%   thought such provision *would* be made

Old-age pensions?

49%   favored them, but
91%   saw them coming anyway

One year later, in October, 1943—a year which had seen the introduction of the Beveridge Report in England and the NRPB Report here—the opinion of business leaders had changed little. Asked what they thought of a "cradle-to-grave" program of minimum security for the United States, they answered thus.[19]

44%   held such a program to be economically impossible and undesirable
15%   thought such a program economically possible but undesirable
21%   granted the desirability of the program but believed it economically impossible, and only
20%   thought a cradle-to-grave security program both possible and desirable

Such is the mood. Upper-income groups and the leaders of the nation's business see in social security—if one may judge by the columnists who speak for them—a variety of evils. The fire-eaters charge a New Deal plot or deplore an approach to "Communism." Still others are opposed to "pet schemes." More sober critics simply do not believe that truly comprehensive social security is compatible with "free enterprise."

But it is abundantly obvious that the rank and file of America does not share in these doubts. To check on the matter, people who had heard of the NRPB Social Security Report were asked shortly after its appearance whether they agreed or disagreed with charges and counter-charges then appearing in the press. First, the arguments against the Plan.[20]

	Agree %
The Plan is too much like Communism............	23
The Plan is an attempt by the President to put over some of his pet ideas during wartime............	28
The Plan is like a big WPA charity and goes against the American system	30
The Plan is filled with crack-brained ideas which could never be carried out........................	26
The Plan is an attempt by a small group in Washington to get more control over the Government........	29
The Plan is just a political move by the President....	26

There you have the opposition. In terms of popular vote they muster never more than 30 per cent.

Now some of the arguments for the Plan.

	Agree %
The Plan would make it possible for everyone to have a fair chance and some opportunity..............	66
It is the duty of the Government to see to it that no one starves...............................	79
We must plan like this now if we are going to do away with unemployment after the war...............	69

And so on.

Why, then, didn't popular pressure force social security through both Houses of Congress in record time? Why the death of NRPB's Plan?

The answer, oddly enough, lies in the almost unconquerable faith of Americans in their own personal futures. The worker in the war plant, the waitress in the hash joint, the parking place attendant—each has faith in his ability to hang on to his job after the war. None believes that social security is his meat. Post-war America will be the land of opportunity. Fifty-nine per cent of the country believes that a young man will have a better chance to get ahead than he did after the last war.[21] Eight in ten of America's workers are expecting to keep their present jobs after the war. Scarcely one in ten expects to be out job-hunting—and they think jobs will be easy to get.[22] Even in war-boom centers like Wichita, Pittsburgh, Portland (Maine), Detroit, and Mobile, only a third of workers are worried.[23] Indeed, workers in those centers believe they will have enough money saved to tide them over if they lose their jobs and have to look for new ones. Sixty-five per cent think they will; only 22 per cent think they won't.[24]

This vision of green post-war pastures has blunted the dramatic personal relevance of social security. Our optimism is such that only a third of the country believed that NRPB's version of comprehensive social insurance would make any difference in their lives.[25] And even among the poor, less than a half felt any personal stake in the Plan.

And so when it came to the matter of whether Congress should act on proposals for social security now or wait till the end of the war, support was lacking. Only 39 per cent of the country favored immediate action.[26]

But in this case it is no matter of throwing out the baby with the bath. Virtually nine people in ten of those who favored waiting until after the war indicated by their reasons that it was expediency and not opposition to the Plan which prompted them.[27] Two-thirds of those not in favor of immediate action, for example, believed that there would be time after the war to consider such questions as social security.

That is the story of the NRPB Plan. The case study of 1943 points this lesson. Our individualistic optimism, our faith in the future—not our opinions of social security—keep us from making social security a *cause célèbre*.

But there will come a time when, if only temporarily, our economic life will again be disrupted. The old visceral fears will return in some measure—the measure depending upon how skillful we are in handling reconversion. When Demobilization Day comes, will we be content with antiquated social security? Will the nation want to return to "normalcy" and the status quo?

The answer is—what normalcy? In 1940, lest we forget, there were 8,000,000 people unemployed in the United States. To that kind of normalcy, few will want to return.

In the Great Depression, the American people learned what social security meant. When the pinch comes again—if the pinch comes again—the demand for better social security will surely grow urgent. We Americans may believe that people are needy because they lack initiative or ability, but when the needy person happens to be me, that's something else again.

The Psychology of Social Security

But American thinking on social security is more than opinion on specific proposals. There is something deeper—almost a "psychology" of social security. Perhaps the best introduction to such a "psychology" is a quick comparison of the American and British philosophies of security.

In Britain the philosophy of social insurance rests on two assumptions: "national minimum" and "common pool." The theory of the national minimum, which goes back to the beginning of this century in British thinking, provides that each citizen, having fulfilled his obligation to the community, shall be protected by the community from the danger of falling below a minimum British standard of living. Should a citizen be menaced by loss of job, misfortune, or old-age, it is the responsibility of the state to protect him from the ravages of abject want. National minimum is the cornerstone of the social-service state.

In the words of Sir William Beveridge, whose Report is the most recent and most advanced statement of national minimum, "My Plan is not simply a plan to develop social insurance; it is a plan to give freedom from want by securing to each citizen at all times, on condition of service and contribution, a minimum income sufficient for his subsistence needs and responsibilities. It interprets, as any modern democracy must interpret, freedom from want to mean, not a claim to be relieved by the State on proof of necessity and lack of other resources, but having, as of right, one's own income to keep one above the necessity of applying for relief. My Plan takes as its aim the abolition of want." * In short, national minimum is not a guarantee of relief. It is a guarantee against relief.

The national minimum is not plush. This is what Beveridge has to say about it. "My Report as a whole is intended to give effect to what I regard as a peculiarly British idea: the idea of a national minimum. The idea of a minimum wage, which we learnt from the trade unions and have embodied in Trade Board Acts, is necessary but is not sufficient. There is wanted also a minimum income for subsistence when wages fall for any reason; a minimum of provision

* Sir William Beveridge, *The Pillars of Security*, New York: MacMillan, 1943, p. 145.

for children; a minimum of health, of housing, of education. . . . But being a minimum only it leaves room and incentive to individuals to add to it for themselves according to their personal capacities and desires." *

Just how *much* room there is for incentive is demonstrated rather dramatically by some figures collected in Canada. People were asked how much money as a very minimum they would need to get along on if they lost their jobs and had no money or property at all.[28] These are the figures. Next to them are the sums which would be granted weekly if the Beveridge Plan were put into operation in Canada.

	Estimate of Canadian public	Beveridge benefits
Single person	$15.00	$4.85
Two persons	20.00	8.08
Three persons	25.00	9.70
Four or more persons	25.00	11.32

Plush indeed.

Now the "common pool." The idea of a common pool keeps national minimum out of the realm of charity. Each person while he is working puts into the common pool. When he is not able to work, he takes out.

It so happens that the Beveridge Plan provides for equal contribution from all to the common pool. Contribution according to the size of income, a more American practice, is not contemplated. But whichever way it is done, the basic principle of communality remains. Psychologically the point is that *I* contribute to *my* insurance against want.

Now in England, where comprehensive social security goes back even beyond the famous Webb Minority Report of 1906, the tra-

* Sir William Beveridge, *op. cit.*, pp. 156-157.

dition of social insurance is taken for granted. Indeed, as early as 1832 a Royal Commission was appointed "to make diligent and full inquiry into the practical operation of the laws for the relief of the poor in England and Wales." Just as in England collective bargaining is a non-controversial topic, so is the idea of social security. England is ahead of us on both scores.

Three other factors are characteristic of the British view. First, the British have known want far more acutely than have we. Whole areas of England spent time between wars on Government dole. Secondly, Britain lost her frontier long before we did ours. Finally, England has had for many years a strong and vocal Labour Party which has assumed responsibility for keeping before the voting public the issue of security.

What of America?

Our first national social security law was passed in 1936. One British authority has remarked, facetiously to be sure, that the NRPB Plan in 1943 should be called not the American Beveridge Plan but the American Webb Minority Report of 1906. Social security is not taken for granted here.

Neither national minimum nor common pool has ever taken root here.

Until the New Deal, no party has espoused systematically the cause of social security. And not until the New Deal has America's labor movement felt secure enough to branch out with fullest vigor into the realm of comprehensive social insurance.

In America, the prevailing conception of social security has been in the past the relief of suffering, not the prevention of suffering. The tradition has been the "means test" to discover whether an applicant is badly enough off to deserve relief.

In America, too, there is the frontier, or at least the frontier tradition. The opportunity to make a "new start" has served as a homespun and self-regulating social security system. But making a new start is not what it was fifty years ago.

American thinking boils down to two principles—one declining, the other growing. The first is "welfare." Where the British talk in terms of "national minimum," we think about "welfare." Welfare in popular thinking has two sides. It is always for the other fellow. And it is something which goes into operation only after the damage has been done.

The Community Chest, the American Red Cross, the myriad of war relief agencies—all of these are testaments to our zeal for welfare. If specific social security measures find more acceptance here than do comprehensive plans, it is because specific measures are familiar expressions of the "welfare mentality."

There was a time, to be sure, when the dispensation of welfare was not regarded as a function of government. It was, rather, a prerogative of "charitable organizations." That is no longer true. Eight Americans in every ten believe that "it is the duty of the Government to see to it that no one starves." [20] Even three-quarters of the nation's business leaders who, as we have seen, are most opposed to Government-sponsored comprehensive social security, realize that if there is a depression, the public will demand relief from the Government. [29]

But with the advent of the ubiquitous social security number in 1936, our opinions have begun slowly to change. Where once social security and welfare were synonymous, now they are beginning to take on different meanings. An old and powerful wine is being poured into new bottles. Social security is coming to mean thrift—thrift sponsored by the Government.

The gradual transition from "welfare" to "sponsored thrift" is more than anything else an index of our growth from the frontier, through the piratical capitalism of the 19th century, to mature industrialism in the 20th. But there is more than history at work shaping our conceptions. A national minimum, for example, in a country as economically and geographically diverse as America, is just too abstract to grasp. Our demography is not suited to the doctrine. After a tour of the Eastern half of the United States, Sir William Beveridge himself admitted as much.*

In the long run, which will prevail—emphasis on welfare or emphasis on sponsored thrift? History, I think, provides its own prediction. There has never been a country which, having tasted social security, did not in due course want more social security and better social security. We want security, we are getting it, and we will want more. Welfare has never meant security—only the perpetuation of insecurity.

The future, however, is not without its perils. Attempts to introduce comprehensive social insurance in the United States will be opposed bitterly by many of the nation's most influential business leaders. From the ranks of the economically secure these leaders will draw powerful support. The fight may be bitter.

But as a wise man once put it, "Ideologies divide, projects unite." Disagree we do on the general "ideological" issue of comprehensive social security. But when the voters are faced with concrete measures, disagreement evaporates. A lesson for the future? Probably that progress in the field of social security may come piecemeal. Put it this way: political *caution* dictates piecemeal progress; political and economic *wisdom* requires comprehensive planning. Is there a half-way house?

* At an informal talk at the Institute for Advanced Study, Princeton, New Jersey, during the summer of 1943.

CHAPTER IX

JOBS FOR ALL: FREEDOM OF OPPORTUNITY

TO the man in the street the first post-war problem is employment. Jobs for war-workers, jobs for the returning soldier, a job for me. Though America listens and reads with interest about our future relations with Russia, about a thirty-hour trip across the North Pole to Moscow in tomorrow's super-clipper, about the boon of penicillin, it is on none of these things that post-war thoughts invariably center. Our curiosity reflects our basic concern. For every one person wanting to know more about maintaining post-war peace, there are three who want to know about jobs and what we are doing to assure them.[1] By comparison, concern about international relations is secondary. Foreign policy does not buy the groceries; a job does.

The lower one goes in the economic scale, the greater the preoccupation with domestic affairs. To the vast numbers of economically insecure, international affairs are hardly in the same realm of urgency with finding a job.[2] So to the average man winning the war and losing a job is a hollow victory, one which cannot be lessened by words. A clever propagandist may, if astute enough, make the American people swallow for a while a foreign policy that runs counter to their wishes. But there is no way of convincing the American people that *unemployment* is "expedient" or "temporarily necessary" or "desirable in the light of difficult circumstances."

To America, employment is survival. It is the promise of a new world, a good society.

THE EMPLOYMENT OUTLOOK

But our preoccupation with jobs does not spell pessimism. The war has raised wages, given jobs to the unemployed. Fat years are a drug. Under its influence we deny the vision of the lean years which may lie ahead. Yet with all our soul we fear that vision. Ours is the bonanza psychosis.

Promises have kindled the fires of hope. A new world of stream-lined splendors, with jobs and houses for all, has been all but promised in the expensive advertisements. Spokesmen of business have painted rosy pictures of the years after war. Tomorrow's world promises an end to drudgery, an easing of old routines with new plastics, television and escape for all. And so, we expect good things. The foundation of "good things" is a job.

But neither the prosperity of war nor the promise of business is solely responsible for America's optimism. There is something else which underlies both: a deep faith in the future of America. Somehow, someone or something will see to it that the story has a happy ending. Who or what that something is will be clearer in the pages which follow.

The dimensions of our optimism go something like this. Only about one in ten people who now hold jobs think that when the war ends they will have to look for new ones.[3] Though there is still the stereotype that wars are "inevitably" followed by depression, depression has come to mean something for the other fellow. And so while a substantial minority expect "a depression," few indeed see *themselves* out of work.[4] Nor are those who are expecting to lose war jobs gloomy about their prospects. Getting a new job will be easy.[5]

From the home front, the tone of hope has spread to the war fronts. Our troops are no less hopeful. American soldiers in Britain were questioned on the matter. Sixty-two per cent say they have old jobs waiting for them when they return. Those jobs, they believe, will still be there. To the remainder, the prospects look good. Only a quarter think their job chances will be poor.[6]

Men and women working in the expanded war industries are somewhat less optimistic. But even in war-boom towns, as we have seen, only about one worker in three expects definitely to be looking for a new job at war's end.[7] Shipbuilding is a case in point, an industry with anything but a rosy future. Shipyard workers in Portland, Maine, and Mobile, Alabama, for example, view their chances this way.[8]

39% expect they will have to look for new jobs,
34% expect their jobs will continue, and
27% aren't sure yet whether they will be out of work at the end of the war.

Ask workers why they think their jobs will continue after the war. One of three answers will emerge. The pent-up demand for consumer goods is the first. We will need cars, iceboxes, washing-machines, clothes—everything. And there will be new products creating demand—air conditioning, television, flivver planes. All these things betoken prosperity.

Reconstruction is the second. America will have to rebuild shattered Europe. That means jobs. In Chapter IV that story was told in detail.

Finally, there is the nostrum of infinite reconvertibility. People need iceboxes, don't they? We're making tanks now. All right, after the war, iceboxes. More jobs.

To America the prospect of reconverting a massive war economy to peacetime is not, obviously, terrifying. Not only is the formula tanks-to-iceboxes; it is tanks-to-iceboxes-in-a-hurry. Americans are accustomed to industrial wizardry. How long will reconversion take? Four in ten of us think it will be finished in a year or less.

Seven in ten expect the job to be finished in two years or less.[9] Miracles for war; why not miracles for peace?

The men who run American industry—the miracle workers—are no exception to the rule of optimism. Fully three-quarters of America's business leaders foresee only moderate or little unemployment during the transition period.[10] "If we are given a break," comments one of the leading executives of a great chemical corporation, "we can do the trick."

The tone is optimism. But that is not the whole story. One group in America—an influential one—does not share the hopes of the majority. Two thirds of that group expect extensive unemployment as an accompaniment of transition.[11] The basis of pessimism among these men is more important than their identity. Hear one of them speak: "Jobs aren't just going to happen after the war. We're going to have to plan. The task is enormous. So far I don't see any evidence of planning that's worth a damn. Congress has been kicking the post-war job problem around like a political football. We'll come to the end of the war and everyone will start scrambling. But you don't reconvert a 150-billion-dollar economy by scrambling."

The man speaking is the vice-president of one of America's great international unions. The group in question is composed of national, regional, and state officials of the A. F. of L., CIO and their affiliates. If their pessimism is out of line with current thinking, their emphasis on planning is not.

For neither do the American people believe in scrambling. Labor leader and average American differ in one respect. The latter takes for granted that leaders will plan. Labor is not convinced. Both regard planning as an essential plank in any program for post-war employment.*

* This chapter was written before the Baruch-Hancock Report on post-war adjustment policies was made public. The subsequent appointment by the President of a Work

Planning for Full Employment

Much nonsense has been spoken about the attitude of Americans toward planning. The expression "planned economy" is, to be sure, a shibboleth. But so is "unplanned economy." John Smith plans his and his children's future as best he is able. The corner druggist plans for his business. General Motors plans. The State plans the roads it will build in the next twenty years. Naturally, the country plans too. We believe in the efficacy of planning—for everybody. The important problem is not whether, as far as the nation is concerned, our economy is "planned" or "unplanned." It is the objective that counts—providing jobs, saving the banks, mapping flood control, protecting the farmer.

In the figure which follows is a sample of opinion on the issue of job planning. The question put was this: "Do you think the Government, business and labor should get together *now* and make plans

OPINION FAVORING LABOR-MANAGEMENT PLANNING TO PREVENT UNEMPLOYMENT

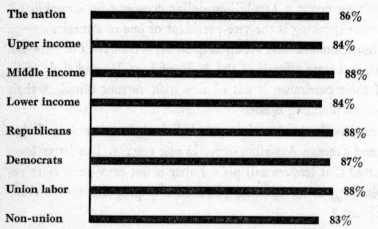

The nation	86%
Upper income	84%
Middle income	88%
Lower income	84%
Republicans	88%
Democrats	87%
Union labor	88%
Non-union	83%

Director to carry out some of the Baruch-Hancock proposals doubtless answers, in part at least, the criticisms levelled at our job-planning efforts by organized labor.

to try to do away with unemployment after the war?" [12] National opinion is overwhelmingly affirmative. No prerogative of the intelligentsia, willingness to plan permeates all groups—the poor, the rich, Democrats, Republicans, union members, unorganized labor.[13]

Such opinions as these are not, by any means, excursions into the realm of sweet idealistic vision. The majority of Americans frankly believe that planning *can* do away with unemployment after the war. The conviction that it cannot is shared by only a quarter of the country.[14]

The test of faith in planning comes when one compares the confidence of key groups in the country. Is the confidence of Democrats a function of trust in the President? Are Republicans, less in sympathy with the Administration, more hard-boiled? In point of fact, both groups feel equally sure that joint planning can do away with post-war joblessness. In the same vein, one might expect the poor, strongly motivated by fear of losing jobs, to be impelled to confidence by wishful thinking. But rich and poor agree on the efficacy of planning.[15]

The result is that the people are well ahead of their Government in demanding that something be done. Long before concrete steps had been taken in Washington to co-ordinate transition planning, the country was on record as favoring creation of an authoritative central agency to carry on this needed work. In June, 1943, for example, the public was asked this question with these results.[16]

"For handling domestic problems like unemployment, the converting of war plants to peacetime use, or the demobilization of soldiers—do you think the Government should set up a central agency *now* with full authority to make plans and with full authority to carry out these plans as soon as the war is over?"

75% favored a central agency
14% opposed it, and
11% had no opinion on the matter.

Several weeks after the public thus expressed themselves, the National Resources Planning Board, the nearest thing to a co-ordinating agency, closed shop for lack of Congressional funds and authorization.*

The desire for centralized planning is by no means a hankering after Government-by-bureaucracy. Planning, yes, but not planning by a clique. Nine in ten of those who want a central agency want to see business, labor, and agriculture represented in the agency's councils.[17] Government is essential, but Government *alone* is not enough.

But neither can business do it alone. That realization is the heritage of the Depression. The nation has faith in the American system of enterprise; it would not, as we shall see in the following chapter, trade it for something else. But we have known a really disastrous depression. We know that when the pillars of the economy begin to crack, business seems as helpless in the face of disaster as any other institution. The Government provides the real bulwark against collapse. Those feelings, bred during the '30s, are part of public opinion today.[18]

"Do you think it will be possible for private industry to employ the great majority of workers after the war, or do you think the Government will have to work out projects to keep many people employed then?"

27% think industry can do it alone
66% think that Government help is needed, and
7% are not sure

Subtly, the heritage of depression follows a rule of primogeniture. To the poor fell the greatest legacy. Those who suffered most are least willing to leave their fate again in the hands of business alone. The lower one goes in the economic scale, the closer one approaches unanimity on the need for Government aid in providing

* Nine months later, opinion and policy got back in phase with the announcement of the Baruch-Hancock Report.

176

jobs. Among the poor, three-quarters hold that view; among the well-to-do, only 49 per cent.[19] At the very top of the economic hierarchy, among the nation's business leaders, opinion takes a different form. Businessmen realize, to be sure, that in the reconversion period, some aid from Government will be essential. After that, say business leaders, industry can look after matters alone.[20] But even business executives know to whom the country will turn if they should fail. Government, not business, will have to clean up the mess.[21]

How Plan for Full Employment?

And so the Government must take its place in planning for full employment. But how? Though most of us would much prefer to work in private industry, our only concrete notion about "Government help" takes the form of public works. When private industry is no longer able to employ, Government steps in and takes up the slack. In a backhand sort of way, it is our own version of "Guaranteed Employment" or "The Right to Work." It is planning by prophylaxis, not by immunization. It happens to be the only kind of employment planning we know about, for we have no backlog of experience with before-the-fact preventive planning. But whatever its current form, the principle of the Right to Work is an American credo. Consider this question.

"It has been suggested that the Government guarantee a real job on useful government work to anybody unemployed after the war until they can find a job in private industry. Would you favor or oppose this plan?"

These are the results.[22]

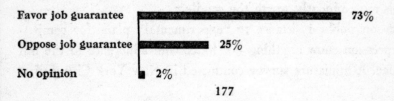

Favor job guarantee   73%

Oppose job guarantee   25%

No opinion   2%

However the politicians choose to draw their lines on the issue, the rank-and-file of both parties are of one mind. Republicans and Democrats may differ in enthusiasm for the Right to Work principle, but both want it. These are the figures.[23]

	Republican voters %	Democratic voters %
Favor Government guarantee of jobs	59	80
Oppose Government guarantee of jobs	36	20
No opinion	5	—

When you get down to cases, the difference of opinion between the rich and poor on the ability of business to provide enough jobs is still there. But despite the difference, majorities of all economic classes line up in favor of an adequate system of public works jobs— "just in case." [24] Confidence in business is one thing; precaution against disaster is yet another. A legacy of WPA jokes notwithstanding, the guarantee of a job on public works when all else fails has become a part of our economic tradition.

But it is an injustice to public opinion to represent public works as its sole cure for unemployment. All peoples are wedded to the familiar until something better is offered. As laymen, we know little of plans whereby prosperity may be guaranteed through credit control and the more subtle devices of deficit financing. The country, doubtless, would be delighted if economists could devise a formula for preventing depression—and with it the need for public works. Certainly we are not averse to experimenting along such lines. The game is too eminently worth the candle.

Tests on public resistance to "experimental" plans for combating depression show anything but hidebound adherence to the old formulae. A miniature survey conducted in New York City during

1943, presented New Yorkers with three plans, admittedly extreme, for combating postwar unemployment.[25] How would they feel about them?

In the first one this idea was presented:

"As you know American industry can produce a tremendous number of things. To keep industry going so that it can provide jobs for everyone, people have to have enough money to buy all the things that industry produces. According to this plan, whenever it looked as if people would *not* have enough money to buy all the things which industry was producing, the Government would lower taxes so that people would have enough money to spend and production would not have to slow down. Would you approve or disapprove of this plan?"

Of every ten people interviewed, six approved, three disapproved, and one couldn't make up his mind.

Then a more radical suggestion.

"As you know, people cannot buy things if the prices are too high. To make sure that people could buy all the things which industry produced the Government would put ceilings on prices to keep them from going too high. Would you approve or disapprove of this plan?"

This time, resistance was even less—83 per cent endorsed the use of price ceilings.

Finally, New Yorkers were asked:

"In the third plan the Government would help small business to keep going in order to compete with big business and to supply more jobs. The Government would lend money to small businesses to keep them going if necessary. Would you approve or disapprove?"

Approval was enormous. For every one person opposed, nine were in favor.

We are willing enough to experiment. We have, indeed—witness our recent history—turned to heterodoxy when our leaders fail to meet crises with sound measures of control. Were that not true,

179

there would have been no "Ham and Eggs," no Townsend. But we are not, let it be said, reckless of tradition. Experimentation will have to proceed within a traditional framework. Balancing a budget is something we believe in.[26] But within the limitations of "soundness" the American people are venturesome. That too is part of their tradition.

Some will say that the public is willing to experiment only when times are bad, that they will refuse to tamper with the economic system in prosperity. That, doubtless, is true in part. But the nation is not confusing a war boom with normal "prosperity." We know that dangers lie ahead. Recall too that the figures presented in this chapter were gathered not during a depression but at a time when employment and production were booming at levels almost undreamed of in the history of American industry.

The Economics of Full Employment

But there is more to full employment than the wish that we have it, or the demand that we plan for it. Bold planning or no bold planning, the economics of employment will still operate. The public has no small place in its operation. The individual—as both consumer and worker—can, by his actions, abrogate the most painstaking planning. Whatever a producer's intent, he is bound by the psychology of the consumer and the demands of the worker. He cannot escape.

There are, then, certain minimum requirements to which the public must conform if full employment is to be the fruit of planning. On certain of these, economists are agreed. In the pages which follow, three are considered.*

* Two extremely provocative books which treat with challenging insight the relation of economics and "the public" are worth mention in passing. John Maynard Keynes, *The General Theory of Employment, Interest, and Money;* and John H. G. Pierson, *Full Employment.*

Post-war Demand

It is obvious, first, that people will have to unfreeze their "capital assets" after the war, spending for consumer goods the billions of dollars which have been stored up in war bonds. On every side we hear of the inevitable, pent-up demand for cars or refrigerators or cribs or nylon stockings.

But the problem of demand can be too facilely oversimplified in the interest of wishful thinking. *Potentially*, there *is* a huge reservoir of demand. That, nobody will deny. But the bland assumption that every Mrs. Jones is just waiting for that new refrigerator is neither safe, obvious, nor a true picture of what Mrs. Jones is really like. Ask American consumers whether they are going to hang on to their savings for a while or spend them right away. Three-quarters will tell you that they plan to hold on to them.[27] Such answers are, of course, cautious. But cautious is what we will be till we see the lay of the land. Consumers will save if times look uncertain, and spend if the promise of prosperity is realized.

Spending has ever been a function of confidence. Undermine confidence, and buying will shrink to the level of bare necessity. It matters not that the chances for prosperity immediately after the war look promising now. Should a wave of scare-saving start as a result of public fear, one of those chances will fail of realization. Reconversion would inevitably be delayed. Time in this case is on the side of disaster. For in economics there are no water-tight compartments; delay in one vital sphere washes out the possibility of gain in others. What remains then is for the government to salvage the debris. So time is eminently of the essence.

But public confidence is not gained by assuring people that everything is going to be all right. The average consumer lives in the present. Prosperity may indeed be just around the corner, but the economic here-and-now gives him his cue. What is done *now* is what he can see. At the present moment confidence in the future is at a high level. To let it deflate would be to beg trouble. The first installment on post-war public confidence can and should be paid now: measures to protect the American worker from unemployment after the war, plans to help business over the transition, joker-proof price guarantees to the farmer. Cheaper substitutes will not do.

But plans are not enough. There will also have to be adequate information. Take, for example, the case of the farmer. Legislation exists which guarantees him a 90-per-cent-of-parity minimum price for his commodities after the war. In spite of its weaknesses, the legislation is there. Yet no systematic effort has been made to bring that legislation to the attention of farmers. Some of them—the big ones—know about it. Most of them do not. And so, 41 per cent of the American farm community expects a price collapse at the end of this war as severe as that after the last.[28] If planning for the future is to have the desired effect of maintaining public confidence, the information problem will have to be tackled more vigorously.

Beyond plans and information, there is still something else. There is "atmosphere." The gloomy defeatism of businessmen faced with Government restriction will do little to create an atmosphere of confidence. Obstructionist party politics on Capitol Hill are in the same category. Arbitrary "regulation," indecision, or compromise at the other end of Pennsylvania Avenue, in their turn, help matters little. Unreasonable demands from any quarter which precipitate disunity must necessarily make the task more difficult. Organized business, labor, and agriculture cannot chuck their responsibility when the shooting stops. If they do, the public will not be easily convinced that refrigerators are more desirable than a hedge against collapse.

Maintenance of Economic Controls During Transition

Demand is one factor. The problem of control is another. Whatever our economic condition after the war, chaos would most assuredly result if, in the interest of appeasing special interests, wartime economic controls were scrapped precipitately. There will, doubtless, be demands that we rid ourselves of the annoyance of price control and rationing as soon as war ends. But the spearhead of such pressure will not be the public. The country knows of the dangers of inflation, the prospect of continuing scarcity. Nine people in ten, consequently, believe that rationing will be desirable for a while after the war.[29] In like vein, fully 75 per cent are in favor of maintaining price controls during the transition period.[30]

But the problem is not so simple as all that. The public wants necessary controls to continue. It is natural, nevertheless, that as we approach peace—for the war will end gradually, and not all of a sudden—the hankering after a simpler economy will become greater. If the period during which controls are needed is a short one, the public can be counted on to give its full support to necessary measures—in spite of pressures operating in the other direction. But if the period of transition is long, if controls must be kept not for months but for a year or two or even three, the average consumer will become more and more skeptical of their necessity. That will be true *unless* the palpable signs of scarcity or inflation are so obvious that they can be kept before the public in unambiguous form. Sum it up this way. We have no love for rationing, and probably don't like price control as a permanent thing; but we dislike unregulated scarcity and inflation far more.

A word about the maintenance of wartime controls as a political issue. It is more than conceivable that there will be those in Congress who, by way of bidding for votes, will demand an end to "Administration-inspired" war regulations at as early a date as possible. Congress has been reluctant enough to support the OPA in wartime; in peacetime, sniping will likely be more violent. However the lines in Congress are drawn—and the chances are that they will follow party alignment—the rank-and-file of voters in each party will not be the force precipitating the split. Republican and Democratic voters alike agree on the issue.[31] The pressure will come from other quarters.

A blanket statement that it will come from farmers or from businessmen is dangerous. Both have a stake in holding the economy in line during transition. Business leaders, for example, are evenly split on the desirability of scrapping price control immediately after the war.[32] What can most certainly be said is that there will be *some* business interests, *some* farm interests, and *some* of the public who will want an immediate snap-back into a spurious normalcy. Congress must not interpret these voices as America.

About the more subtle forms of wartime control—allocation of raw materials, fiscal and tax regulations on business, and the like—there is no public opinion. Not only does the public have no opinion, it has no knowledge. These are questions which the man in the street gladly leaves to the experts. Insofar as such questions turn into general issues—"Government" versus "Business," for example—the public will have a piece to speak. But that is the subject of the next chapter.

Re-patterning American Industry

Population shifts during periods of wartime production cast their shadows ahead into the peace that follows. It is a truism that the geographical distribution of heavy industry for war production is not adequate for the more balanced industrial pattern of peacetime. Reconversion to "normal" production will require extensive "remigration." It will also require shifting of workers from one type of job to another. The war worker in the powder plant will not be loading howitzer shells for the rest of his life. And some ghost towns will result—if not immediately after the war, then two or three years later. Evolving a new pattern for industry is the third economic problem in which the public must play a part.

Although economists can tell us in only rough terms how many people will have to move from one place to another or from one kind of job to another, there are some hard facts which have already emerged.* We know that many of the over-crowded industrial areas created by the war will have to contract as war ends. We know, too, that the number of people working in highly improved manufacturing plants is far greater now than post-war conditions will require. And so, men will be moving from Wichita, from Mobile, from factory to filling station, from shipyard to dairy farm.

There should be no particular difficulty in shifting workers from one kind of job to another. Temporary unemployment may occur, but an efficient U. S. Employment Service and an adequate vocational training program can cut the time down to a minimum. Some skills—particularly in manufacturing—will be lost in the shuffle, but in terms of the long haul it has always been true that times of upheaval leave technological wastage behind.

The problem of "remigration," too, though obviously more difficult of solution because of the scope of the dislocation involved, can be handled easily if there is proper planning. It has never been difficult to get workers to leave a place where there is no job for one where there are plenty of jobs. Were that not so, war-swollen communities would never have come into being, nor would ghost

---

* For a discussion of the migration aspect of industrial reconversion see J. S. Bruner, "How Much Post-war Migration?" *American Journal of Sociology*, July, 1943. The Bureau of Labor Statistics of the Department of Labor has compiled a set of estimates on probable shifts in employment from one industry to another.

towns. The same will hold after the war. The migrant populations of cities like Portland (Maine), Mobile, Los Angeles, Wichita, Atlanta, Pittsburgh, Buffalo, and Detroit will be as ready to leave as they were to come, if and when jobs give out. Workers in these communities feel this way about it.[33]

"If you lose your present job after the war would you be likely to move away from here to find work?"

36% say they would move away
58% would stay on, and
6% can't decide

It is, of course, impossible to convert results such as those above into round millions. Nor is it necessary to do so. Certainly all people who *would* move if they lost their jobs are not going to have to move. All that need be said is that there is a large potential force of workers who would be available for re-patterning America's industry. The question now is whether we are wise enough to effect the re-patterning with a minimum of human and industrial debris.

MANDATE FOR THE FUTURE

Any policy for guaranteeing full employment in the United States will be subject to the most rigid test which public opinion can provide. For the public knows both what it wants and what it has been promised. We are agreed that employment is the biggest problem facing us. If the test will be rigid, it will also be swift. It requires only a few months of mass unemployment to convince the public that its leaders have failed.

The Government has a mandate from the people. The public wants jobs. It is counting on business and Government to work out plans—bold ones if need be—to that end.

It is with the people's mandate that we have been concerned in this chapter. In summary, the mandate reads like this.

First. Planning for transition is essential. To drift chaotically into transition is at once economic suicide and a failure to keep faith with the people.

Second. The very minimum of planning is the provision of "guaranteed jobs" for those to whom unemployment will be the inevitable consequence of shifting from wartime to peacetime production. Because there is the feeling that business will be unable to absorb all workers during transition, the Government must provide a system of public works.

Third. Like all successful efforts, the effort to provide jobs should be undertaken co-operatively by business, government, and labor. The nation has faith in our ability to abolish unemployment through joint planning.

Fourth. Planning for full employment should be centralized in an agency which has both the power to plan and the power to execute.

Fifth. Planning should be courageous, aggressive. Rationing, price control, subsidies to small business, fiscal controls—we are willing to accept any or all of these and more if they are necessary steps in averting depression.

That is the mandate. Failure to heed it will reflect on business as well as on the Government. This is the economic fork in the road. If we go in the wrong direction, we may never have the privilege of another try under the present economic system. People want jobs. The system that produces jobs is the system that they will have.

CHAPTER X

THE FUTURE OF FREE ENTERPRISE

SOME years ago, there appeared on America's billboards a poster of Uncle Sam, sleeves rolled to the elbows. Behind him loomed a landscape of great factories. Blazoned across the front of the display was the slogan, "WHAT'S GOOD FOR BUSINESS IS GOOD FOR YOU." Since those days the display has changed and the words have varied. But the thought is still the same. Institutional advertising now sings the virtues of "Free Enterprise."

Behind the billboards and the expensive advertisements is a conflict which must inevitably beset all industrial democracies. Can business, in a developed industrial economy, strike a happy balance between profit and the public interest? Can that balance, if attained, be perpetuated without the intercession of a higher authority? And, if intercession there must be, what are its limits? The New Deal has heightened the drama of these questions. But they are not new. As long as there has been enterprise, there has been the problem of regulating it in the public interest. Enterprise has never been free. While enterprise exists, the problem of controlling it will also exist.

But though the problems are not new, their most recent manifestation has something of a new twist—at least for America. The shock of the Depression has done what "left" propaganda was never able to accomplish: "Free Enterprise" has become a political issue. With the tremendous development of modern communication, that issue has now been placed squarely before the public. The nation

188

is being asked—indeed, urged—to choose between Free Enterprise and Something Else.

How the public is to choose is not made clear by either side. A vote against the New Deal is represented by some political casuists as a vote *against* Something Else *in favor* of Free Enterprise. That maneuver, cheap as it is, has served only to push the issue of free enterprise closer to the center of the political arena. Free Enterprise is now having its debut as a major political issue in America. There will, of course, be no official takers for the opposite point of view—for Something Else. Yet takers or not, a public issue is slowly emerging. Where before, our economic system has been taken for granted, it is now beginning to acquire a question mark.

What does this demand for a "public decision" mean to the man in the street? Is the average American thinking in the terms set for him by the ad-writers, the publicists, the political whipper-uppers?

In America "business" is taken for granted. It has its problems, it makes its mistakes, is capable of abuses. Bluntly, business is making a living, making products, selling things. It helps people by giving them jobs, or raises, or Christmas bonuses, or a profit. It hurts people when it keeps prices artificially high, or fakes its claims, or uses unfair methods to squeeze the little fellow. Above all else business is rarely thought of as Business. When it is Business with a capital B it evokes an ideological aura, creates dissension. As business with a small b, it is good; that's how we make our living.

As far as free enterprise is concerned, this much can be said: It is so obvious that we have no word for it. To the public, Free Enterprise is not the word for free enterprise in fact. Hardly three Americans in ten know what the expression "Free Enterprise" means.[1] But everybody knows what free enterprise is.

What is it? It is people starting a business, running shops, taking profits with the losses, working in offices, hoping to be boss, taking a flier on the market. This kind of free enterprise is perfectly capable of taking care of itself—except when it steps on somebody's toes. For doing business also means following the rules. The rules change with circumstances. The rules ultimately are the government. They are there to protect us from ourselves. They are also there to protect us from Business with a capital B.

Now Government. Americans are just as capable of reciting its shortcomings as they are capable of reciting the shortcomings of Business. Maybe more so. But we do not fear Government. The cry that Government with a capital G is trying to usurp the prerogatives of Business with a capital B is capable of dividing the country into violent pros and antis. But when it comes to a specific government regulation of a specific business practice, the aura dissolves in a cleansing bath of American common-sense. People expect government to see to it that business follows practices which are not harmful to the community. Government acts as a guardian. It acts as a guardian not only because that is the tradition, but because government is subject to the people's will in a way which business cannot be. There are times—wartime is a good example—when government must take an active part in business. Crisis or abuse is the signal for government action. When there are neither crises nor abuses, government must leave business alone. But there is always *some* crisis, *some* abuse.

Finally, government is neither a colossus nor is it monolithic. People see business, labor, and agriculture participating in its councils. They believe, as we have seen, that co-operative effort by all of these groups must go into planning for employment. On general principle, a majority of Americans believe too that labor, business, and agriculture should have even more of a say in formulating the nation's domestic and international policies.[2]

That is the common-sense view. It is the view which prevails when the discussion is of government with a small g and business with a small b. It is the view which has made free enterprise possible. As far as the public is concerned, it is a subject about which there need be no undue controversy. It is only when the talk turns to Business, Government, and Free Enterprise in capitals that tempers grow shorter. Only when events push the public from lower case conceptions of the economy to a preoccupation with capital letters, will America be thinking in the terms set for it in the expensive advertisements about Free Enterprise.

Because of this dichotomy, the discussion in the pages which follow will be on two levels—lower case and capital letters. The latter, vague and seamed with prejudice, serves to divide us. The former is the psychological cement in our economy. Consider first the ideological issue: Government and Business.

The Ideology of Government Control

If you ask the country a question like this one, you split it down the middle.[3]

"When we get back to peacetime conditions, do you think the American people will be better off if the Government has more control or less control over Business than it had before the war?"

35% want more control
38% want less control
12% want about the same control, and
15% have no opinion or hold some qualified view.

Neither side has a very clear idea of what it stands for; each is convinced of its rightness.

Any issue which raises the problem of Government control in such general terms will split the country along the same cleavage lines. There are two requirements: that the issue be general and that it be vague. Figures will vary a little one way or another, depending on the wording of the question and the embroidery on the issue, but always the split will be close to even. Here are some examples. The National Resources Planning Board suggested in its Report for 1943 that Government and Business go into partnership in certain vital industries connected with war production when the war is over. The country was asked its opinion.[4]

48% favored the plan
38% opposed the plan
14% had no opinion

Another example. Should Government and Business get together and make plans for preventing unemployment after the war? Virtually nine in ten people agree that they should.[5] The objective is more important than the participants. Now confront the public with this problem.[6]

"How would you like to see this co-operation get started—would you like to see business and labor take the lead and draw up plans for the government to follow, or would you like to see the government take the lead and make plans for business and labor to follow?"

36% want the government to lead
36% want business and labor to lead
20% would prefer to see them work as equals, and
8% have no opinion on the matter

Again there is the familiar split. Who are the people on each side of the fence? Roughly speaking, this can be said of them. On the left side of the fence, in the ranks of those who favor Government control, one finds *more* of these groups:

The less well-to-do
Democrats
Urban dwellers
The young

192

On the right side of the fence, those who protest Government control, there are *more* of these:

> The middle and upper income groups
> Republicans
> The inhabitant of the small town or small city
> People past their youth

But the fence is no barricade between proletariat and elite. All Democrats are not on the left; neither are all city-dwellers. Nor are all the well-to-do on the right. More important, *one side of the fence does not consider itself Left, the other side Right.* There is still the fact that nine Americans in ten consider themselves members of the middle class.[7]

The figures which follow give a more accurate picture of the line-up. The question at issue is whether the Government should have "more or less control of Business after the war."[8]

	More control %	Less control %	No opinion %
Politics			
Republicans	14	66	20
Democrats	43	29	28
Age			
Under 30	46	27	27
30-49	35	37	28
Over 50	30	44	26
Occupation			
Executive	23	54	23
White collar	27	48	25
Manual workers	47	23	30
Farmers	35	39	26
Income			
Upper income	22	57	21
Middle income	34	37	29
Lower income	50	20	30

	More control	Less control	No opinion
	%	%	%
Color			
White	33	40	27
Negro	55	14	31
Sex			
Men	36	44	20
Women	35	32	33
Education			
Grade school	40	29	31
High school	35	40	25
College	28	49	23

A thumbnail sketch of a typical adherent of Government control and one of his opposite number in the ranks of the opponents would be as interesting as it is impossible. But some of the elements which go into the thinking of people on both sides of the fence can be outlined.

The Adherents of Control

On the one hand there is the unsophisticated view of Government, something of a Great White Father complex. The Government protects, provides relief, lends seed money to the small farmer. Government to the one-third of a nation who are "ill-housed, ill-fed, ill-clothed" is that. A South Carolina share-cropper, being interviewed, consistently used the expression, "The Government, he . . ." To that man, the Government was the only power pledged to his protection. The pronoun was no semantic accident. The slum dweller, the seasonal worker, the mill hand in the company town, are in the same boat. When the issue is Government control, they will predominate in the ranks of those who are all for it. Government control is protection.

But this view is neither the only nor the most important expression of the desire to see Government act as a strong regulator. The

194

philosophy of the New Deal has had a tremendous influence too on the thinking of the middle and lower middle classes in America. Few have forgotten what it meant to have the Government close the banks when disaster seemed imminent. We may not like the red tape of "so much Government" but we like the feeling that someone is looking out for our bank deposits. And we like somebody to guarantee a minimum wage, decent hours, and tolerable working conditions.

And so there has emerged, if not an ideology, then a coherent philosophy of the role of Government. Government is the bulwark against disaster, the shield against abuse. To provide for the poor, to protect the weak from the strong, to guarantee the rights and privileges of the little man, and to see that hardship is kept at a minimum—those are its functions.

None of this means Government "ownership"; people would object to having the view called even a mild form of socialism. We still want private enterprise, the chance to own what we can get fairly. This is middle class liberalism, not proletarian revolution. And as for the New Deal, it pledged itself to the removal of the *abuses* of private enterprise, not to the removal of private enterprise itself. The professional alarmists might well go out and conduct a few interviews themselves among some "New Dealers."

Finally, there is nothing all-or-none about the view which accepts the necessity of "more government." Neither is it a plea for "all government," and most certainly it is not a commitment to support every proposal for government regulation.

The Opponents of Control

Social service is the objective of government control as its adherents view it. Individualism and the frontier tradition are the hall-marks of the view that Government should be kept at a minimum. Rather than pinning their faith on the efficacy of "outside" regulation, the opponents of control look to the ability of individual men and private endeavor to work out equitably their own destinies.

Extreme statements of the view—rare, to be sure—condemn even social security as a dangerous form of coddling. But again, these matters are relative. Just as "more Government" does not mean "all Government," so "less Government" does not mean "no Government." That there are abuses to be rectified and that there are crises to be weathered remains a truism for both sides. Both agree that Government must play its role in these domains. But as to what is an abuse and what is a crisis, there will be differences of opinion. The differences are of degree, not of kind.

Viewing the matter in terms of American tradition, the "less Government" view takes its life from the belief in what economists call vertical mobility. Men can get ahead if they have what it takes, rise to the top. "Freedom of opportunity" is the new phrase for it. If people oppose "too much Government" it is not because they despise helping the weak but, rather, that they are intent upon giving the strong and able their chance. There are, to be sure, the cheap few who use dishonestly the slogan of opportunity in the interest of opportunity for the few. Yet the deeply sincere and thoroughly American faith in the initiative of individuals cannot be dismissed by pooh-poohing the prostitution of its symbols.

A word about faith in vertical mobility. There is no way of knowing about its history in public opinion. The proclamations of statesmen are no guide to the public mind. But whatever it once meant, "the chance to rise" is no longer cast in the classic lines of Horatio Alger. To the lower third of the nation, opportunity means the opportunity to be secure and self-sufficient—not to be a bank president. If the middle class is dreaming about bank presidencies, they are certainly not verbalizing those dreams. As the American economy approaches maturity, economic aspirations become more sober. But though hopes are not extravagant, they are still there, still hopes. Insofar as regulation and control of the economy appear to threaten the fulfillment of those hopes, regulation and control will be anathema to the ambitious.

And so, the ideological difference between those on either side of the fence is not irrevocably profound. Both want private enterprise. One emphasizes security and social service; the other, opportunity. Nor have the differences yet led, except in rare instances, to bitter partisanship. Hatred for the New Deal there is, to be sure. On the other side there is resentment over fat profits, cost-plus, and the rest.

But to say that the battle lines are drawn between the Left and the Right would be so much nonsense. There is the *potential* for such a split in public opinion. That cannot be denied. One important element in the potential is the role of government. If, as one writer has contended, we are moving toward the "Europeanization of America" with a sharp line between Right and Left—and the battle over Free Enterprise is a symptom that we are—then the issue of government control may be an ideological spearhead. That is the story on the level of capital letters.

RESOLVING THE CONFLICT

The existence of division would be more important were it not true that it can be dissolved by getting down to cases. Abstractly we either like or we don't like Government control—and that's that. But prejudice, where *specific* issues are concerned, is subordinated to hard-headed common-sense. Given a situation and an objective, our opinion on the role of the Government is compounded of our estimate of the gravity of the situation and the importance of the objective. If the situation is grave and the objective important, we are willing to take what steps are necessary—including government domination. Expediency comes first, then ideology.

Wartime is, of course, the classic case. The situation is clear; so too the objective. Strong government is not only approved; it is demanded. Tradition be damned. A man and womanpower draft? [9] Yes. Drafting women for the armed services? [10] Yes. Compulsory forty-eight-hour week? [11] Again, yes. Is it necessary in order to win the war? Then do it.

When post-war problems approximate the clarity of crisis and objective which characterizes war problems, the same manner of thought can be expected. One such problem—jobs—is fast approaching that degree of clarity. Others may follow. Insofar as post-war economic sailing is smooth, little support for stringent government regulation will develop. But if the going is rough, the crises are clear, the demand will be strong and loud.

The cases, then, will be crucial—not the ideology. Two have been discussed in preceding chapters—employment and social security. Both bring the issue of government control into sharp focus. Here we consider several others, crucial for the same reasons. Failure to handle them properly will bring us that much closer to a knock-down, drag-out fight over Business and Government with capital letters.

Disposing of Government-owned Plants and Facilities

The first is the disposal of fifteen billion dollars' worth of war plants and facilities built by the Government during the war. Shall they be sold by the Government? If so, to whom and under what conditions? The problem is new. But the background is old. We do not approve of the Government's owning and operating factories. The men who work in factories, who might be expected to feel more disposed toward government ownership, feel the same way. Ask them whether they would like to see the Government own and operate electric companies, coal mines, and automobile factories. This is what you find: [12]

10%   want the Government to own and operate automobile factories
23%   feel the same way about electric light companies
19%   favor government ownership of coal mines

On principle, we do not even like *legitimate* government operations to compete with private business save in certain special instances. The nation, for example, approves heartily of public works as a means of taking up slack in employment. But as strongly as we approve of government-operated public works, that strongly do we disapprove of these projects being given over to tasks which would compete with private business. [13]

Yet when it comes down to the matter of plant disposal something else gets added. In the first place there is an outlay of fifteen billion taxpayer dollars for the factories. Perhaps more important, the problem is so vaguely complex that our feelings get clouded by the old Business versus Government controversy. The nation has been asked this question, for example. [14]

"As you know the Government has spent about 15 billion dollars during the last couple of years in building war plants and factories. At the present time, these plants are owned by the Government, but run by private companies. What do you think the Government should do with these plants after the war?"

Presented with four alternatives, opinion divides this way:

50% { 4%   would give the plants to the companies that now run them
      46% would sell them to the companies that now run them
37% { 11% would have the Government go into partnership with the companies that now run them
      26% would keep the plants and let the Government run them
      13% have no opinions

So the split is close to even: 37 per cent are on the left—wanting plants kept outright or controlled through partnership by the Government; on the right are 50 per cent who would either give or sell the plants back into private ownership. As might be expected, the faces on each side of the fence are familiar. More Republicans, more well-to-do want to see the plants in private hands; Democrats and the less well-off predominate on the other side.[15]

Add the element of the Government's taking a possible loss on those plants whose options have not been taken by operating companies—the excess plants, so to speak—and the issue is still unresolved. That, too, fails to bring the matter down to the bedrock of cases. What should the Government do with these "excess" plants? The question was put this way:[16]

"As you know the Government has spent about 15 billion dollars in the last couple of years building war plants and factories. At present these plants are owned by the Government but run by private companies. These companies have the right to buy the plants from the Government if they want to. Suppose they don't want to buy the plants, what should the Government do—sell them to the highest bidder, or take them over and run them itself?"

37%   would sell to the highest bidder
46%   would have the Government take over
17%   have no opinion

With the new factor added, the balance swings toward Government —but again the split is close to even. Again too the same faces appear on opposite sides of the fence.[17]

So long as the issue remains on a general level, the balance of public opinion remains in doubt. But just suppose the problem of plant disposal should assume more meaning than just "Government versus Business." Suppose, for example, the post-war years are such that jobs must be provided for large numbers of idle workers. A proposal is made that the Government lease or operate these plants to create jobs. How would the public stand? For jobs, of course. Or suppose that there is a boom, that plants cannot produce enough goods for the market. It is proposed that the Government sell immediately those plants on which options have run out so that business might produce the needed goods. How would the public stand then? For goods, of course. The crux of the matter—if the matter is ever to be resolved and brought from the level of generalities—is not whether the Government should or should not sell, but what can be accomplished by selling. Those are the determinants of opinion on concrete cases. To the extent that they operate, opinion will be polarized along lines of expediency and not prejudice. Should the issue remain abstract, as it now is, the public will continue to make up its mind according to vague predilections for Government or Business.

Finally there looms the question of plant disposal and monopoly. To whom shall the plants be sold? To the big man or the little? To the question of monopoly and industrial "giantism" we turn next.

Post-war Monopoly

In theory, Americans have a strong distaste for monopoly—for the "evils of bigness." In practice, that distaste makes itself felt only when the monopoly in question pinches. When there is no pinch, the awareness that there is a monopoly recedes. We may even come to admire the "bigness" and "efficiency" of what amounts to monopoly. We like so many things: competition, bigness, super-efficiency, small business, the underdog, industrial giants like Ford and Henry Kaiser. We should like, of course, to have all of them. And we are not by any means convinced that we cannot.

But the dislike of monopoly is not, in spite of all this, just an abstract antipathy, based on a mysterious prejudice. America is in aspiration, if not in fact, a land of "small business." In terms of dollar volume, small business is no longer supreme. But in the sense that "free enterprise" requires for its existence the competition of many enterprises, bidding against each other, small business is still the backbone of the economy. Yet more potent than the bare statistics of dollar volume and the theory of small enterprise is the psychological support in the country for small business. Recall, for example, how popular is the idea of Government aid to small business forced to compete with big rivals (Chapter IX). For small business is within the reach of Everyman. It is more than a fact; it is a symbol of middle-class aspirations, and America is a land of the middle-class. To those aspirations monopoly is a threat.

Our opinion, therefore, on whether Government should take steps to control monopolistic practices are clearcut in the extreme. When one asks the public about regulation of monopolies, the answers come out like this: [18]

85% favor anti-monopolistic measures by the Government,
12% oppose such measures, and
3% have no opinion on the matter.

Applied to the problem of disposing of Government-built plants after the war, the small-business dream guides the public in the traditional direction. Should the Government make special provisions so that big companies will not be able to buy more than their fair share of Government-owned plants to the detriment of small businesses who may also want to buy a share? The answer is overwhelmingly, "Yes." [19] Small business must be protected. Sum it up this way: are you in favor of Government protecting small business? Yes, I am in favor of small business.

But again, bigness *qua* bigness is not necessarily a basis for suspicion or dislike. We oppose monopolies which hurt the consumer or the small competitor. We oppose them for their evils, not for their bigness. Where bigness serves a special purpose, it is preferred to smallness. It is doubtful whether many Americans would vote to have General Motors broken up into several hundred small companies producing motor cars competitively. Recall too that a majority of Americans would rather have our "infant" synthetic rubber industry built up after the war in spite of higher prices for tires, than go back to the old system of importing crude (Chapter III). The synthetic rubber industry is not, by any stretch of the imagination, a stronghold of small business.

The opinions of the public and those of America's business leaders differ little on the question of competition and monopoly. There are but five executives in a hundred who believe that a better economic future can be guaranteed through less competition. The general feeling is that a 1939 level of competition is still a healthy condition for business.[20] That holds for the economy as a whole; it holds also when executives are asked about competition in their own particular line of business.[21]

Yet in spite of a desire on the part of executives to keep competition alive, there are few people in industry who expect small business to have smooth sailing during the post-war years. The small producer had a tough time before the war, an even tougher time during the war production boom. Not a quarter of the country's leading executives think that matters will improve much after the fever of war production has passed.[22] If the prediction of the business experts turns into fact, small business is going to need all the support the public seems ready to give it.

To view the matter in broader terms, our industrial picture today might be quite different had not the American people felt the urge to protect the small from the big. Yet, inevitably, control of the

American economy has been more and more concentrated in the hands of fewer people. Technological advancement in a capitalistic economy, though not dictating such concentration, certainly favors it. In the future, we are told, technological discoveries made in the heat of war research, will revolutionize production processes still further, will force former competitors into combination for the exploitation of new processes. It is conceivable too that the means of distribution will improve to the extent where the small retailer—and retailing is the citadel of small enterprise—will be forced from his already precarious position by the chain and the "giant market." Just as they have in the past, people will ask for protection from their government. Doubtless, they will get some protection. And the greater the pressure, the greater will be the demand for protection.

The desire for protection is the desire of the middle class to keep its aspirations intact. It is the need to feel some equity in the economy—or some chance for equity. Equity is, after all, the translation of democracy into economic terms. Down at the bedrock, it is the sense of equity that makes people want a system of free and private enterprise. Destroy the chance for equity, and you destroy concern over whether Giant Amalgamated Oil Company belongs to the three or four hundred people who own a controlling block of stock or belongs to the Government.

If it is inevitable that the control of business is to become more concentrated with the march of new discovery, then it is equally inevitable that the dream of free enterprise will become a dream of the few and not of the many—unless one condition is fulfilled. Can an economy of huge combines provide a substitute for equity? Profit sharing? Some form of labor-management co-operation in planning and conducting business? If it cannot and if enterprise is to be limited to the great, then we are rapidly approaching the end of the era of private industry. That is why monopoly is, perhaps, more than just another of our economic problems.

The Spirit of Post-war Taxation

If disposing of Government-owned plants and controlling industrial "greatness" are two looming exercises in Government regulation, then the structure and spirit of post-war taxes is a third. The question, I think, can be stated this way. Free enterprise requires incentive and the exercise of risk. In financial jargon, incentive and risk spell "venture capital," which means just what it sounds like. Any tax structure which is either punitive with respect to risk or excessive with respect to "profit" reduces the amount of available venture capital and throws business into either a slump or dependence on a source of capital which is not under private control (the Government). Penalties on risk or expropriation of profit, moreover, create an atmosphere in which business cannot operate freely, cannot expand to its fullest limits, and cannot provide the number of jobs which otherwise might be provided.

That is one side of the story. The other side is the principle of taxation in accordance with the ability to pay, a familiar tradition in America. The conflict is this: when does over-solicitousness for one principle slight the other? Do lenient taxes on profits represent a violation of the principle of taxation according to ability to pay? Must a light tax burden on low income brackets mean, necessarily, that the availability of venture capital will be that much lessened by taxes on business? The ultimate answer is, of course, for the economists, not the public. But the public will help decide the kind of answer that gets embodied in our *tax statutes* this year, next, and the year after. Congress has ever been mindful of the constituency in such matters.

What about the public? Certainly people want taxes which are based on ability to pay. Just as certainly, they do not approve of taxes which hurt business. That much is obvious. But Americans know that the next ten years or so will mean high taxes. The war needs paying for, and the man in the street is not fooling himself into thinking otherwise. Nine in ten Americans are expecting to yield up good sums of money during the next ten years for high taxes.[23] If, indeed, the country *is* paying high taxes during the post-war years, it is very improbable that there will be much sympathy for those who complain of heavy taxes on business or on the rich.

That is the background. But it is not all. Sympathy for the tax troubles of others or no sympathy, we do have our prejudices about "good" and "bad" kinds of taxation. We do not, first of all, like taxes which limit the amount of money any *individual* is allowed to earn in a year.[24] Progressive taxation is one thing; but a ceiling on income is too restrictive.

The jump from the individual to the corporation is a big one. On the matter of limiting *corporate* profit, the public takes a completely different position. Corporate profits *should* be limited. That goes by way of being control of the kind of Business with a capital B. Take this question as an example.[25]

"There have been many suggestions made recently about the kinds of control Government should have over business after the war. One of them is that the government should see to it that companies are limited to about 10 per cent profit during the year on their investment. If a company is making more than 10 per cent profit it should be required to lower its prices or increase the wages it pays. Would you agree or disagree?"

Seven Americans in ten say, "Yes."

But if the public is sure that it does not like juicy post-war profits for business, business executives are, naturally, just as sure that corporate taxes will have to be lowered if ever the economic going gets rough after the war. That is the majority view among business leaders.[26] It foretells one source of future conflict over taxes.

There can, really, be no final answer. The public does not feel kindly toward the plea that corporate profits are too heavily taxed. It will feel less so if we continue to pay a good fraction of our personal earnings for taxes. At the same time business is convinced that high corporate taxes are a bane to good business and, in the long run, a threat to private enterprise. The public will not sit idly by while corporations are taxed less and they are taxed more. Nor will business sit idly by and see opportunities lost through lack of available capital. A compromise, doubtless, will be struck. In which direction it will incline will very likely depend on who happens to be living in the White House during the post-war years. Which is still another reason why "Free Enterprise" and "Government Control" happen to be in the middle of the political arena.

THE PROSPECTS

The fight over "government control" has already started. It is inevitable that it will become more bitterly contested as the unifying cement of war crumbles. What the future holds, not even the political prophets are daring to say. War's end may be "farewell to reform." It can, just as likely, be the birth of the New Reform. But whether *laissez faire* is dying or gaining new life is not the refrain of this chapter. That is for the economists to say.

All that can be said here is that there is a conflict in public opinion, a conflict between those who want more Government and those who want less. The dimensions of that conflict and the roster of combatants we have sketched here. One final fact remains to be said.

Fifteen years ago, before the Great Depression and before the

New Deal, it is doubtful whether the public would have granted the inevitability of strong and active government in the realm of business. But history conditions us. We have become accustomed to ever-increasing activity by the Government in the field of economics. The tempo of increase has become a part of our thinking about the world in which we live. So now, all of us—whether we like it or not—are expecting more control, more regulation of business by Government. Leaders of the nation's business, though they will fight it, see, in the post-war years, less freedom for business than before the war.[27] The nation too sees an increasing role for Government. Asked whether they expect to see more or less regulation in eight basic industries after the war—public utilities, farming, railroad, oil, banking, steel, milk distribution, and auto manufacturing, few indeed are the Americans who see an abatement in regulation.[28]

What, then, is the future of free enterprise? It depends for its existence upon a public opinion willing to see it free. Freedom for the few may kill the public's support for the present form of "Free Enterprise." But that is far in the future. For the present, we are willing and eager to live with our economic system. As far as the public is concerned there are only two alternatives—that enterprise remain at the same stage of freedom it enjoyed before the war, or that it be even more regulated in the public interest. Nobody—save the quixotically nostalgic—wants to return to the mythical "good old days" of Hoovervilles before the New Deal.

There is something prophetic about a people's expectations, a key to what they are prepared to accept. The nation is expecting more Government regulation in the future. They see that trend not because they think there is anything inexorable about the growth of Government power, but because they see problems to be solved. If there is more regulation, it will be because regulation is necessary in the public interest—to provide jobs, control monopoly, save the small businessman. Gradually the slogan of "As Little Government as Possible" is coming to read "As Much Government as Necessary." That is the pragmatic approach, very American. In the postwar 20th century, it will probably be good horse sense.

CHAPTER XI

THE CASE OF THE RETURNING SOLDIER

THE returning soldier is to the American people more than a fact-to-be. He is at once a symbol and an alarum. As a symbol he is the sentimental cynosure around which our interests in domestic post-war problems center. We talk anxiously of jobs. But "jobs for the returning soldier" is the expression most fraught with emotion. So too social security for the returning soldier, a decent America for the returning soldier, and the rest. But these are the flag-wavings, the hero-worshipings. The hero gloss will wear off when eleven million ubiquitous Johnnies come marching home, tired, human, and deadly sick of war. In all wars, the soldier has been a hero. But hero worship has never counted for much in assuring the run-of-the-mill heroes a place in the post-war sun. After the last war, was not England to be made a "land fit for heroes"?

What counts is that the returning soldier this time is also an alarum; a pang to the conscience, a dread to the wayward politician, a nightmare to the businessman. We know only vaguely and fearfully what eleven million men looking for work can mean. The politician knows how many votes are 11,000,000. But most important is that to most of America this returning soldier is not just Joe Doakes, but our son, our father, our cousin, or that young fellow next door.

THE PROBLEM OF JOBS

First comes his job. The vision of ex-servicemen tramping the streets we do not like. Eager as we are to get men back into civilian life, our concern is such that we would rather see the men released gradually with jobs than willy-nilly without. Take this question as an example.[1]

"Which do you think it would be better for us to do—to release soldiers from the army as soon as the war is over, or to release them only when a job can be found for them?"

58% favor release when a job can be found
33% favor immediate release, and
9% have no opinion on the matter.

We mean what we say. Even if some men must be kept on in the army six months or more after the war, there would still be eight in ten who would prefer gradual demobilization to "dumping."[2] Our feelings about unemployed soldiers are strong.

But all this is a keynote, not the whole story. The whole story, stated simply, goes like this: *Any measure which protects the soldier from post-demobilization unemployment is better than any measure which does not.* The opinions cited above are significant because they show to what drastic extremes the American people are ready to go to make sure that the returning soldier has work when he comes home. It matters not that people are optimistic about the chances soldiers have of getting jobs (Chapter IX). In spite of all optimism, we are still not so rash as to take reckless chances.

It goes without saying, of course, that recourse to slow and prolonged demobilization is hardly the most popular method of fighting unemployment. There are other, less drastic, proposals which muster far more enthusiastic support. Few people would demand that soldiers be kept in the army for six months awaiting jobs if a better means of protecting them from hardship were offered.

Dismissal pay for soldiers is one of such "less drastic" proposals. Long before action was considered seriously by Congress the American people had gone on record as favoring such legislation. A plan whereby discharged soldiers could receive substantial additional pay after dismissal was sponsored by eight in ten Americans a full year before legislation.[3] When legislation reached the floor of Congress, the nation not only gave it a public blessing, but expressed willingness to pay any higher taxes that might be required.[4]

But knowing how Americans feel about the relative desirability of a job *versus* a relief check, one need scarcely indulge in inference to understand why they want something more than dismissal pay for men mustered out of service. If we are willing to have the army hold men for as long as six months in the interest of getting them placed in jobs, naturally we are eager to have other devices used to see that soldiers find work. Such provisions as Section 8a of the Selective Service Act providing for the return of men to their old jobs are, of course, popular.[5] Yet we also know that there are more than a few men who will not be covered by Section 8a. For these men, something else will have to be worked out.

The nation assumes—and rightly—that the government will make some effort to serve as an employment agency for demobilized soldiers. The public is vaguely aware of plans. Three in particular have been made known. The first is the principle of Selective Service in reverse. Within the Selective Service system there is a Re-employment Division charged with the task of finding work for soldiers in the communities from which they were drafted. The plan calls for special members of local draft boards to undertake the responsibility of getting in touch with prospective employers in the community. During the period of war-boom prosperity, Selective Service in reverse has been successful in placing those men discharged for medical or other reasons. Whether the same success will mark the more crucial post-war phase of re-employment is a moot point. At any rate, Selective Service in reverse is one proposal.

Another is the United States Employment Service, an agency with a long background in job placement. Finally, there has been talk of setting up a new government bureau with more power than the United States Employment Service whose sole function it would be to find work for demobilized soldiers.

How does the public feel about it? Sooner or later one of three plans will become *the* plan for demobilization. They have some decided ideas on the matter. When the three alternative plans mentioned above are presented to the public, these are the reactions.[6]

16% favor local draft boards acting "in reverse,"
37% want a new agency with more power than USES, and
47% would like to see re-employment handled by the USES.

Reasons given for these opinions tell an interesting story. We have nothing against draft boards. In point of fact, the great majority of Americans believe they have done a splendid job—as draft boards.[7] People prefer agencies whose sole function is employment (USES or some new agency) for the same reason they prefer the dentist and not the hardware merchant when their teeth ache. As one cab driver in Chicago put it to an interviewer, "What does the draft board in our part of town know about getting my kid brother a job when he gets out? I don't know much about this getting-soldiers-a-job business but for my money I'll take the kind of outfit whose job is getting people jobs and I'd give them some say about it. I like this idea of a new employment agency set up by the Government to do the job. That's how I look at it."

To sum it up, what America wants for its demobilized soldiers is an employment agency—a real, professional one—that is second to none, one with either a background of experience or one with power to do something besides merely give advice. If all these characteristics could be combined, all the better. As we approach

"D-day" the demand for such an agency will, doubtless, grow stronger.

Even so, the "getting-soldiers-a-job business" does not end when an employment agency comes into being. The agency should have a special weapon. That weapon is the right of the veteran to first choice of available jobs. Consider this question.[8]

"After the war do you think soldiers should be given first choice of the jobs that are open or do you think everybody should have an equal chance to get jobs?"

64%   want soldiers to have first choice
33%   favor "first come, first served"
 3%   have not made up their minds

Yet, inevitably, special privilege for one group—even returning heroes—means stepping on the toes of another. Enthusiasm for a job priority system, for example, is greatest among those with secure jobs and plenty of seniority. But among those just making a start— the age group 20-30—enthusiasm is less noticeable. To this younger group, working mostly on defense jobs which may fold up after the war, the soldier with priorities is a threat. Though a *majority* of the young are not opposed, it is significant that *half* the population between twenty and thirty years of age are.[9]

To be sure, the negative opinion of young civilians will probably cut little legislative ice, nor will it dissuade employers from giving preference to men with a service record and release papers. Yet it does highlight a serious problem on which action still remains to be taken. An army of unemployed civilians is no less calamitous than an army of jobless servicemen.

Still another evidence of the extent to which America is ready to go in giving special job rights to soldiers is our attitude toward the post-war rights of working women. During 1943, for example, this alternative was proposed to a cross-section of the public.[10]

"Do you think that women who are working now ought to be made to give up their jobs to returning soldiers after the war is over?"

82% agreed
13% disagreed
5%   had no opinions

To those who say the mass of American women would rise in arms against such a proposal, the following figures are offered.[11]

80% of men want men to have first choice of jobs, and
83% of women want men to have the first choice.

America may no longer believe that a woman's place is in the home. But more important, we believe even less that a man's place is on the street without a job. Values in every culture are relative. There remains, too, the fact that, in numbers and in spirit, far more women are the wives and mothers of soldiers than are breadwinners. It goes without saying, of course, that none but a scanty handful would permanently deny women who want to, the right to work. In this instance, that general principle is not at stake. Here it is simply a matter of first choice in emergency. Men for jobs, women and children for lifeboats—both are biases, both the norms of the culture in which we live.

There is, finally, one more precaution against post-demobilization unemployment. It is a stop-gap. Whatever other guarantees there are for servicemen, there should also be a job guaranteed by the Government—presumably on public works—at which they may work until regular employment is found. Since "Government projects" are an accepted method of combating joblessness, their use as an aid to unemployed soldiers is favored by an overwhelming majority of Americans.[12] If all else fails, there will still be something to fall back on.

Jobs are the *first* problem for the soldier. We want that problem faced boldly—not only in terms of bold planning for the home front in general, but also in terms of special assistance to the men home from war. But we do not stop there. He should have more than a job.

A Job, Plus . . .

The young soldier, uprooted from civilian life while still in school, should be given every chance to go back to school with the Government's help if necessary, when he comes back. To the public, that, too, is a responsibility of government. It is not a controversial issue. Nine in ten Americans agree.[13] The question of how much the Government should pay and for how long, we leave to the good judgment of legislators. That the help given be adequate is the only requirement set.

There has been some concern among educators that Federal legislation providing educational aid to soldiers will invade the rights of states to control education within their borders. On that problem the public has this to say: Control of the schools should stay in the hands of local and state governments.[14] In the realm of education, we feel strongly about states' rights—and local rights. But as for Federal aid being given to local schools, the public sees no objection.[15] Certainly, the provision of *Federal* aid for soldiers in schools controlled by *States* makes us no less enthusiastic for such aid.

Education is one of the "extras" due servicemen. In the same spirit the public would like to see granted to the ex-soldier the means of making a start for himself in the economic life of the community. Eight Americans in ten would like, for example, to see instituted a system of low-interest, long-term loans extended to men who would like to get into business or buy into a farm.[16] It is a middle-class proposal for middle-class aspirations. But the rich and poor, and the rank-and-file of both parties are heartily in favor of it. The spirit is not one of boondoggling. People with no close relatives in the armed services feel hardly less intense about it than their neighbors with sons in uniform.[17]

All these things we are willing to do. They go by way of being legitimate aid to the returning soldier. Cross the border into the realm of pork-barreling, and the American people do not cross with you. After the soldier has found a steady job, he is on his financial own. Take this as an example.[18]

"Do you think that when a soldier has found a steady job after the war, the Government should pay him more money as a bonus, or do you think that unless he is wounded the Government's responsibility should end when he gets a steady job?"

25%   favor paying a bonus
71%   oppose a soldier's bonus
 4%   have no opinion

Bonuses, thanks to our history, do not mean "aid" to soldiers. They mean, straight and simple, a raid on the Treasury. And so, even among those groups where support for a bonus might be expected, only scant minorities favor them. Thus, among the poor, who have traditionally benefited, scarcely a third can be counted among the adherents of bonuses. Nor does the presence of a close relative in the armed services affect opinion. Those with and those without close relatives in the Army and Navy are virtually unanimous in condemning the bonus.[19]

The matter can be summed up thus: The American people are ready and willing to give to soldiers those opportunities which go beyond the mere possession of a job. Such opportunities are legitimately theirs. Outright gifts and bonuses not directly related to the struggle of the soldier to find his place in civilian life are no more legitimate now than before.

The Thorns in the Bed of Roses

But in spite of laudable public support for all necessary aid to the soldier, still there are bound to be problems. Some of the problems have their roots in the structure of American politics. Others derive from the cold and inexorable logic of military and economic events. The military problems—simpler and more immediate—come first.

Two things are true about this war that have not been true in the past. The first has to do with the cessation of fighting. World War II will not come to an end all of a sudden. The strategy of the war has given priority to the European theater. That phase will, likely, be over first. Some troops fighting in Europe will be shifted to Asia. Others will be demobilized. The families of men fighting through the last stages of the Pacific war may feel jealousy and resentment toward those already demobilized. Inevitably, those demobilized first will get the first crack at available jobs.

The plight of the latecomers to the post-war feast has hardly been discussed publicly. If the war is followed by a boom lasting several years, perhaps no problem will arise. But intelligent planning cannot take as its basis the rosiest possible estimate of future conditions. Supplying work for the first wave of "demobilizees" does not solve the whole problem of post-war joblessness among servicemen. The public is not yet aware of what may some day become a disheartening fact. But when the good job they hoped their own son might get goes to somebody out of the Army a year before, they will become aware of it soon enough. We face a critical problem in public relations, a crisis in planning.

A second problem which grows from the military exigencies of modern warfare is the place of America's military personnel in the many armies of occupation needed at the end of the war. Inevitably,

Americans will be serving in such armies. Inevitably, too, American families will be restive while their sons and brothers are kept on for occupation duty after the neighbor's son has come home and settled back into civilian life.

Although the public will not be called in to decide which American soldiers are to serve in the armies of occupation, the average man does have some definite ideas about what is, and what is not, a fair and wise method of holding men for occupation duty. Cognizance of these will make the Army's public relations job that much easier. The ideas are flexible—compounded of two common-sense elements. The first has to do with military necessity; the second with fairness.

Military authorities need not fear that Americans do not have a sense of what is necessary. Take, for example, the matter of a man's service record. Shall the armies of occupation be made up of men who have been in the Army for some time, men skilled in military "know-how"; or should the choice be men fairly new to the Army? If fairness were the sole criterion, the public would want to see men with more years of service released first. But that is not the case. For each five people who prefer veterans in the army of occupation, there is only one who would choose inexperienced personnel.[20]

When neither necessity nor fairness is clear-cut, the decisions made by the military will stand in somewhat greater danger of running into public resentment. The special problem of the young soldier and the old presents a typical case. From the parents of young men in the army may come the plea that youths should not be held for occupation duty. Uprooted before making a start in life, they must be brought back to civilian pursuits just as quickly as possible lest they become another "lost generation." Just as loud will be the chorus claiming that the older men, already committed to family responsibilities, should be released in the interest of reducing civilian hardship to a minimum. Both sides have compelling arguments. An adequate decision would, of course, require Solomon-like sagacity. Turning to the public affords small guidance, for the nation is equally split on the matter—as many wanting the young men out first as wanting the older ones.[21]

In the end, perhaps, the matter may be settled by a system of volunteering—if volunteering could provide the right numbers of men in the right theaters of operation. That the American people would favor such a method of selecting men for occupation duty—though not by an overwhelming majority—is to be expected. The balance is six to four in favor.[22]

The General Staff doubtless has its plans for occupation, and those plans will and should be put into effect whether the public agrees or disagrees. Yet the opinions of the public on these matters do provide one guide to the military. Public opinion is flexible. It has ever been mindful of problems of military necessity, and, having seen necessity, has given support. Many of the actions of the military the public has taken on faith. That is as it should be.

But as the war draws to a close, peacetime conceptions will again assert themselves. More questions will be asked; more answers expected. That does not mean that the American people will no longer be willing to sacrifice. The end of the war need not spell a snap-back into complacent normalcy (see Chapter II). One thing which the military can do to keep alive a spirit of willing co-operation in the civilian population is to provide, wherever security permits, the reasons for decisions made regarding the choice of personnel for the armies of occupation. If there is the demand from some quarters that men be chosen through volunteering and, at the same time, such a method is not feasible, it is the responsibility of the Commander-in-Chief, or his spokesman, to tell why a system other than volunteering is being instituted. The same goes for the problem of younger and older men. The public is willing to listen, is eager to listen.

These are military problems. The march of events will, in good time, settle them. There are other, political problems which are neither so clear-cut nor so easy of solution. At their root lies a fear of the returning soldier as a factor in American politics.

One final comment about the returning soldier and politics. Most working politicians, one judges, see the "returned" soldier in the image of the old American Legion. Congress has already echoed to the refrain that "the boys want to find things as they left them." The hopes of some and the fears of others are that the new Legion will stand, as did the old, for the "good old times" and ultra-conservatism. Insofar as America's legislators—both on the national and state levels—operate on such an assumption, the voice of the soldier will be confused with the voice of the "professional veteran." Nobody knows for sure yet what our citizen-soldiers stand for politically.

There are other evidences pointing to a distaste for unbridled social individualism among our fighting men. Many of them knew only one of three things before induction—either a war-boom job, or a precarious depression job before that, or unemployment still earlier. Virtually all of them grew up in a depression. Soldiers may be hankering after those comforts of civilian life which formerly they had taken for granted. But such hankerings are neither actual nor presumptive proof of political leanings. K rations have a way of inducing nostalgia without so much as touching social and political convictions.

In conclusion, the case of the returning soldier reduces to something very simple. Everybody wants to give him a break. Of good intention there is an abundance. In that we are united. The danger comes, not from intention, but from the fact that the returning soldier is a political as well as an economic and moral issue. In the end, public pressure will get him his due. If it does not come from his mother, brother, and father, then it will come from the returning soldier himself. With public opinion in its present mood, it is not a matter of "yes or no," but, rather, of "when and how."

THE PROSPECT

THERE are ninety million adults in this country. This book has been their story. It is not all happy, not all sad. The public is neither an angel nor a devil. The story is not finished; it will never be finished. The public is ever growing. Into what is it growing? What are the prospects?

The public is common sense. It is people—people with visions ahead of their times, people with hankerings after the past, people absorbed in the present.

Americans shun the doctrinaire, because the doctrinaire is alien to the ways of common sense. When we think of the great international and domestic issues, we do not think as theorists. People are concrete. War and its causes are not abstract military-economic chess. War is somebody being greedy. War is sons being drafted. War is casualty lists. War is having your life disorganized. And peace is not a theory of high level employment nor a system of international commitments. Peace is a job. Peace is people sitting around a conference table making sensible decisions—without guns. Peace is having children and sending them through school. Peace is a Sunday drive in the country.

The public appraises the world in these concrete terms. It does no good to explain the intricacies of, say, deficit financing to the people without first reducing—or raising—the discussion to the level of everyday life. What is important is that people sense the great issues in terms of their own common sense.

That is public opinion. When people are uninformed about great issues it is because they fail to see the relation of world trade to a Sunday drive in the country. It is because they fail to see the relation of tin in Malaya to somebody being greedy. If the public is to be informed, it will take more than pamphlets and lectures about how the League works, more than speeches by great statesmen about world markets. The challenge of the future is to make people realize their own personal stake in what heretofore has been "the affairs of state," the responsibility of the few.

Deep inside all of us is the knowledge of why we fight, what we want. That too is our common sense. Again, it is not for doctrine, not for ideology. We fight for self-protection, yes. But we also fight for some common-sense practices which, for lack of a better name, we call "decency." A military man, General Somervell, put the matter this way: "We fight for the simple things; for the little things that are all-important. We fight for the right to lock our house doors and be sure that no bully with official sanction will break the lock. We fight for town meetings, for the soap-box in the public square, for the high school debating team, for open doors to cathedral and church and synagogue. We fight for schools built on a foundation of books, not bayonets. We fight for the country editor and the metropolitan daily and for the editor's right to say the wrong thing if he thinks it's right. We fight for the right to organize for any decent purpose; for labor; for employers; for the Grange and the Legion and the ladies' literary club, and for the Lodge meetings in full regalia on Tuesday nights. We fight for our candidate for sheriff and for the other fellow's candidate and for the right to be sorry we elected him and say so. We fight for free radio, for the right to listen to what we want to and turn off what we don't want. We fight for the right to work at jobs of our own choosing; to read the books which we want to read, to listen to music that pleases us without regard to the race or nationality of the composer.

We fight for the high privilege of throwing pop bottles at the umpire."

These are the signs that there still exists a way of life which we expect, which we need. This is the structure of everyday life in America—the chance for freedom, for individuality, even for happiness.

That is the way things have been up to now. Our common sense has been able to grasp the complexities of the world, been able to translate them into the concrete terms of experience. At times, the public has failed because it has been unable to translate the new issues into the old thoughtways. The new issues, the issues of the world after the war, are going to be more complex, more abstract than they have ever been. Technology has made life easier, yes. Just as truly, it has made life infinitely more difficult. We are being deprived of the security of the craftsman, of the quiet of the valley. Leisure and unemployment have been the rewards of the new technology. We have yet to learn how to use the one wisely and control the other. In the political sphere, the town meeting has gone, but the international organization is coming. Will we use it wisely?

The challenge of the future is to keep democracy with its effective public opinion and at the same time to enjoy the fruits of the increasing complexity of modern life. If mass production and the new marvels of science mean that the creativeness of the individual is to be stultified and subordinated to the "managerial elite" then technological discovery will have been in vain. If, again, the establishment of a system of international security and co-operation means that the machinery of government controlling man's destiny has been further removed from the control of the individual, then too, the game in the long run will not have been worth the candle.

Neither of these consequences is inevitable. We can have a consummate technology and a breathtaking array of modern appliances

225

and still retain the creativeness of the individual, so necessary for the functioning of democracy. Nor need the establishment of the most thoroughgoing internationalism mean less political power for the individual. To have our technology, our internationalism, we will also have to have a public capable of coping with them—in short, a public as well-informed as modern communication can make it. But if we are to have our cake and eat it, we cannot leave the development of an informed public opinion to luck. Such a public comes not by blind chance, but by hard, painstaking, and often frustrating effort.

In recent years we have heard much of the Common Man and of faith in the Common Man. One might even say that we have become smug about him. It has become the fashion to treat the Common Man as if he were a finished product. That is a fiction. The Common Man is still evolving. He will always be evolving. It is his world, his to warp, or be warped by; his to control, or be controlled by. Recent history has shown us all too tragically that the Common Man can be made into a fighting robot at one extreme or a paragon of creativity at the other. And it is not by chance that history finds him at one extreme or the other. We can go in either direction. It is up to us.

What are the prospects? We stand at the crossroads. In tomorrow's world the public cannot stay where it is. It must go one way or the other. If it comes to understand its stake in the world, if it is active and creative in its demands, then it will be the Great Arbiter, the counterpoise in the democratic process. If, through the irresponsibility of its leaders, it is allowed to sink into apathetic dependence upon the experts, then the end of effective democracy is in sight.

But though we are at the crossroads the future is bright. Today, thanks to the development of mass communication, the American public is probably better informed and more strongly bulwarked by convictions on the great issues than it has ever been in its history. On that score there is ground for rejoicing—but scarcely reason for smugness. If the future is to continue bright, two conditions must be fulfilled. There must first be ceaseless effort to inform the man in the street, to inform him honestly and in the language of common sense. But as important, we must improve the methods whereby the public makes felt its will. For the conduct of national and international affairs we cannot go back to the town meeting. But we must, if we are to survive as a democracy, recapture more and more of its spirit. What makes democracy is people. The mandate from the people must be heard, must be heard constantly.

APPENDIX

IN this Appendix will be found the detailed material upon which the text statements concerning public opinion findings are based. Each entry gives the approximate date on which a question was asked, and the name of the polling organization responsible. Where the exact wordings of the questions do not appear in the text they are reproduced in the Appendix. The same rule is followed with respect to percentage results of questions. Thus the Appendix is not a self-contained summary of poll results but a supplement to the text.

The Appendix is subdivided into chapters corresponding to chapters in the text. The numbers preceding each entry in the Appendix correspond to the numeral superscripts scattered throughout the text.

Certain abbreviations have been used throughout to designate various polling organizations. These can be listed as follows:

AIPO   —American Institute of Public Opinion
                (operating in the United States)
NORC —National Opinion Research Center
                (operating in the United States)
OPOR —Office of Public Opinion Research
                (operating in the United States)
FOR   —Fortune Poll
                (operating in the United States)
CIPO   —Canadian Institute of Public Opinion
                (operating in Canada)
BIPO   —British Institute of Public Opinion
                (operating in Britain)
FOR-BR—Fortune Poll of Britain
                (operating in Britain)
APOP   —Australian Public Opinion Poll
                (operating in Australia)

The procedures followed in public opinion polling, by now fairly well standardized, are easily described. In order to get an accurate miniature of the total population, all major regions of the country must be covered; interviewing must be done in cities of different size; a correct proportion of men and women, rich and poor, young and old, workers and farmers, Republicans and Democrats must be polled.

Because polls are conducted on a miniature of the population and not on the population as a whole, they are subject to something known as "sampling error." The size of this error is a function of two things: the number of people included in the miniature sample, and the extent to which the miniature corresponds in all crucial respects to the population of the country as a whole. The major polls, the results of whose work are reported herein, interview between 1500 and 3500 people on each survey. Constant check is kept on the degree to which these miniature populations correspond to the population as a whole. For such miniatures, "sampling error" is fairly small. Stated in the simplest statistical language, the extent of error can be summarized as follows: If a poll question were repeated on 100 miniature samples of the United States, in 95 cases out of 100, the results obtained would not vary more than 6 per cent for samples of 1500 people and not more than 4 per cent for samples of 3500 people. In interpreting poll results in this book, the size of this sampling error should always be considered.

INTRODUCTION

—1. Right now, lots of people are interested in post-war problems. Which interest you more—*international* problems (like a new league of nations and an international police force) OR *domestic* problems (like full employment and production)? (OPOR, 11-43.)

	Per cent
International	16
Domestic	53
Both	26
No opinion	5

CHAPTER I

—1. Question wording and results as indicated in text. (OPOR, 11-42.)

—2. Do you think it was a mistake for the U. S. to enter the last World War? (OPOR, Trend.) Results as indicated in text.

3. Are you a member of a church? (AIPO, 10-42.) Results as indicated in text.

4. Question wording and results as indicated in text. (FOR, 8-38.)

5. Are your sympathies with either side in the present Spanish Civil War? (AIPO, 5-37.)

    Yes 21%, *No, or don't know enough about it* 79%

6. Which side do you sympathize with in the Spanish Civil War—the Loyalists or Franco? (AIPO, 12-38.)

    Loyalists 30%, *Franco* 10%, *Neither or no opinion* 60%

7. Should Congress change the Neutrality Act to permit shipment of arms to the Loyalists in Spain? (AIPO, 1-39.)

    Yes 17%, *No* 66%, *No opinion* 17%

8. Question wording as indicated in text. (AIPO, 10-35.)
     Yes 28%, *No* 67%, *No opinion* 5%
9. Asked of 28 per cent who favored U. S. joining with others to stop aggression, on #8, directly above: Which measures would you favor? (AIPO, 10-35.)

	Per cent
Economic and non-military measures only	65
Military measures if necessary	31
No opinion	4

10. If war in Europe is averted through the League of Nations, do you believe the United States should join the League? (FOR, 1-35.)
     Yes 30%, *No* 57%, *No opinion* 13%
11. Do you think the cause of world peace will be hurt if the League of Nations is dissolved? (AIPO, 12-37.)
     Yes 29%, *No* 45%, *No opinion* 26%
12. Should President Roosevelt call a world disarmament conference? (AIPO, 4-37.)
     Yes 25%, *No* 56%, *No opinion* 19%
13. Would you favor a conference of the leading nations to reduce the size of all armies and navies at this time? (AIPO, 2-39.)
     Yes 39%, *No* 51%, *No opinion* 10%
14. Question wording as indicated in text. (AIPO, 7-37.)
     Yes 67%, *No* 25%, *No opinion* 8%
15. Do you think England and France will have a war against Germany within the next twelve months? (AIPO, 9-38.)
     Yes 44%, *No* 36%, *No opinion* 20%
16. Do you think there will be a general European war anyway (in spite of Munich) in the next few years? (FOR, 1-39.)
     Yes 66%, *No* 16%, *No opinion* 18%
17. Hitler says he has "no more territorial ambitions in Europe." Do you believe him? (AIPO, 10-38.)
     Yes 6%, *No* 74%, *Don't know* 20%
18. If there is another general European war, do you believe the U. S. can stay out? (AIPO, 12-36.)
     Yes 60%, *No* 36%, *Don't know* 4%
19. Do you think the United States will go into the war in Europe or do you think we will stay out of the war? (AIPO & OPOR, Trend.) Results as indicated in text.
20. Do you think Hitler's claims to Danzig are justified? (AIPO, 8-39.)
     Yes 10%, *No* 62%, *No opinion* 28%
21. Would you like to see England, France, and Poland agree to Germany's demands regarding Danzig? (AIPO, 8-39.)
     Yes 9%, *No* 68%, *No opinion* 23%

22. Do you think Hitler's claims to the Polish Corridor are justified? (AIPO, 8-39.)

    Yes 10%,   *No* 61%,   *No opinion* 29%

23. Which country or countries do you consider responsible for causing the present war? (AIPO, 9-39.)

	Per cent
Germany................	81
England &/or France......	3
Versailles Treaty..........	4
Others..................	6
Don't know.............	6

24. Do you think the U. S. should declare war on Germany *at once* and send our Army and Navy abroad to help England, France, and Poland? (AIPO, 9-39.)

    Yes 9%,   *No* 88%,   *No opinion* 3%

25. Which of these two things do you think it is more important for the United States to try to do: To keep out of war ourselves, or to help England win even at the risk of getting into war? (OPOR, Trend.) Results as indicated in text.

26. If Germany and Italy defeat England in the present war, do you think Germany and Italy would start a war against the U. S. within the next ten years? (OPOR, 3-41.) Results as indicated in text.

27. Do you think that, if England falls, Germany will soon be in control of all of our trade and foreign markets? (OPOR, 3-41.) Results as indicated in text.

28. Do you think that, if Germany wins the war, we will have to keep up and pay for such a strong national defense that people in this country will be poorer than they are now? (OPOR, 3-41.) Results as indicated in text.

29. If Germany defeats England in the present war, do you think you will be as free to do what you want to as you are now? (OPOR, 3-41.) Results as indicated in text.

30. Which side do you think will win the war—Germany and Italy or England (and France)? (OPOR & AIPO, Trend.) Results as indicated in text.

31. Which of these statements is closer to the truth? (OPOR, Trend.)

    1. England (and France) are now fighting mainly to keep their power and wealth.

    2. England (and France) are fighting mainly to preserve democracy against the spread of dictatorship.

Results as indicated in text.

32. Do you think America's failure to join the League of Nations was partly responsible for the present troubles in Europe? (AIPO, 9-38.)

    Yes 17%,   *No* 62%,   *No opinion* 21%

33. If the U. S. had joined the League of Nations do you think it would have prevented the war? (AIPO, 7-41.)

    Yes 20%, *No* 56%, *No opinion* 24%

34. Do you think the fact that the U. S. did not join the League of Nations after the last war is largely responsible for this war? (AIPO, 12-42.)

    Yes 22%, *No* 52%, *Don't know* 26%

35. Which of these reasons come closest to describing your own idea as to the real cause of the present European war? (FOR, 12-39.)

Per cent

The German people always want to have their own way even if that brings a war	6
Hitler's greed for land and lust for power	54
Germany's (or Hitler's) desire to regain all possessions lost in the last war	20
The Treaty of Versailles—it was unfair to Germany	10
England and France are trying to keep Germany from becoming a really strong power	6
The same old hatred between the peoples of Europe	11
The over-population of Europe—a war is needed to thin them out	2
Other	3
Don't know	5
	117 *

    * Total more than 100%; multiple answers allowed.

36. Have you heard or read about the 8-point program which Roosevelt and Churchill drew up at their recent meeting? (AIPO, 8-41.)

    Yes 75%, *No* 25%

37. Have you heard or read about the Atlantic Charter? (AIPO, 1-42.)

    Yes 23%, *No* 77%

38. Asked of those who had heard of the Atlantic Charter: Can you tell me briefly any of the main provisions of the Atlantic Charter? (AIPO, 1-42.)

    4% of the total population could name one or more provisions.

CHAPTER II

1. Which of these countries do you think has done the most toward winning the war so far—Russia, China, Britain, or the U. S.? (AIPO, 6-43.)

    Russia 30%, *China* 5%, *Britain* 11%, *U. S.* 46%, *No opinion* 8%

2. Question wording and results as indicated in text. (AIPO, OPOR, Trend.)

3. After the war, do you think the United States should play a larger part, about the same part, or a smaller part in world affairs than it did before the war? (FOR, Trend.)

	Dec., '41	June, '43
	%	%
Larger	59	77
Same	18	12
Smaller	10	4
Don't know	13	7

4. See #2, this chapter. (AIPO, 6-43.) Results as indicated in text.

5. See #2, this chapter. (OPOR, 11-43.)

	Take active part
	%
Upper income	87
Middle	75
Lower	58

6. See #2, this chapter. (AIPO, OPOR, Trend.) Results as indicated in text.

7. "Interventionists" on #2 of this chapter were asked the two questions indicated in the text with these results: (OPOR, 6-42.)

Would the expense of an international police force be justified?

Yes 93%, *No* 3%, *No opinion* 4%

Would co-operation be worth while if we became involved in entangling alliances?

Yes 61%, *No* 20%, *No opinion* 19%

8. "Isolationists" on #2 of this chapter were asked the two questions indicated in the text with these results: (OPOR, 6-42.)

If war threatens should we still stay out?

Yes 57%, *No* 28%, *Other* 7%, *No opinion* 8%

If living standard is lowered should we still stay out?

Yes 61%, *No* 20%, *Other* 6%, *No opinion* 13%

9. Which of these seems better to you—for us to win the war first and then think about the peace, or to start thinking now about the kind of peace we want after the war? (FOR, OPOR, Trend.)

	June, '42 (FOR)	Aug., '43 (OPOR)
	%	%
Start planning now	33	59
Wait till after war	59	38
Undecided	8	3

10. Should the government take steps now, before the end of the war, to set up with our Allies a world organization to maintain the future peace of the world? (AIPO, OPOR, Trend.) Percentages based on those with opinions. 12% were without opinions in Dec., '42; in Nov., '43, less than 1%.

	Dec., '42 %	Nov., '43 %
Yes	73	81
No	27	19

11. After reading to respondents the Fulbright Resolution, interviewers asked: Do you want your Congressman to vote for or against this resolution? (AIPO, 6-43.)

For 78%, *Against* 9%, *No opinion* 13%

The vote of the House of Representatives on September 21, 1943:

For 92.5%, *Against* 7.5%

After the passage of the Fulbright Resolution but before the adoption of the Connally Resolution, this question was asked: Would you like to see the United States Congress take a vote now to find out how Congressmen feel about the United States joining some kind of union of nations? (NORC, 9-43.) Percentages based on those with opinions. 8% were without opinions.

Yes 71%, *No* 29%

12. After this war if two countries have a disagreement, do you think it would be better if they tried to settle it themselves, or do you think it would be better if some kind of organization worked with them to try to settle the disagreement? (NORC, 9-43.)

Themselves 26%, *Organization* 69%, *No opinion* 5%

Which one of these comes closest to expressing what you would like to have the U. S. do after the war? (FOR, 3-44.)

	Per cent
A. Enter into no alliance and have as little as possible to do with other countries	13
B. Depend only on separate alliances with certain countries	8
C. Take an active part in an international organization	68
D. No opinion	11

13. To insure world peace, which do you think will work better—a league of nations or military alliances between strong nations? (AIPO, 5-36.) Percentages based on those with opinions. Data on those without opinions not available.

League 37%, *Alliances* 63%

14. If a union of nations is formed after the war, do you think it would be a good idea or a bad idea for the United States to join it? (NORC, Trend.) Results as indicated in text.

A longer perspective on the development of opinion is provided by another question: Would you like to see the United States join a league of nations after this war is over? (AIPO & OPOR, Trend.)

	Yes %	No %	No opinion %
October, 1937 *	26	53	21
May, 1941	37	39	24
June, 1942	60	22	18
November, 1942	55	20	25
October, 1943	62	17	21

* The question read at that time: Would you like to see the United States join the League of Nations?

The smaller favorable percentage polled by this question is the result of using the unpopular symbol "league of nations." For further discussion of point, see text.

15. If a union of nations is formed after the war, do you think it would be a good idea or a bad idea for the United States to join it? (NORC, 9-43.) Results as indicated in text.

16. Which one of these statements comes closest to what you would like to see us do when the war is over? (FOR, 6-43.)

	Per cent
A. Take an active part in some sort of international organization with a court and police force strong enough to enforce its decisions....	57
B. Try to keep the world at peace but make no definite agreements with other countries.......................................	25
C. Stay on our side of the oceans and have as little as possible to do with Europe and Asia.....................................	13
No opinion	5

17. See #16, this chapter. Asked of business leaders only. (FOR, 10-43.)

	Per cent
A.	71
B.	23
C.	5
No opinion	1

18. Asked of the 84 per cent of the population not opposed to joining a union of nations after the war, #14, this chapter: If the United States has only the same amount of power in the union as (Great Britain) (Russia) (Germany), would you be in favor of our joining it or against our joining it? (NORC, 1-43.)

	Great Britain %	Russia %	Germany %
Favor	62	55	28
Oppose	13	18	46
No opinion	9	11	10
	84	84	84

19. Do you think countries should get together in a union of nations to decide how big an army, navy, and air force each country can have? (NORC, 9-43.)

    Yes 77%, *No* 17%, *No opinion* 6%

20. If the United States does join with other countries in a union of nations, would you be willing to have the union decide how big an army, navy, and air force the United States should have? (NORC, 9-43.)

    Yes 70%, *No* 24%, *No opinion* 6%

21. As you know, Congress has the power to make laws about problems that may come up between states. Do you think a union of nations should have power to make laws about problems that may come up between countries in the union? (NORC, 9-43.)

    Yes 76%, *No* 13%, *No opinion* 11%

22. Do you think it would be a good idea for countries to get together in a union of nations to decide how trade between countries should be handled, or do you think each country should handle trade any way it wants? (NORC, 9-43.)

    Union decide 65%, *Each country decide* 29%, *No opinion* 6%

More recent research confirms the fact that Americans are willing to give the new organization of nations strong teeth. Consider this question: If a general international organization should be set up, which of these things do you think it should and should not be organized to do? (FOR, 3-44.)

Prevent any member country from starting a war of its own against an outside country.

Should 79%, *Should not* 7%, *Don't know* 14%

Decide which country is right if two members get into a dispute.

Should 76%, *Should not* 8%, *Don't know* 16%

Decide what taxes individual member nations must pay to support the organization.

Should 70%, *Should not* 9%, *Don't know* 21%

Decide what military strength each member nation can have.

Should 69%, *Should not* 14%, *Don't know* 17%

Regulate the rights of airplanes from one member nation to land on airfields in other member nations.

Should 61%, *Should not* 14%, *Don't know* 25%

Have a permanent military force of its own, *stronger* than any single nation.
Should 54%, *Should not* 23%, *Don't know* 23%
Decide what tariff rates should be charged by member nations.
Should 45%, *Should not* 23%, *Don't know* 32%
Decide which side is right if a civil war breaks out in a member nation, and support that side.
Should 43%, *Should not* 32%, *Don't know* 25%
Decide minimum standards for working conditions in member countries.
Should 32%, *Should not* 45%, *Don't know* 23%

23. People who think they've found out why the League of Nations failed are now preparing for a new union of nations if we win the war. Nobody can say for sure whether a new union would end all wars or only lead to worse ones. In order to try out a union of nations as a possible way of preventing wars, would you yourself be willing or not willing: (NORC, 1-43.)

. . . to stay on a rationing system in this country for about five years to help feed the starving people in other countries?
Willing 82%, *Not willing* 14%, *No opinion* 4%

. . . for part of the American Army to remain overseas for several years after the war to help establish order?
Willing 75%, *Not willing* 19%, *No opinion* 6%

. . . to consider most of our lend-lease materials as aid to the Allies and not expect any payment for them?
Willing 41%, *Not willing* 49%, *No opinion* 10%

. . . to pay more taxes for a few years while the new union was being organized, even if people in other countries couldn't afford to pay as much?
Willing 64%, *Not willing* 28%, *No opinion* 8%

. . . to give up our Army, Navy, and Air Force if all other nations would do the same?
Willing 41%, *Not willing* 55%, *No opinion* 4%

. . . to allow foreign goods to come into this country and compete with things we grow or make here—even if the prices were lower?
Willing 28%, *Not willing* 62%, *No opinion* 10%

. . . to forget reparations—that is, not try to collect any money from Germany or Japan to pay for what the war has cost us and our allies?
Willing 28%, *Not willing* 64%, *No opinion* 8%

24. Do you think the cause of world peace will be hurt if the League of Nations is dissolved? (AIPO, 12-37.)
Yes 29%, *No* 45%, *No opinion* 26%

25. See #14, this chapter. Compare the two trends presented in that place. At any given time, sentiment for a "union of nations" is more favorable than sentiment for a "league of nations." (AIPO, OPOR, NORC, Trend.)

26. Should the countries fighting the Axis set up an international police force after the war is over to try to keep peace throughout the world? (AIPO, OPOR, Trend.) In August, 1939, the wording of the question differed slightly from later wordings: Would you like to see the U. S. join in a movement to establish an international police force to maintain world peace? Results as indicated in text.

27. See #26, this chapter. (OPOR, 9-43.) Results as indicated in text.

28. See #26, this chapter. (OPOR, 9-43.) Results as indicated in text.

✓29. There has been a lot of discussion about how the international police force should work. Which one of these plans do you like best? (OPOR, 9-43.)

> A. The international police force should police only the Axis countries to see that they do not build up strong armies or attack neighboring countries.
>
> B. The international police force should police the Axis countries and should also keep the small countries all over the world from going to war with each other.
>
> C. The international police force should see to it that no country prepares to make war on other nations. It should police the Axis countries and the small countries but it should also have the power to stop big countries like the United States, Russia, and Great Britain from going to war.

Results as indicated in text.

30. Asked of the 79 per cent in favor of a police force, #29, this chapter: Do you think all the countries now fighting Germany and Japan should have soldiers in the international police force, or do you think some of these countries should not? (OPOR, 9-43.) Results as indicated in text.

31. If leading nations of the world agree to disarm, should the United States also agree to sink all of its warships and destroy all of its war materials? (AIPO, 10-42.)

> *Yes* 11%, *No* 87%, *No opinion* 2%

32. After the war is over, do you think every able-bodied young man should be required to spend one year in the Army, Navy, or Air Force when he reaches military age? (AIPO & OPOR, Trend.) Results as indicated in text.

33. After the war, do you think we will be able to end all wars between nations, or do you think there will always be big wars? (NORC, 8-43.)

	Per cent
Can end all wars..........................	27
Depends on type of peace after this war......	7
Always be wars............................	57
Qualified and no opinion..................	9

34. Do you think there will probably be another big war during the next 25 to 30 years, or do you think there is a fairly good chance to avoid it? (FOR, 6-43.)

Per cent
Chance to avoid........... 62
Another war.............. 31
Don't know............. 7

Let it be said that we think our chances for preventing war are better than they have been before. Asked, "Do you think chances of a permanent peace after this war are better than they were after the last war?" 66% answered "yes." (AIPO, 10-42.)

35. After Germany and Japan have been beaten and disarmed, do you think all the nations should agree to disarm gradually, so that after about 25 years, *no nation* would have a big army or navy, or do you think it would be better for the United States to have a big army and navy all the time for our protection? (OPOR, 9-43.)

Per cent
Gradual disarmament........... 26
Big U. S. armed force.......... 68
No opinion................... 6

36. Asked of those favoring large U. S. armed force on #35, this chapter: If a strong international police force were set up to keep the peace, would you still be in favor of having a large American Army and Navy all the time for our protection? (OPOR, 9-43.)

Yes 57%, *No* 9%, *No opinion* 2% = 68%, total per cent favoring large armed forces for our protection.

37. Asked of those favoring a police force on #26, this chapter: However large the United States Army will be after the war, do you think the international police force should be larger, smaller, or about the same size? (OPOR, 9-43.) Results as indicated in text.

38. Question wording as indicated in text. (NORC, Trend.)

	Feb., '42 %	July, '42 %	Jan., '43 %	June, '43 %
Give up land hard to defend.....	9	7	8	9
Keep only pre-war land.........	39	33	41	35
Get new bases.................	31	41	37	42
Get all the land we can.........	13	11	9	10
No opinion...................	8	8	5	4

39. Would you favor or oppose letting the United States Air Force and Navy
40. use bases in Australia after the war? Should it be a permanent right or a lease, say, for 25 years? (APOP, 5-43.)

	Per cent	Per cent
Favor		77
On lease	47	
Permanent	23	
Undecided	7	
	77	
Oppose	15	
No opinion	8	

41. The treaty that ended the last war created a number of small countries such as Poland, Czechoslovakia, Iraq, Lithuania, Latvia, and Finland out of territory formerly part of larger nations such as Germany and Russia. In the light of subsequent events, do you think this was a good or a bad thing? (AIPO, 10-42.)

   Good 33%, *Bad* 58%, *No opinion* 9%

42. Which country do you think *should* have the most to say about what kind of peace there should be? (FOR, 4-42, 9-42.) Results as indicated in text.

43. Which country do you think actually *will* have the most to say about the peace? (FOR, 4-42, 9-42.) Results as indicated in text.

44. As a result of this war, do you think the U. S. will be more powerful, less powerful, or have about the same amount of power as before the war? Will Russia? Germany? Britain? Japan? China? Italy? (FOR, 7-42.)

	More %	Same %	Less %	Don't know %
United States	73	17	4	6
Russia	57	17	7	19
China	55	21	8	16
Britain	25	28	34	13
Italy	1	8	77	14
Japan	2	3	86	9
Germany	1	2	89	8

45. Some people say that a strong international police force would be a threat to this country, because it might try to make us do things we don't want to do. Do you agree or disagree? (OPOR, 9-43.) Results as indicated in text.

46. A comparison of those who see a threat in the international police force and those who do not, see this chapter, #45. Each group was asked whether it was in favor of setting up an international police force, see this chapter, #26. (OPOR, 9-43.)

	Group seeing threat in police force %	Group seeing no threat in police force %
Favor police force..............	56	89
Oppose police force............	34	6
No opinion	10	5
	100	100

47. Would you tell me which of these you personally would favor as the best way to have peace treaties approved after the war? (AIPO, 8-43.)

	Per cent
Approval *only* by the President...........................	7
Approval by President and *majority* of *whole Congress*........	54
Approval by President and *two-thirds* of *Senate*..............	25
No opinion	14

CHAPTER III

1. What is your understanding of the term "reciprocal trade treaties"? (AIPO, 12-43.) Results as indicated in text.

2. Should the U. S. try to develop its own industries to the point where it does not have to buy any products from foreign countries? (FOR, 9-39.) Results as indicated in text.

3. After the war should the U. S. try to develop its own industries to the point where it does not have to buy any products from foreign countries? (OPOR, Trend.) Results as indicated in text.

   The shift in opinion toward international trade obtained by the use of the trend question noted above is confirmed by the use of different question wordings. Consider this question: After the war, which of these things do you think the United States should do? (AIPO, 12-43.)

	Per cent
Trade a lot with foreign countries even if this permits some foreign goods to sell here at a lower price than our goods..............	60
OR, Refuse to trade with foreign countries and let our people pay the higher prices for these things produced here..............	21
No opinion	19

4. See #3, this chapter, for question wording. (OPOR, 4-43.) Results as indicated in text.

5. See #3, this chapter, for question wording. (OPOR, 4-43.)

	1940 vote	
	Republican	Democrat
	%	%
For self-sufficiency	38	47
For trade	57	48
Don't know	5	5

6. Question wording and results as indicated in text. (OPOR, 6-42.)
7. After the war would you be willing to pay a higher price for all rubber products so that the new synthetic rubber factories in this country can compete with natural rubber from abroad? (AIPO, 10-43.)

Yes 53%, *No* 23%, *Qualified* 5%, *No opinion* 19%

8. Asked of a cross-section of the State of Colorado: Which one of these three ideas comes closest to what you think our government should do about letting goods from other countries be sold in the United States: (NORC, 5-43.)

Per cent

A. The United States should not let any foreign goods come into this country at all, so things made or grown here won't have to compete with foreign products we don't need............... 10

B. The United States should put a tax on most foreign goods which come into this country so that they can't hurt the business of American producers who make or grow the same things at a higher cost... 71

C. The United States should let foreign goods come into this country without being taxed, so that American people who buy things can get them cheaper and save money..................... 12

Don't know 7

9. Asked of 81% in Colorado who favored some form of trade restriction: In peacetime do you think we have so much of some products that it helps us to sell or trade them to other countries or not? (NORC, 5-43.)

Helps 70%, *Does not help* 7%, *No opinion* 4%

Asked of 70% who said it helps on #9: In order to send the products we don't need to other countries, do you think it's necessary or not necessary to let other countries send us certain products that compete with things produced here? (NORC, 5-43.)

Necessary 43%, *Unnecessary* 23%, *Depends* 1%, *Don't know* 3%

10. Question wording and results as indicated in text. (NORC, 5-43.)
11. Question wording and results as indicated in text. (NORC, 5-43.)
12. Question wording and results as indicated in text. (OPOR, 1-43.)
13. Question wording and results as indicated in text. (AIPO, 10-42.)
14. Question wording and results as indicated in text. (AIPO, 1-44.)
15. Question wording and results as indicated in text. (AIPO, 1-44.)

16. Question wording and results as indicated in text. (AIPO, 1-44.)
17. Question wording and results as indicated in text. (AIPO, 1-44.)
18. Question wording and results as indicated in text. (AIPO, 1-44.)

CHAPTER IV

1. Which country of the United Nations do you think has made the greatest single contribution towards winning the war? (BIPO, 4-43.)
   Britain 42%, *Russia* 50%, *China* 5%, *U. S.* 3%

2, 4. Do you think the nations now getting lend-lease materials from us will repay us for these materials either in money or goods, or will not repay us at all? (AIPO, 3-43.)
   Will pay 29%, *Will not pay* 60%, *Not sure* 11%
   Do you think they should repay us? (AIPO, 3-43.)
   Should pay 73%, *Should not pay* 21%, *Not sure* 6%

3. What would you like to see done about the war debts European countries owe the United States—try to collect them in full, reduce them, or cancel them entirely? (AIPO, 8-38.)
   Collect in full 59%, *Reduce* 23%, *Cancel* 9%, *No opinion* 9%

5. Do you think we are getting anything at all in return for the supplies and war materials we are sending England? (NORC, 7-43.)
   Yes 54%, *No* 28%, *Don't know* 18%
   Asked of 54% answering "yes" to #5, above: What are we getting? (NORC, 7-43.)

	Per cent
INTANGIBLES (co-operation, friendship, giving us time to prepare, keeping war from America, etc.)	39
TANGIBLES (money, supplies, guns, island bases, etc.)	20
	59 *

   * Per cent exceeds the 54 per cent since a few people named both tangibles and intangibles and have been classified twice.

6. Asked of those who, on #5, this chapter, indicated that we were receiving something in return for lend-lease shipments to England: Do you think this enough to get in repayment for what we're sending England, or do you think we should get something more? (NORC, 7-43.)
   Enough 56%, *Pay more* 28%, *Qualified* 4%, *No opinion* 12%
   Asked of those who, on #5, this chapter, indicated that we were not getting anything in return for lend-lease to England or who were not sure whether we were or not: Do you think the United States *should* expect to get anything in return for what we're sending England? (NORC, 7-43.)
   Yes 74%, *No* 15%, *Qualified and no opinion* 11%

7. See #5, this chapter. (NORC, 7-43.) Results as indicated in text.
8. Asked of those in favor of collecting for lend-lease after the war: If shipments of war material to England will save any American lives, shall we consider the war materials paid for in full or not? (NORC, 5-43.) Results as indicated in text. Colorado survey.
9. Asked of those in favor of collecting for lend-lease after the war: If collecting the repayment would help cause a depression in England, in the long run would we be better off to collect and cause a depression, or not to collect? (NORC, 5-43.) Results as indicated in text. Colorado survey.
10. If after the war people in some of the countries of the world are starving, do you think the United States should help feed the people in these countries? (NORC, 7-42.)

    Yes 74%, *Qualified* 19%, *No* 5%, *No opinion* 2%
11. Would you be in favor of continuing food rationing for a while after the war if this were necessary to feed people in countries which have been hard hit by the war? (OPOR, 4-43.)

    Yes 92%, *No* 6%, *Not sure* 2%
12. Do you think it will be necessary or unnecessary for the government to continue rationing food while we are getting back to peacetime conditions? (NORC, 4-43.)

    Necessary 62%, *Unnecessary* 30%, *Don't know & Qualified* 8%
13. Question wording and results as indicated in text. (FOR, 6-43.)
14. See #13, this chapter, for question wording. (FOR, 6-43.) Results as indicated in text.
15. Do you think that after this war there will be a moral responsibility on the United States to see that every person in the whole world is well fed? (AIPO, 10-42.)

    Yes 40%, *No* 52%, *No opinion* 8%
16. If we do send money and materials [to other countries after the war] do you think this will result in a lower standard of living here, or that it will so increase trade that this country will be more prosperous than ever? (FOR, 6-43.) Results as indicated in text.
17. See #16, this chapter. (FOR, 6-43.) Results as indicated in text.
18. As a result of the war, do you think some countries are going to need help to get back to their normal way of life? (NORC, 9-43.)

    Yes 97%, *No* 2%, *Don't know* 1%
19. Asked of the 98% thinking other countries would need help or were not sure about it on #18, this chapter: Which of these things do you think they [the countries which will need help after the war] will probably need? (NORC, 9-43.) Results as indicated in text.
20. Asked only of the 98% who thought other countries would need our help or who were not sure about it on #18, this chapter: Do you think the United

States should try to produce more of these things [food, clothing, medicines, machinery, etc.] than we need ourselves so we can help other countries? (NORC, 9-43.)

Yes 88%, *Qualified* 3%, *No* 5%, *No opinion* 2% = 98%

21. Asked only of the 93% not opposed to the U. S. producing more goods for other countries during reconstruction, #20, this chapter: If the United States does help other countries, do you think we will have to pay more taxes than if we don't help them? (NORC, 9-43.)

Yes 57%, *No* 26%, *Don't know* 10% = 93%

22. Asked only of the 93% not opposed to the U. S. producing more goods for other countries during reconstruction, #20, this chapter: If it *does* mean that we have to pay taxes to help other countries, would you be willing to help them or not? (NORC, 9-43.)

Willing 73%, *Unwilling* 10%, *Qualified* 7%, *No opinion* 3% = 93%

23. Asked only of the 93% not opposed to the U. S. producing more goods for other countries during reconstruction, #20, this chapter: Do you think we should try to help all countries which need help or just some countries? Which countries do you think we should not try to help? (NORC, 9-43.)

	Per cent
Help all countries	51
Exclude Axis	35
Exclude some allies or neutrals	3
No opinion	4
	93

CHAPTER V

1. What foreign country do you feel most friendly toward? (FOR, 10-35.)
   England 29%, *France* 5%, *Germany* 4%

2. Which of the European countries do you like best? (AIPO, 12-36.) (Percentages based on those who could choose. Data on those who could make no choice not available.)

	Per cent
England	56
France	11
Germany	8
Ireland	4
Finland	4
All others	17

3. What foreign country do you like best? (AIPO, 1-37.)

Per cent

England 31
France 6
Germany 3
Canada 2
Ireland 2
All others 13
No choice 43

4. Which European country do you like best? (AIPO, 6-39.)

Per cent

England 43
France 12
Finland 4
Switzerland 4
Sweden 4
All others 18
No choice 15

5. Asked of workers only: Which of these countries do you feel friendliest toward—England, China, or Russia? (FOR, 2-43.)

Per cent

England 43
China 28
Russia 14
No choice 17
                    ———
                    102 *

* Some respondents chose
more than one country.

6. Do you think the British are doing all they possibly can to win the war? (OPOR, Trend.) Results as indicated in text.

7. Some people say the British are largely to blame for getting us into the last war. Do you agree or disagree? (OPOR, 6-42.)

Agree 39%, *Disagree* 43%, *No opinion* 18%

8. Do you think the British will try to have more to say about the peace that follows this war than the United States? (AIPO, 10-42.)

Yes 62%, *No* 34%, *No opinion* 4%

9. Do you think that Russia will try to have more to say about the peace that follows this war than the United States? (AIPO, 10-42.)

Yes 31%, *No* 62%, *No opinion* 7%

10. Which of these statements do you think is closer to the truth: England is now fighting mainly to preserve democracy against the spread of dictatorship; or, England is now fighting mainly to keep her power and wealth? (OPOR, 8-43.)

Democracy 30%, *Power* 35%, *Both* 23%, *No opinion* 12%

11. Question wording and results as indicated in text. (OPOR, 6-42.)

12. After the war is over do you think England can be depended upon to co-operate with us? (NORC, 11-42.) Results as indicated in text.

13. Do you think we should continue to co-operate with England after the war? (NORC, 11-42.) Results as indicated in text.

14. Do you think the United States will continue to co-operate with England after the war? (NORC, 11-42.) Results as indicated in text.

15. Question wording and results as indicated in text. (AIPO, 8-43.)

16. See #15, this chapter. (AIPO, 8-43.) Results as indicated in text.

17. After the war is over do you think we should or should not have free trade with the British Empire (the United States)? (FOR, 4-42, FOR-BR, 8-42.) Results as indicated in text.

18. After the war is over do you think we should or should not allow the people of the British Empire and the people of the United States to live and work in either country without immigration restrictions? (FOR, 4-42.)

Yes 23%, *No* 63%, *No opinion* 14%

19. As a result of this war, do you think the U. S. will be more powerful, less powerful, or have about the same amount of power as before the war? Will Russia? Britain? China? (FOR, 7-42.) Results as indicated in text.

CHAPTER VI

1. Should the U. S. sell war materials to Russia? (AIPO, 8-41.)

Yes 71%, *No* 22%, *No opinion* 7%

2. In the present war between Germany and Russia, which side would you like to see win—Germany or Russia? (AIPO, 6-41.)

Russia 73%, *Germany* 4%, *Neither* 18%, *No opinion* 5%

3. If you had to choose, which kind of government would you prefer to live under—the kind ir Germany or the kind in Russia? (OPOR, Trend.) Results as indicated in text.

4. Do you think we should continue to co-operate with Russia after the war? (NORC, 11-42.)

Yes 80%, *No* 8%, *No opinion* 12%

5. Do you think the United States will continue to co-operate with Russia after the war? (NORC, 11-42.)

Yes 78%, *No* 7%, *No opinion* 15%

6. Do you think Russia can be trusted to co-operate with us when the war is over? (OPOR & AIPO, Trend.) Results as indicated in text.

7. See #6, this chapter, directly above. (OPOR & AIPO, 1-44.) Results as indicated in text.

8. Did you know that the United States, Great Britain, and Russia held a conference in Moscow recently? (NORC, 11-43.)

    Yes 80%, *No* 20%

9. Asked only of those who had heard of the Moscow Conference: Did the Moscow Conference produce greater or smaller results than you expected? (AIPO, 11-43.)

	Per cent
Greater	43
Smaller	8
Same as expected	14
No opinion	35

10. Asked only of those who had heard of the Moscow Conference: Will you tell me in general something of the things that were decided at this conference? (NORC, 11-43.)

	Per cent
Correct answers	51
Incorrect	11
Don't know	38

11. Asked only of those who had heard of the Moscow Conference: Do you think all three countries will stick to these agreements after the war? (NORC, 11-43.)

    Yes 56%, *No* 23%, *Not sure* 21%

12. Do you think Russia ought to have as much to say as the United States about the peace that is made with Germany? (NORC, 9-43.)

    Yes 75%, *No* 17%, *No opinion* 8%

13. After the war should the U. S. and Russia make a permanent military alliance, that is, agree to come to each other's defense immediately if the other is attacked at any future time? (AIPO, 8-43.)

    Yes 38%, *No* 41%, *No opinion* 21%

14. If Germany is knocked out of the war first, do you think Russia will continue fighting and help us beat Japan, or not? (NORC, Trend.)

	Sept., '43 %	*Nov., '43* %
Yes	35	49
No	40	31
Don't know	25	20

(November figures, showing an increase in confidence in Russia as an ally against Japan, probably reflect the influence of the Moscow Conference.)

15. Do you expect that Russia will want about the same kind of peace that we do or that she will make demands that we can't agree to? (FOR, 6-43.) Results as indicated in text.

16. After the war do you think Russia will or will not try to bring about Communist governments in other European countries? (FOR, 6-43.) Results as indicated in text.

17. Some observers believe that if Russia is largely responsible for defeating Germany, all Europe may go communistic after the present war. Do you agree or disagree with this? (AIPO, 10-42.) Results as indicated in text.

18. Question wording and results as indicated in text. (AIPO, 10-42.)

19. Asked only of those who felt Russia could not be trusted after the war (34 per cent, see #6, this chapter): Why do you think Russia will not co-operate with us when the war is over? (AIPO, 8-43.)

	Per cent
Russia not interested in co-operating......................	24
(Hasn't been sitting in on military conferences, Russia out to help herself, past record shows she is not interested in the rest of the world, etc.)	
Too great a difference between Russia and the West............	21
(Different forms of government, different ideals, different kinds of people, etc.)	
Russia is just a bad moral risk..............................	45
(Russia and Russians can't be trusted, Stalin is vicious, you can't do business with Communism, etc.)	
Other reasons	5
Could give no reasons	5

20. Do you think Russia will want more territory after the war than she had before the war started? (NORC, 11-43.)

Yes 59%, No 24%, No opinion 17%

21. Do you think Russia *should* have more territory than she had before the war? (NORC, 11-43.)

Yes 27%, No 56%, No opinion 17%

22. If Russia wants some land that belonged to Poland before the war, do you think that the United States and other Allied countries should try to stop her from getting it? (NORC, 11-43.)

Yes 39%, No 38%, No opinion 23%

CHAPTER VII

1. Do you, personally, hate the German people? Do you, personally, hate the Japanese people? (AIPO, 5-42.) Results as indicated in text.

2. Do you think orchestras and bands in this country should stop playing German music? (AIPO, 10-39.)

   Yes 8%,　*No* 86%,　*No opinion* 6%

3. Do you think American colleges and high schools should stop teaching the German language? (AIPO, 10-39.)

   Yes 11%,　*No* 83%,　*No opinion* 6%

4. See #1, this chapter. (AIPO, 5-42.) Results as indicated in text.

5. In the war with Germany, do you feel that our chief enemy is the German people as a whole, or the German Government? (OPOR & AIPO, Trend.) Results as indicated in text.

6. In the war with Japan, do you feel that our chief enemy is the Japanese people as a whole, or the Japanese Government? (OPOR & AIPO, Trend.) Results as indicated in text.

7. From the words on this card, which seem to you to describe the German people best? Select as many as you wish and call off the letters and words that go with them. (OPOR, 7-42.) Results as indicated in text.

8. From the list of words on this card, which seem to you to describe the Japanese people best? Select as many as you wish and call off the letters and the words that go with them. (OPOR, 7-42.) Results as indicated in text.

	Per cent		*Per cent*
Hardworking	69	Artistic	21
Intelligent	24	Conceited	1
Ordinary	18	Lazy	6
Radical	2	Unimaginative	10
Warlike	4	Treacherous	4
Practical	23	Aristocratic	9
Cruel	3	Ignorant	22
Rude	2	Dull	10
Brave	48	Religious	33
Arrogant	1	Progressive	14
Quick-tempered	4	Sly	8
Impossible to characterize.	12	Honest	42

9. From the list of words on this card, which seem to you to describe the Chinese people best? Select as many as you wish and call off the letters and words that go with them. (OPOR, 7-42.)

10. Which of the following statements comes closest to describing how you feel, on the whole, about the people who live in Germany (Japan)? (NORC, Trend.)

The German people will always want to go to war to make themselves as powerful as possible.

The German people do not like war, but they have shown that they are too easily led into war by powerful leaders.

The German people do not like war. If they could have the same chance as people in other countries, they would become good citizens of the world.

No opinion.

Results as indicated in text.

11. Which country do you think we can get along with better after the war—Germany or Japan? (AIPO, 2-44.)

Germany 74%, Japan 4%, No opinion 22%

12. See #11, this chapter, directly above, for wording. (AIPO, 2-44.)

	Geographical differences	
	Far West	New England and Middle Atlantic
	%	%
Germany	74	69
Japan	5	3
No opinion	21	28

13. See #11, this chapter, for wording. (AIPO, 6-43, 2-44.)

	Racial differences			
	Negro %		White %	
	(6-43)	(2-44)	(6-43)	(2-44)
Germany	30	39	70	76
Japan	22	9	7	4
No opinion	48	52	23	20

14. Do you have definite feelings of like or dislike for Japan? (FOR, 10-37.)

Like 5%, Dislike 31%, Neutral 64%

15. Why do you think Japan is fighting the United States? What are the underlying reasons? (AIPO, 12-41.)

	Per cent
Urged by Germany	48
Wants control of Far East	30
Needs raw materials	6
Angered by our embargo	5
Angered by aid to China	5
Miscellaneous	10
Don't know why	12
	116 *

* Percentages total more than 100 since multiple answers were permitted.

16. Question wording and results as indicated in text. (AIPO & OPOR, Trend.)

17. If the German Army did overthrow Hitler, do you think this would mean that the German people would or would not control the government? (AIPO, 1-43.)

   Would 21%, *Would not* 60%, *Don't know* 19%

18. Suppose that the German Army gets rid of Hitler, gives up all the countries Germany has conquered, and offers to make peace—if that happens, should we make peace, or should we continue the war until the German Army is completely defeated?* (AIPO, 10-43.)

   Make peace 23%, *Fight on* 72%, *No opinion* 5%

19. Can you tell me who General Giraud is? Can you tell me who General de Gaulle is? (AIPO, 2-43.)

   29% identified Giraud correctly
   37% identified de Gaulle correctly

20. Some people say it will be a better peace if the Allies make the peace terms with Germany, Italy and Japan as soon as possible after the fighting is over. Others say it will be a better peace if the Allies stay in Germany, Italy, and Japan for a few years and then make the peace terms. Which side do you agree with? (NORC, 7-42.)

	Per cent
Peace right away	32
Wait a few years	54
Qualified	1
No opinion	13

21. Do you think the peace treaty after the war was too easy or too severe on Germany? (AIPO, 6-37.) Percentages which follow are based only on those who had opinions. 22 per cent were without opinions.

   Too easy 41%, *Too severe* 30%, *About right* 29%

22. In the treaty that ended the last war, were the Germans dealt with fairly, too severely, or not severely enough? (AIPO, 10-42.) Percentages which follow are based only on those who had opinions. 6 per cent were without opinions.

   Too easy 49%, *Too severe* 29%, *About right* 22%

23. If Germany is defeated by England (and France), should the peace treaty be more severe on Germany or less severe than the treaty at the end of the last war? (After U. S. entry into the war, the wording was changed to read:) When the war is over, should the peace treaty be less severe or more severe than the treaty at the end of the last war? (AIPO, Trend.) Results as indicated in text.

   *By way of background, in February, 1940, 75% of the American public felt that the warring nations should negotiate a peace (AIPO), in April, 1941, 48% still thought so (AIPO), while in June, 1941, the figure dropped to 41% (AIPO).

24. Assuming that Germany loses this war, do you think she will, if she can, start as soon as possible preparing for another war? (AIPO, 9-43.) Results as indicated in text.

25. We have listed a number of things here that might be done with Germany when we are victorious. Do you think the United Nations should or should not: (FOR, 1-44.)

    a. Abolish the Nazi Party?

        Should 88%, *Should not* 3%, *No opinion* 9%

    b. Completely demobilize the German Army and keep them from having any army again?

        Should 77%, *Should not* 13%, *No opinion* 10%

    c. Govern Germany with an occupation force for several years?

        Should 73%, *Should not* 11%, *No opinion* 16%

    d. Break Germany up into smaller states?

        Should 29%, *Should not* 41%, *No opinion* 30%

    e. Prevent the Germans from rebuilding their steel, chemical, and automotive industries?

        Should 31%, *Should not* 53%, *No opinion* 16%

    f. Make German labor rebuild devastated areas in other countries at the rate usually paid prisoners of war?

        Should 46%, *Should not* 32%, *No opinion* 22%

26. How should we treat the German people after the war? (OPOR, 7-42.) Results as indicated in text.

27. If we win the war, which of these things comes closest to what you think should be done with Germany? (FOR, 6-43.)

	Per cent
Set up a United Nations council to rule Germany for ten years or so, and eventually make her adopt a democratic government and see that she sticks to it.	37
Bring to trial and execute all found to be leading Nazi officials....	31
Make Germany use all her available men, money and materials to rebuild the damage done in other countries.	27
Set up an international government to rule Germany for one hundred years	21
Do nothing to Germany but see to it that she stays within her own boundaries	13
Carve Germany up and divide her among some of the United Nations	11
Kill a Nazi for every person killed by the Germans in occupied countries	4
No opinion	7
	151 *

* Percentages exceed 100 since multiple answers were permitted.

28. German Nazis are telling the German people that if they lose the war they may all be killed by the people of the countries they have conquered. Should we tell the German people that we will protect them from such vengeance? (AIPO, 10-42.)

   Yes 63%,   No 35%,   No opinion 2%

29. How much do you think the Allies should TRY to make Germany, Italy, and Japan pay toward what the war has cost the Allies? (NORC, 7-42.) Results as indicated in text.

30. Asked only in Colorado: Some people think that trying to collect the cost of the last war from Germany was one of the main causes of Hitler's coming into power. Do you agree or disagree? (NORC, 5-43.) Results as indicated in text.

31. Asked only in Colorado: See #29, this chapter, for wording. (NORC, 5-43.)

	Per cent
As much as possible	52
None	10
Some between	30
No opinion	8

32. Asked only in Colorado: If making Germany pay for some of our cost of the war would bring about a depression in Germany, in the long run would such a depression hurt our trade so much that we'd be worse off to collect, or not? (NORC, 5-43.) Results as indicated in text.

33. Asked only in Colorado: If Germany is made to give up almost all the land she took since 1930 and if Hitler and the other Nazi leaders are punished, should we try to make Germany pay for what the war has cost us, or not? (NORC, 5-43.) Results as indicated in text.

34. In general, after the war is over, do you feel that Germany should be broken up completely so that she will never again be able to rise as a unified nation, or that Germany's military and political leaders only should be overthrown and the German people allowed to build a new nation? (AIPO, 10-42.) Results as indicated in text.

35. What do you think should be done with Germany as a country after the war? (AIPO, BIPO, CIPO, APOP, 12-43.)

	U.S. %	Britain %	Canada %	Australia %
Supervision or control by allies	44	43	40	59
Break her into small states	21	31	35	11
Rehabilitation and re-education	17	10	12	9
Miscellaneous and don't know	18	16	13	21

36. Question wording and results as indicated in text. (NORC, 7-42.)

37. Asked of the 73 per cent favoring U. S. entry into an organization of nations: Do you think Germany (Japan, Italy) should be in this union? (NORC, 1-43.)

	Germany %	Japan %	Italy %
Yes	44	40	52
No	21	28	15
Qualified and No opinion	8	5	6
	73	73	73

38. Asked only of those willing to join a union of nations or not sure about it (83 per cent): If the United States has only the same amount of power in the union as Germany, would you be in favor of our joining a union of nations or against it? (NORC, 1-43.)

For 34%, *Against* 54%, *No opinion* 12%

39. After the war is over, how should we treat the Nazi leaders in Germany? (AIPO, 6-42.) Results as indicated in text.

40. Asked of the 73 per cent favoring occupation on #25, this chapter: Some feel that the best way to make Germany into a good nation is to govern her by an occupation force for at least ten years and maybe longer, while others feel that Germany should be governed only until the Nazis are crushed and a new government set up. With which do you agree? (FOR, 1-44.)

Ten years 55%, *Until Nazis crushed* 38%, *No opinion* 7%

41. Question wording and results as indicated in text. (AIPO, 12-42.)

42. After the war should three or four million German men be sent to Russia to help rebuild destroyed cities there? (AIPO, BIPO, 1-44.) Results as indicated in text.

CHAPTER VIII

1. It has been said that there will always be people in the United States who do not have the kind of food, clothing, and housing they need. Do you think there always will be or not? (NORC, 4-43.)

Will 83%, *Will not* 12%, *Qualified & No opinion* 5%

2. Asked of those who answered "will be" on #1, this chapter, directly above: What do you think is the main reason for this? (NORC, 4-43.)

	Per cent
Lack of initiative in individuals	39
Lack of ability in individuals	42
Economic or political system	12
Miscellaneous	17
Don't know	5
	115*

* Per cent exceeds 100 since some respondents gave more than one reason.

3. As you may know, under the present Social Security Law workers in certain occupations have to save money so that when they are too old to work they will receive money from the Government, like insurance. Do you think this is a good idea or a bad idea? (NORC, 4-43.) Results as indicated in text.

4. The Social Security Law requires some workers to save money so they will get money from the Government in case they lose their jobs. Do you think this is a good idea or a bad idea? (NORC, 4-43.) Results as indicated in text.

5. After the war do you think the Government should provide free medical care for all who need it and can't afford it? (OPOR, 3-43.) Results as indicated in text.

6. Would you favor or oppose a law providing money for the support of students under 18 who had ability but were unable to afford an education? (OPOR, 3-43.) Results as indicated in text.

7. It has been suggested that the Government provide a real job on useful government work to anybody unemployed after the war until they can find a job in private industry. Would you favor or oppose this plan? (OPOR, 3-43.) Results as indicated in text.

8. Question wording and results as indicated in text. (OPOR, 3-43.) *23 per cent* were unable to make a choice among the four proposals.

9. Question wording as indicated in text. (OPOR, 6-43.)

	Straight compensation %	Public works %	No opinion %
National..........	15	76	9

	Per cent favoring public works %
By income	
Upper	74
Middle..........................	80
Lower	74
By politics	
Republicans	77
Democrats	78

10. Asked of war workers in Wichita, Pittsburgh, Mobile, Buffalo, Portland (Maine), Los Angeles, Atlanta, Detroit: As you know, your employer now pays a three cent tax to the Government on every dollar he pays you. This is to provide unemployment compensation for you in case you lose your job. Would you be willing to start now to pay the Government an additional three cents out of every dollar of your wages so that you could get more money later in case you lost your job? (OPOR, 2-43.)

   Yes 65%, *No* 30%, *No opinion* 5%

11. If you were assured complete medical and hospital care for yourself in case of accident or illness (except dental care, would you be willing to pay: (AIPO, 12-38.)

	Per cent
$3.00 a month	48
2.50 a month	49
2.00 a month	61

12. To provide which of the following things do you think the Federal Government should and should not collect enough taxes after the war? (FOR, 7-42.)

	Should %	Should not %	No opinion %
Medical care for everyone who needs it	74	21	5
An old age pension for every citizen over 65	74	22	4
Jobs for everyone who is able and willing to work but cannot get a job in private employment	68	25	7
Compensation for everyone unable to find work	58	34	8

13. Have you heard or read of a new plan announced by the President, for social security after the war? (OPOR, 3-43.)

	Yes %	No %
3-15-43	58	42
3-25-43	35	65

14. Question wording and results as indicated in text. (OPOR, 3-43.)

15. See #14, this chapter, directly above. (OPOR, 3-43.) Results as indicated in text.

16. See #14, this chapter. (OPOR, 3-43.) Results as indicated in text.

17. Asked only of the country's leading business executives, CIO leaders, and A. F. of L. leaders: Do you feel that the National Resources Planning Board plans for post-war demobilization and security recently announced by the President, or some alternative plan for handling such problems should be acted upon now by Congress, or do you think that Congressional action should wait till the end of the war? (OPOR, 4-43.) Results as indicated in text.

18. Asked only of business leaders: After the war, do you think the Federal Government should or should not provide for medical care, old-age pensions for everyone, and job insurance? Do you think it will provide any or all of these? (FOR, 9-43.) Results as indicated in text.

19. Asked only of business leaders: Do you think a cradle-to-the-grave program of minimum security for all in the U. S. is: (FOR, 10-43.)

   Impossible and undesirable,
   Economically possible but undesirable,
   Desirable but impossible, or
   Economically possible and desirable.

   Results as indicated in text.

20. Asked of people who had heard of the NRPB Plan: I am going to read you what some newspapers have said about the Plan. Please listen to each comment carefully and tell me whether you agree or disagree with it. (OPOR, 3-43.) Comments and results appear in text.

21. On the whole, after the war do you think the average young man will have more opportunity, about the same opportunity, or less opportunity to get ahead than a young man had after the last war? (FOR, 6-43.)

   More 59%, *Same* 17%, *Less* 15%, *Don't know* 9%

22. Asked only of people now full- or part-time employed: Do you think your present job will continue after the war or do you think you will have to find a new one? (AIPO, 3-43.)

	Per cent
Keep present job	79
Look for new job	13
Not sure	8

23. Asked of war workers in Wichita, Mobile, Pittsburgh, Los Angeles, Buffalo, Portland (Maine), Atlanta, Detroit: After the war is over, do you expect to be able to keep your present job or will you have to look for a new job? (OPOR, 2-43.)

	Per cent
Keep present job	50
Look for new job	35
Not sure	15

24. Asked of war workers in Wichita, Mobile, Pittsburgh, Los Angeles, Buffalo, Portland (Maine), Atlanta, Detroit: By the end of the war, do you expect to have enough money saved up to tide you over in case you lose your present job? (OPOR, 2-43.)

   Yes 65%, *No* 22%, *Not sure* 13%

25. Asked of people after they had been told about the major provisions of the NRPB Social Security Report and informed of its universal coverage: Do you think that this new social security plan for after the war would help you personally or wouldn't it make much difference as far as you yourself are concerned? (OPOR, 3-43.)

259

	Help me %	No difference %	No opinion %
National	34	58	8
By income			
Upper...........	20	79	1
Middle	27	65	8
Lower	45	45	10

26. Do you think Congress should consider the new social security plan suggested by the President at the present time, or should Congress wait until after the war? (OPOR, 3-43.)

   Now 39%, *Later* 52%, *Not sure* 9%

27. Those who on #26, directly above, believed that Congress should wait till after the war were asked for their reasons. (OPOR, 3-43.)

	Per cent
Too busy with war now; time afterwards..........	67
Too early to give problems mature thought........	19
May not be able to afford plan after war...........	6
No need for plan now or after war..............	2
Can't tell how long war will last.................	3
Vague reasons	3

28. If you (or your husband) found yourself out of a job tomorrow, and had no money or property at all, what is the least amount of money that you (or your immediate family) could get along on? (CIPO, 5-43.) Results as indicated in text.

29. See #21, Chapter IX.

CHAPTER IX

1. Is there anything you would like to know about our plans for after the war? (NORC, 2-43.) (Those who were interested in knowing something about plans for after the war, 58%, name these things.)

	Per cent
Domestic	
Domestic economic affairs	60
Domestic political affairs	7
Position of the Negro	2
International	
Formulating and maintaining peace..........	24
World reconstruction	7
Other and miscellaneous	15
Not ascertainable and other	5
	120 *

* Total percentage exceeds 100 since multiple answers were permitted.

2. Right now, lots of people are interested in post-war problems. Which interests you more—*international* problems (like a new league of nations and an international police force) OR *domestic* problems (like full employment and production)? (OPOR, 11-43.)

Per cent choosing "domestic"

National 53
Upper income 36
Middle income 47
Lower income 60
Very poor 64

3. Asked only of people now full- or part-time employed: Do you think your present job will continue after the war or do you think you will have to find a new one? (AIPO, 3-43.)

U. S. public
%

Keep present job 79
Look for new job 13
Not sure 8

4. For the first year or two after the war, which one of these things do you expect: enough jobs for everybody, some unemployment, or a lot of unemployment? (NORC, 4-43.)

Per cent

Enough jobs 33
Some unemployment 31
Lots of unemployment 32
No opinion and qualified........ 4

5. Asked of the 13 per cent of workers who thought they would be looking for a new job after the war, #3, this chapter: Do you think you will have any difficulty finding a new job? (AIPO, 3-43.)
    Yes 17%, *No* 58%, *Don't know* 25%

6. Asked of American enlisted men stationed in Great Britain: Do you have a definite job ready for you when you return after the war? (BIPO, 9-43.)

Per cent

Yes.......................... 62
No 27
Plan to continue in school........ 3
Don't know 8

Asked of those who said "No": Do you think it will be hard to find a job? (BIPO, 9-43.)
    Yes 24%,   *No* 56%,   *Don't know* 20%

7. Asked only of war workers in Portland (Maine), Pittsburgh, Detroit, Mobile, Los Angeles, Wichita, Atlanta, Buffalo: After the war is over do you expect to keep your present job or do you think you will have to look for a new job? (OPOR, 2-43.)

	Per cent
Keep present job	50
Look for new job	35
Don't know	15

8. See #7, this chapter. (OPOR, 2-43.) Results as indicated in text.
9. After the war about how long do you think it will take for war plants to be changed back to making peacetime goods, and to get the armed forces back into civilian life? That is, about how long will it take to get back to peacetime conditions? Just your own best guess. (NORC, 4-43.)

	Per cent
One year or less	41
One to two years	29
Two to five years	18
Over five years	5
No opinion	7

10. Asked only of business leaders: As you see things developing now, do you think the country will experience extensive unemployment, moderate unemployment, or no unemployment at all in the period immediately following the war during which industry will be reconverting to peacetime production? (OPOR, 3-43.)

	Per cent
Extensive unemployment	27
Moderate unemployment	63
No unemployment	10

11. #10, this chapter, directly above, asked of state, regional, and national leaders of organized labor. (OPOR, 3-43.)

	Per cent
Extensive unemployment	62
Moderate unemployment	33
No unemployment	5

12. Question wording and results as indicated in text. (OPOR, 6-43.)
13. See #12, this chapter, for question wording. (OPOR, 6-43.) Results as indicated in text.
14. Do you think government, business, and labor, by making plans now, *can* do away with unemployment after the war? (OPOR, 5-43.)

Yes 57%,   *No* 26%,   *No opinion* 17%

15. See #14, this chapter, for wording. (OPOR, 5-43.)

*Per cent who believe planning can
abolish post-war unemployment*

Democrats 59
Republicans 55

Upper income 53
Middle income 61
Lower income 55

16. Question wording and results as indicated in text. (OPOR, 6-43.)

17. Asked of the 75 per cent favoring the creation of a centralized agency to co-ordinate and direct domestic post-war planning, #16, this chapter: Do you think this agency should be made up entirely of government representatives, or do you think it should also have members who represent other groups like business, labor, and agriculture? (OPOR, 6-43.)

Per cent
Government alone 9
Other groups 87
No opinion 4

18. Question wording and results as indicated in text. (OPOR, 6-43.) Pretty much the same results, though more detailed, were obtained to the following question, asked nine months later: Which of these comes closest to expressing your ideas of what the government should do to avoid periods of unemployment after the war? (FOR, 2-44.)

Per cent

Let business and industry work out the problem without any government interference at all 15

Depend mainly on business and industry to create enough employment normally, and just provide work at those times when industry cannot employ everyone 32

Carry on continuously a program of public works, enlarging it during periods of unemployment and reducing it when there are plenty of jobs .... 35 } 74

Carry on large government works all the time, even if business and industry find it difficult to get enough workers in good times.. 7

Don't know 11

The beauty of these figures is that they indicate clearly that Government help is wanted while, at the same time, underlining the fact that business initiative is also wanted.

19. See #18, this chapter, directly above. (OPOR, 6-43.)

*Per cent who believe government
help needed for full
employment*

Upper income 49
Middle income 66
Lower income 72

20. Asked of business leaders only: Allowing for a period of reconversion, do you believe reasonably full employment after the war can be maintained by private business? (FOR, 10-43.)

   Yes 74%, No 22%, No opinion 4%

21. Asked only of business leaders: If we have a depression after the war, what do you think is likely to be the reaction of the American public? (FOR, 10-43.)

Per cent

Demand relief from government.................... 72
Rapid growth of political labor party................ 41
Grin and bear it................................. 29
Rioting and disorder.............................. 12
Rise of new type of leader like Huey Long or Coughlin.. 12
Vote Socialist or Communist....................... 7
All others 11
                                                  ——
                                                  184 *

   * Per cent totals more than 100 since multiple answers were permitted.

22. Question wording and results as indicated in text. (OPOR, 3-43.)
23. See #22, this chapter. (OPOR, 3-43.) Results as indicated in text.
24. See #22, this chapter. (OPOR, 3-43.)

*Per cent favoring government
projects to provide post-
war jobs*

Upper income 56
Middle income 68
Lower income 83

25. Asked only in New York City: I am going to read you some plans that have been proposed to make sure that we have full employment in the United States after the war. Would you tell me after each plan whether you would approve of it or disapprove? (OPOR, 2-43.) Plans and results as indicated in text.

26. Asked of business leaders only: With which of these statements are you more nearly in agreement? (FOR, 10-43.)

Per cent

There is no difference between private and government debt. In both cases, current budgets should be balanced just as soon as possible; otherwise ruin follows............................ 86

Provided we have an expanding national income, it is not necessary to fear the expansion of government debt in the way that we fear an unbalanced private or business budget................... 14

The same question or one of equal complexity cannot, of course, be asked of the general public, yet past public opinion on the matter of balancing the budget and keeping government spending at an economic level indicates that the view of businessmen, expressed below, reflects the view of the public.

27. Asked of the 82 per cent of Americans who own war bonds or war stamps: As you see things now, do you expect to spend a good part of this money (in war bonds or stamps) right after the war for things you need, or do you expect to save the money for a while? (OPOR, 5-43.)

Per cent

Spend right away.............. 11
Save for a while............... 73
Don't know................... 16

28. Asked only of farmers: Do you think there will be such a big drop in farm prices after the war that farmers will be as badly off as they were after the last war? (OPOR, 10-43.)

Yes, 41%, No 47%, Don't know 12%

29. Would you be in favor of continuing food rationing for a while after the war if this were necessary to feed people in countries that have been hard hit by the war? (OPOR, 4-43.)

Favor 92%, Oppose 6%, No opinion 2%

30. Do you think ceiling prices, established to keep prices from going too high during the war, should be kept on for a while after the war? (OPOR, 5-43.)

Yes 75%, No 15%, No opinion 10%

31. See #30 and #29, this chapter, on post-war food rationing and price control. (OPOR, 4-43, 5-43.)

	Per cent favoring post-war	
	Food rationing	*Price control*
Republicans	91	72
Democrats	93	77

32. Asked of business leaders only: After the war, do you think price ceilings in general should be abolished immediately in the interests of a free economy, or maintained until adequate consumer stocks are built up? (FOR, 10-43.)

Abolished immediately 52%, Kept till goods exist 47%, No opinion 1%

33. Question wording and results as indicated in text. (OPOR, 2-43.)

CHAPTER X

1. Will you tell me in your own words what you understand by the term, "free enterprise"? (AIPO, 10-43.)

    Correct 26%, *Doubtful* 8%, *Don't understand term* 66%

2. It has been suggested that labor should have more to say about the government's financial, domestic, and international policies. Do you agree or disagree? Should farmers have more to say about these policies? Should businessmen? (AIPO, 10-43.)

	Labor %	Farmers %	Businessmen %
Agree	45	63	58
Disagree	38	23	26
Not sure	17	14	16

3. Question wording and results as indicated in text. (NORC, 4-43.)

4. The President has suggested recently that business and government go into partnerhip after the war in vital defense industries like airplanes and shipbuilding on which the government has already spent a great deal of money. Would you favor or oppose such a partnership between government and business? (OPOR, 3 to 6-43.) Results as indicated in text.

5. See #12, Chapter IX. (OPOR, 6-43.)

6. Question wording and results as indicated in text. (OPOR, 6-43.)

7. Which income group do you feel that you are a member of—the middle income group, the upper income group, or the lower income group? (OPOR, 6-41.)

    Upper 5%, *Middle* 87%, *Lower* 8%

8. See #3, this chapter. (NORC, 4-43.)

9. After finding out what each person can do, should the government have the power to tell each citizen what to do as his part in the war and require him or her to do it? (AIPO, 10-42.)

    Yes 67%, *No* 24%, *No opinion* 9%

10. Do you favor drafting single women between the ages of 21 and 35 to serve in the WACS, WAVES, or other similar branches of the armed services? (AIPO, 7-43.)

	National total %	Women aged 21 to 35 %
Yes	45	58
No	48	36
No opinion	7	6

11. Would you favor or oppose a law requiring workers connected with war industries to work at least 48 hours a week? (AIPO, 11-42.)

    Yes 78%, *No* 12%, *No opinion* 10%

12. Asked of a national cross-section of factory workers: After the war is over, would you like to see the government own and operate electric light companies (automobile factories, coal mines), only regulate them, or leave them alone? (FOR, 2-43.)

	Leave alone %	Regulate %	Own %	No opinion %
Automobile factories.......	56	23	10	11
Electric companies.........	39	30	23	8
Coal mines	35	34	19	12

13. Asked of the 78 per cent not opposed to government public works for combating post-war unemployment: If the Government has to do one of these four things to get them all (unemployed ex-servicemen) jobs, which one would you choose? (NORC, 4-43.)

	Per cent
A. Start some government projects which would not compete with private business	51
B. Start some government projects which would compete with private business	8
C. Take over and run some private businesses.................	8
D. Give money to some businesses so they can hire more people....	22
Qualified and no opinion................................	11

14. Question wording and results as indicated in text. (OPOR, 5-43.)
15. See #14, this chapter, directly above. (OPOR, 5-43.)

	Per cent in favor of selling plants
Republicans....................	66
Democrats.....................	41
Upper income	61
Middle income	54
Lower income	35

16. Question wording and results as indicated in text. (OPOR, 6-43.)
17. See #16, this chapter, directly above. (OPOR, 6-43.)

	Per cent favoring sale to highest bidder
Republicans....................	58
Democrats.....................	33
Upper income	66
Middle income	42
Lower income	23

18. There have been many suggestions made recently about the kinds of control government should have over business. One of them is that the government should see to it that businessmen do not get together and make agreements to keep prices up at higher levels than they would be normally. Would you agree or disagree? (OPOR, 6-43.) Results as indicated in text.

19. As you know, the government has spent about 15 billion dollars during the last couple of years in building war plants and factories. At the present time these plants are owned by the government but run by private companies. After the war they will be sold by the government. If it looks as if a few big companies, because they have money on hand, are going to buy most of these plants, do you think the government should take steps to see that small businesses can buy these plant too, if they want to? (OPOR, 1-44.)

   Should 80%, *Should not* 7%, *No opinion* 13%

20. Asked of business leaders only: Do you think that, as compared with 1939, business in the U. S. after the war needs about the same amount of competition within business, more competition, or less competition? (FOR, 10-43.)

   More 19%, *Same* 76%, *Less* 5%

21. Asked of business leaders only: In your own business field, do you think after the war it would be a good thing if there were about the same number of competitors as now, more competitors, or fewer competitors? (FOR, 10-43.)

   More 12%, *Same* 74%, *Less* 14%

22. Asked of business leaders only: After the war do you believe that small manufacturers will have about the same opportunity, less opportunity, or the same opportunity? (FOR, 10-43.)

   More 23%, *Same* 45%, *Less* 32%

23. Do you think that we are likely to have high taxes during the next ten years? (AIPO, 10-42.)

   Yes 95%, *No* 5%

24. When the war is over, do you think it would be a good idea or a bad idea for us to have a top limit on the amount of money any one person can get in a year? (OPOR, 4-43.)

   Good idea 40%, *Bad idea* 51%, *No opinion* 9%

   A similar question, asked by *Fortune* in 7-42, using this wording: "After the war, do you think there should be a law limiting the amount of money any individual is allowed to earn in a year?" drew 60 per cent opposed to limitation on incomes. It is possible that the war years with their heavy tax loads have influenced our opinions somewhat.

25. Question wording as indicated in text. (OPOR, 6-43.)

   Agree 68%, *Disagree* 20%, *No opinion* 12%

26. Asked only of business leaders: In the event of a new depression, what one or several of these means would you advocate to alleviate it? (FOR, 10-43.)

	Per cent
Economy by government departments...............	77
Lower corporate taxes............................	62
Co-operative credit and employment effort by business...	54
A huge public works program......................	27
A spread-the-work program........................	24
Liberalization of consumer credit...................	18
Liberalization of bank credit......................	15
Government subsidies to business...................	3
Greater government regulation of business...........	1
Devaluation of the dollar.........................	1
All others.......................................	13
	295 *

* Percentage total exceeds 100 since multiple answers were permitted.

27. Asked only of business leaders: After the war, do you think business will have: (FOR, 10-43.)

	Per cent
Less freedom than in 1939.............	63
About the same	23
More freedom than in 1939...........	14

28. After the war is over do you think there will be more, the same, or less government regulation of: (FOR, 12-41.)

	More %	Same %	Less %	Not sure %
Public utilities	46	23	8	23
Farming	40	28	13	19
Railroads	39	26	10	25
The oil business	38	20	10	32
Banking.................	36	35	6	23
The steel business	35	19	13	33
Milk distribution	33	27	9	31
Auto manufacturing	31	22	20	27

(Averaging replies for all eight industries, and excluding those with no opinions, the "average expectation" with respect to post-war regulation is as follows:)

	Average expectation %
More regulation	51
Same regulation	34
Less regulation	15

CHAPTER XI

1. Question wording and results as indicated in text. (OPOR, 6-43.)
2. Asked of those who prefer gradual demobilization with a job guarantee to immediate demobilization: Suppose some of these men have to stay in the Army for six months or more before they get jobs. Do you still think it would be better to keep them in the Army until jobs are found for them? (OPOR, 6-43.)

    Yes 87%,   *No* 9%,   *Not sure* 4%
3. It has been proposed that soldiers who are discharged after the war is over be kept on Army payrolls for a time until they can find jobs. Do you approve or disapprove of this plan? (OPOR, 3-43.)

    Approve 79%,   *Disapprove* 18%,   *No opinion* 3%

    Asked of those who approve: For how long?

	Per cent
Less than six months	5
About six months	40
About a year	23
Over a year	5
Until employed	6
	79

4. A bill in Congress provides that members of the armed forces be given a certain sum of money by the government when they leave the service. Do you approve or disapprove of this idea? (AIPO, 1-44.)

    Approve 90%,   *Disapprove* 7%,   *No opinion* 3%

    Asked of those who do not disapprove:

    a. Here are the amounts that have been proposed:

      For servicemen who have served outside the U. S.

      $500 for 18 months or more
      $400 for 12 to 18 months
      $300 for less than 12 months.

      For servicemen who have served only in the U. S.:

      $300 for 12 months or more
      $200 for less than 12 months.

    Do you think these amounts are too large, too small, or about right?

    Too large 4%,   *Too small* 13%,   *About right* 70%,   *Qualified and no opinion* 13%

    b. Would you, personally, be willing to pay higher taxes in order to make these payments possible?

      Yes 79%,   *No* 13%,   *No opinion* 8%
5. Should every person who now holds a job formerly filled by a man in the

armed services be required to give it up when the serviceman returns? (AIPO, 1-44.)

   Yes 66%,   No 17%,   Qualified and no opinion 17%

6. Which of these plans for helping soldiers and others get jobs after the war do you like best? (OPOR, 6-43.)

Per cent

   I. Local draft boards should be responsible for finding jobs for returning soldiers from their districts after the war is over.... 14

   II. The U. S. Employment Service which is now helping people get jobs in war industries should be responsible for finding people jobs in peacetime industries after the war........... 41

   III. A new government agency should be set up with branch offices in all important towns and cities. This employment agency should have the power of making all companies notify them of any job openings. Anybody who wanted to could register with the agency and be told about jobs that were open........... 33

   No opinion 12

7. Do you think the draft is being handled fairly in your community? (AIPO, 12-43.)

   Yes 75%,   No 25%

8. Question wording and results as indicated in text. (OPOR, 6-43.)

9. See #8, this chapter, directly above. (OPOR, 6-43.)

*Per cent willing to give
soldiers first choice
of jobs*

Under 30 years 51
Age 30-40 64
Over 40 years 69

10. Question wording and results as indicated in text. (OPOR, 4-43.)

11. See #10, this chapter, directly above. Results as indicated in text. (OPOR, 4-43.)

12. If there aren't enough jobs after the war for all the men now in the armed services do you think it should be up to the government to guarantee jobs for them or not? (NORC, 4-43.)

   Up to Gov't 74%,   Not up to Gov't 22%,   Qualified and no opinion 4%

13. It has been suggested that returning soldiers be given a chance to go back to school at the government's expense if they want to after the war is over. Would you favor or oppose a law which provided schooling for soldiers after the war is over? (OPOR, 3-43.)

   Favor 86%,   Oppose 11%,   No opinion 3%

14. Do you think that public school systems should be mostly controlled by the

Federal Government, or mostly controlled by each State Government? (NORC, 6-42.)

Federal Gov't 19%, *State Gov't* 67%, *Qualified and no opinion* 14%

15. Would you be in favor of or be against having the Federal Government turn over a certain amount of money to the states every year for their schools? (NORC, 11-43.)

Favor 69%, *Oppose* 18%, *Qualified or no opinion* 13%

16. In Canada the government has provided that any soldier who wants to can borrow money at very low interest from the government to buy a house or a farm or a business. Would you approve or disapprove of a law of this kind in the United States? (OPOR, 6-43.)

Approve 81%, *Disapprove* 13%, *No opinion* 6%

17. See #16, this chapter, directly above. (OPOR, 6-43.)

	Per cent favoring loans for soldiers
Upper income	73
Middle income	81
Lower income	82
Republicans	76
Democrats	85
Those with close relatives in armed services	91
Those without close relatives in armed services	75

18. Question wording and results as indicated in text. (OPOR, 6-43.)

19. See #18, this chapter, directly above. (OPOR, 6-43.)

	Per cent favoring a soldier's bonus
Upper income	13
Middle income	16
Lower income	32
Those with close relatives in armed services	30
Those without close relatives in armed services	23

20-22. As you know, some soldiers are going to be kept on in the Army to occupy enemy countries after the war. If you were in charge of choosing these men, which soldiers would you pick? (OPOR, 6-43.)

a. Older men or younger men?

	Per cent
Older	39
Younger	36
No difference	18
No opinion	7

b. Men who volunteer or men the Army chooses as best?

Per cent
Volunteers.............. 57
Army's choice 36
No opinion 7

c. Men who have been in the Army a few years or men who are fairly new to the Army?

Per cent
Veterans 69
Fairly new 13
No opinion 18

INDEX

INDEX

INDEX

INDEX